WAR AT THE
WALL STREET JOURNAL

WAR AT THE *WALL STREET* JOURNAL

Inside the Struggle to Control an American Business Empire

Sarah Ellison

HOUGHTON MIFFLIN HARCOURT

BOSTON   NEW YORK   2010

For information about permission to reproduce selections from this book,
write to Permissions, Houghton Mifflin Harcourt Publishing Company,
215 Park Avenue South, New York, New York 10003.

www.hmhbooks.com

Library of Congress Cataloging-in-Publication Data
Ellison, Sarah.
War at the Wall Street journal : inside the struggle to control an American
business empire / Sarah Ellison.
p. cm.
ISBN 978-0-547-15243-1
1. Wall Street journal. 2. Dow Jones & Co. I. Title.
PN4899.N42W28 2010
071'.3—dc22   2009046266

Book design by Brian Moore

Printed in the United States of America

DOC 10 9 8 7 6 5 4 3 2 1

Excerpts from "Family Dynamics: Behind the Bancrofts' Shift at Dow Jones—
Mounting Pressure from Dissident Wing Raises Odds of a Sale," by Matthew
Karnitschnig, Sarah Ellison, Susan Pulliam, and Susan Warren (June 2, 2007),
and from Richard F. Zannino's letter to the Dow Jones board are reprinted by
permission of Dow Jones & Company.

For Jesse

Contents

Cast of Characters

THE BANCROFTS

Clarence Barron, Bancroft patriarch, early Dow Jones owner

Hugh Bancroft, Clarence Barron's son-in-law, early
   Dow Jones president

Jessie Cox, Clarence Barron's granddaughter

Jane Cook, Clarence Barron's granddaughter

Hugh Bancroft Jr., Clarence Barron's grandson

Jane MacElree, Jessie Cox's daughter

Bill Cox Jr., Jessie Cox's son

Jean Stevenson, Jane Cook's daughter

Martha Robes, Jane Cook's daughter

Lisa Steele, Jane Cook's daughter

Christopher Bancroft, Hugh Bancroft Jr.'s son

Hugh Bancroft III, Hugh Bancroft Jr.'s son

Bettina Bancroft, Hugh Bancroft Jr.'s daughter

Elisabeth "Lizzie" Goth Chelberg, Bettina Bancroft's daughter

Leslie Hill, Jane MacElree's daughter

Michael Hill, Jane MacElree's son

Tom Hill, Jane MacElree's son

Crawford Hill, Jane MacElree's son
William Cox III, Bill Cox Jr.'s son

ADVISERS

Michael Puzo, Hemenway & Barnes attorney, Bancroft trustee
Jim Lowell, financial adviser to Hemenway & Barnes on
   Bancroft accounts
Roy Hammer, Hemenway & Barnes attorney, Bancroft trustee,
   Dow Jones board member
Michael Elefante, Hemenway & Barnes attorney, Bancroft trustee,
   Dow Jones board member
Martin Lipton, partner at Wachtell, Lipton, Rosen & Katz, adviser
   to Bancroft family

THE MURDOCHS

Rupert Murdoch, News Corp. chairman/CEO
Wendi Deng Murdoch, Rupert Murdoch's wife
Prudence MacLeod, Rupert's eldest daughter
Elisabeth Murdoch, Rupert's daughter
Lachlan Murdoch, Rupert's elder son
James Murdoch, Rupert's younger son
Grace Murdoch, Rupert's daughter
Chloe Murdoch, Rupert's youngest daughter

ADVISERS

Andrew Steginsky, independent money manager, adviser to
   Rupert Murdoch

DOW JONES & COMPANY

Peter Kann, former Dow Jones CEO, president, and *Journal*
   publisher
Karen Elliott House, former *Journal* publisher
Paul Steiger, former *Journal* managing editor
Richard Zannino, former Dow Jones CEO

Marcus Brauchli, *Journal* managing editor

Gordon Crovitz, *Journal* publisher

Irvine Hockaday, Dow Jones board member

Frank Newman, Dow Jones board member

Peter McPherson, Dow Jones board member

Harvey Golub, Dow Jones board member

Lewis Campbell, Dow Jones board member

William Steere, Dow Jones board member

Bill Grueskin, *Journal* deputy managing editor for news coverage

Paul Gigot, editorial page editor of the *Journal*

Nikhil Deogun, *Journal* editor

Martin Peers, *Journal* editor

Paul Ingrassia, president of Dow Jones Newswires

Joseph Stern, Dow Jones general counsel

James Ottaway, Dow Jones board member

Richard Beattie, chairman of Simpson Thacher & Bartlett, adviser
to Dow Jones's independent directors

NEWS CORP.

Gary Ginsberg, News Corp. EVP of global marketing and
corporate affairs

Lon Jacobs, News Corp. general counsel

David DeVoe, News Corp. CFO

Roger Ailes, chairman/CEO of Fox News Channel and Fox
BusinessNetwork

Leslie Hinton, former executive chairman of News International

Robert Thomson, former *Times* of London editor

James Bainbridge Lee Jr., JPMorgan Chase banker, adviser to
News Corp.

Blair Effron, Centerview Partners, adviser to News Corp.

WAR AT THE
WALL STREET
JOURNAL

Prologue

G AIL GREGG WALKED confidently up the gangway to join
the small gathering on Barry Diller's yacht on a warm August night in 2007. Yet when she saw Rupert Murdoch,
nemesis of her husband, *New York Times* publisher Arthur Sulzberger Jr., she forgot the promise of the evening and almost threw
herself into the Hudson River.

The tabloids would note the party briefly, but this event wasn't designed for mentions in columns with boldface names. No press passes
had gone out to humble journalists. The powerful would mingle privately, exchanging pleasantries and tidbits, setting up potentially
useful future exchanges. Relationships would evolve quietly under
the setting sun. Yet beneath the clinking of cocktail glasses something else was taking place, namely, the latest phase of a competition
involving the future of two of America's most important publications
and a battle for supremacy over who would control what the nation
read, thought, and believed.

The guests aboard Diller's beautiful 118-foot cruiser knew that reality was the creation of the highest bidder. Their media empires didn't
merely report the news; they chose and shaped it. Yet tonight's stated
purpose was not strictly business: at the top of the agenda was the
viewing of Diller's new IAC/InterActiveCorp headquarters from the
water, with a tour to follow. Diller, a comfortable host and a bit of a

showman, had arranged things a week or so earlier. The evening light would perfectly showcase the rather controversial building, designed by architect Frank Gehry to evoke eight wind-whipped sails ready to glide out onto the river. But the strange and graceful edifice was no one's notion of the big news story on that particular evening.

In the wee hours of that morning, Rupert Murdoch had secured a $5 billion deal to buy Dow Jones & Company and the *Wall Street Journal* from the Bancrofts, one of the country's last remaining newspaper families, who had owned the company for 105 years through thirty-three Pulitzers. The only other time Dow Jones had been purchased was for $130,000 in 1902 by Clarence Barron, whom some called the originator of financial writing but whom the Bancrofts referred to as "Grandpa." The founder of the Boston News Bureau, he had purchased the company with a $2,500 down payment loan from his wife, Jessie Waldron, whose cooking the five-foot-five, 330-pound patriarch had enjoyed as a longtime guest at Ms. Waldron's boarding house.

The purchase had ensured that the later generations of the Bancroft family were bonded together, however reluctantly or tentatively. Without it, the Boston-based clan would feel like "just another rich family," a status the elders in the clan were reluctant to embrace. As the generations progressed, their relationships grew ever more tenuous. Murdoch's money would allow them to be rid of one another. It would allow him something else entirely: the $5 billion purchase of the "daily diary of the American dream" was the likely culmination of his controversial career, which had helped shape the century. The paper would become the flagship of his News Corporation.

The seventy-six-year-old Murdoch, his auburn-dyed hair receded halfway back his head, his brow permanently creased as his smile emerged from the crevasses that lined his face, looked relaxed and vibrant in the stifling summer heat. He accepted congratulations in his softly accented Australian mumble. For almost two decades he had coveted just these plaudits. But the question of whether the purchase was actually a triumph would be avidly debated in the Hamptons and elsewhere as the summer came to its close. Some called his timing all but laughable, given the print medium's sorry state. Most noted that the man who had always indulged his penchant for what he called "populist" papers had now steered himself into an impossible challenge—engineering the subtle metamorphosis of a beloved, sophisticated publication with a dwindling audience in the midst of the scariest media moment in recent memory.

Murdoch, worth $9 billion and ranked thirty-third on the *Forbes* list of the four hundred richest Americans that year, remained an awesome competitor. His challenges were just beginning. After capturing the *Journal* with a motley team of advisers and his shareholders' cash, he faced an inevitable battle with its staid newsroom along with emerging calamities that would transform what had seemed a trifle in his mammoth empire into a drain on his business—and his reputation.

Gail Gregg held a unique position as the first lady of Murdoch's biggest competitor, the Sulzberger clan who controlled the *New York Times*. She and her husband had fallen in love when they were both young aspiring journalists, in the days when, thanks to Woodward and Bernstein, journalism was steeped in romanticism. After Nixon's fall, reporting was glamorous; the country had loved the Fourth Estate. The adoration was short-lived.

It was no longer easy to enjoy being a member of America's most powerful publishing dynasty, reigning as Manhattan's all-but-official royal family. Online competitors mocked the self-importance of the once unassailable *Times* from cyberspace as the accountants forecast the demise of the entire newspaper industry.

Many of the other guests at the dinner party were also under siege and uncertain. Technology was upending the old monopolistic industry models, which had made newspapers one of America's great businesses. Media companies were collapsing as the nation fell out of love with publications upon which they once depended. Readers' patience was wearing thin. They had continued to subscribe to papers they perceived as lifeless, drained by their corporate owners of local muckraking, voice, excitement, individuality. Scores of papers across the country were closed or clinging to diminished existence, though the news—wars, terrorism, economic disaster—was more epochal than ever.

Even the proud Sulzbergers seemed insecure. Gail's entrance to the festivities didn't cause the guests to look up as quickly as it once would have. Yet, despite her earlier temptation to brave the waters of the Hudson, she was too tactful to make any sort of scene. Instead, as she spied Murdoch, she slipped off her shoes so she wouldn't scuff the gleaming white deck of the yacht, pulled her lips into a smile, and made her way on board.

The year had been terrible for the *Times* with an ever diminishing paying readership and plummeting ad revenues. (The company would end up mortgaging its new headquarters, taking a usurious loan from Carlos Slim Helú, a Mexican billionaire.) Still, the Sulzbergers saw themselves as survivors. Among old-fashioned American journalism's most serious advocates, they were nearly unapproachable, closely engaged in the business, influential with editorials and endorsements, and involved in a modernization of the paper. But would they, too, be unseated? Would Murdoch or another usurper set his sights on their old Grey Lady? Would his ownership of their rival, the only other truly nationally influential paper, damage the *Times* by forcing it to become more commercial, or further weaken its already addled business?

For three anxiety-ridden months, Gail and Arthur had watched Murdoch struggle to snatch up the *Journal*. Throughout the pummelings of his earlier takeover battles, the press baron always seemed buoyed by his jousts with the "old guard" who disdained his screaming headlines and pulpy stories. But Murdoch's outsider status was yesterday's cliché. He had been a media titan around the globe for nearly half a century. Some may have seen his latest move as a brash upstart's most recent triumph over tradition—a view Murdoch encouraged—but it was much more complicated. Many of the Bancrofts, in fact, had come to see him as not a spoiler or a corrupter, but a savior.

The Sulzbergers begged to differ. Gail still called Murdoch "dreadful." It didn't matter that his instincts might just keep their medium alive. Those same instincts, they feared, would debase the country's dialogue. They knew that perhaps one (maybe two) strong survivors would become America's national newspaper or newspapers. Murdoch believed that the race would be between his own new flagship publication and the *Times*.

The medium still fascinated Murdoch, who had come from a newspaper family and inherited his first, the *Adelaide News*, as a twenty-one-year-old fresh from Oxford. Within a few years he was acquiring (the *Sydney Daily* and *Sunday Mirror*) and in 1964 launched Australia's first national paper, the *Australian*. Forty-three years later, he controlled the 20th Century Fox movie studio, the Fox television and "fair and balanced" Fox News empire, the BSkyB and Sky Italia satellite businesses, and now the *Journal*.

Murdoch had inherited his taste for politics from his father, Keith, who, after having lost out to a rival reporter for the assignment to cover Australian troops in World War I, wrote a passionate letter critiquing the Gallipoli campaign. Frustrated with the censorship that didn't allow the press to report on the actual events at Gallipoli, he delivered the letter directly to the Australian prime minister. Though riddled with errors, the lacerating memo helped bring about the dismissal of the commander in chief of the campaign and, some say, the end of the campaign itself. Historians credit his letter with a greater impact on the events at Gallipoli than any articles published in the press.

Murdoch, like his father, didn't hide behind rules of journalistic objectivity; he wasn't too bothered by the occasional mistake. Murdoch was unafraid to use his media outlets, particularly his tabloid papers, as instruments of influence. In fact, he measured the success of his papers by their influence. In Britain, he achieved his greatest impact with the *Sun*. With nearly eight million readers, the *Sun*, in addition to its topless Page Three girls, carried more weight in its home country than almost any other paper in the world. It had steered the 1997 British parliamentary election to Tony Blair after Murdoch, alienated from Prime Minister John Major, led the Thatcherite British tabloid in an energetic campaign for the Labour candidate, who then won the election for prime minister in a landslide. The move shocked British Conservatives into nearly apoplectic fury. That was fine. Murdoch was no fan of pussyfooting in public, in private, or in print.

The *Journal's* conservative editorial page made it a natural *Times* antagonist; Murdoch would apply his predatory tactics to create an even tougher competitor to the more liberal institution. The *Journal* was the heartland's choice, but TV news programs, other newspapers, and magazines took cues from the *Times*. That rankled Murdoch, who sensed Sulzberger's politics on that paper's every page. The old posture of objectivity, Murdoch believed, was just a way to con *Times* readers into imbibing left-leaning perspectives. His *Journal*, never more feisty, would launch an old-fashioned newspaper war with guerrilla warfare and terrorist techniques. The battle for the future was on.

Born into privilege, Murdoch was Oxford-educated and pampered, but none of it showed. He revealed little and seemed the natural enemy of the overblown or lavish. He treated six palatial homes—in New York, Los Angeles, London, Long Island, Carmel, and Beijing—as more convenience than excess. The accouterments of wealth weren't what he was about. For Murdoch, the great game was its own reward; there was always the next move. There was a bit of theater to it all, and he went along with it, but he didn't put himself on display as an authoritative TV or social presence. He kept at the battle day by day and told his employees (there were almost sixty thousand) to call themselves pirates.

The Australian's conquest of Manhattan had begun in the 1970s when he snatched up the liberal *New York Post* and changed its political philosophy. He then moved on to *New York* magazine, where nearly all the staff walked out rather than face the new owner's reinvention of their magazine. Once, his breach of the Dow Jones fortress would have been unthinkable, but a series of lucky coincidences had given him his opening, and he had seized it.

Nearly eighty years after Clarence Barron's death, his family, to whom he left an estate of $1.575 million in 1928 ($19.4 million in 2009 dollars), had little in common with "Grandpa." None worked at his company or shared his passion for the business. (His last words were "What's the news? Are there any messages?") They lived off family trusts set up in the 1930s by Barron's adopted daughter Jane after she was widowed. Most of the money was tied up in the family business. Jane's three children, Jessie Cox, Jane Cook, and Hugh Bancroft Jr., who had lived comfortably off the fortune, entertained in their Boston Back Bay mansions and tended their horses. (Hugh, Jessie, and Jane died in 1953, 1982, and 2002, respectively.)

Their sparring heirs formed the three branches of the family—each with a roughly equal share of the family fortune—who had faced down Murdoch. His $5 billion, $60-a-share offer boosted the value of the original Bancroft fortune by over half a billion dollars, enough to allow the thirty-five adult members of the family to envision a few more years in the lifestyle to which they had become accustomed. But the family had been deeply divided by the offer and was even further torn apart now that the decision had been made.

Rupert Murdoch was a suitor more similar to their founder, Barron, than any of the Bancrofts would have liked to admit. (The year of his death, Clarence Barron broke with Dow Jones's late founder Charles Dow's decree that the *Journal* never endorse a political candidate and called for a vote for Herbert Hoover.) Like Murdoch, Grandpa Barron had multiple residences and an elaborate entourage. He traveled with sixty pieces of luggage, a secretary, a chauffeur, and a male nurse who buttoned his pants and tied his shoes for him since his girth prevented such exertions.

As his company passed through the generations, Barron's descendants turned their lack of interest into a virtue, protecting their precious heirloom with a policy of noninterference. "Leave it to the professionals" became the mantra. Such benign neglect worked as long as the family had a clear leader, and for much of the newspaper industry's halcyon years that leader was Barron's granddaughter Jessie Bancroft Cox—irreverent, boisterous, and horsey in the Boston way. As her family gathered in April 1982 at Manhattan's '21' Club to celebrate Dow Jones's hundredth anniversary, the round grandmother entertained with characteristic stories—she once caught future president Franklin Delano Roosevelt trying to cheat her in a game of mahjong. She had lived her life in Boston and spent the summers a short drive away at the family's lavish twenty-eight-room summer home, "The Oaks," on Cohasset Harbor, complete with tennis courts, a boat dock, and equestrian-inspired china that acknowledged Jessie's passion for horses. The house, originally designed by Barron as a wooden Victorian, had been torn down after his death by his son-in-law Hugh Bancroft, who rebuilt it in brick as a wedding present for his daughter Jessie. She had entertained President Eisenhower there and hosted elegant equestrian events, helping create what the local historian in Cohasset called "an illustrious chapter" in the town's history. At the time of the dinner at the '21' Club, Dow Jones was at the height of its success and power. Jessie's son, William Cox Jr., called the *Journal* "the best damn paper in the country."

But that evening, Jessie was in a foul mood. As a Bostonian and a sports fan, she had developed a strong affection for the hometown baseball team. The Red Sox had lost six out of the last ten games and she was upset about the losing streak. When another dinner guest mentioned the losses, she responded angrily.

"What the fuck's the matter with my Red Sox?" she cried, promptly knocking against the adjacent table before falling to the floor. She was rushed past her stunned relatives and died shortly afterward. With her died any remaining cohesion in the Bancroft family, and the "professionals" slowly adopted an ever more powerful role, dictating many of the family's financial decisions. That was until thirty-two-year-old Elisabeth Goth, the great-great-granddaughter of Clarence Barron, descended from the Hugh Bancroft branch of the family, decided to join forces with her third cousin Billy Cox III, Jessie's grandson, to challenge "the professionals."

Despite their occasional eruptions, the Bancrofts had become one of the lesser-known dynasties, lacking the blood rivalries of the Kentucky Binghams, the visibility and influence of the DC Grahams, and the social cachet of the California Chandlers. At the start, after the early sizing up, Murdoch may have wished for better sport, but he would learn that where money and New Englanders are concerned, the process of seduction takes more than a few clambakes.

The Bancrofts believed in the *Journal* name. Unambitious, a bit panache-deprived, they remained dedicated to their paper, from a distance. They never bowed, as others had, to the conglomerates, which would have stripped the publication of its identity and then puzzled over its failure. Unlike Murdoch, however, the family allowed their paper to espouse political views with which they disagreed whole-heartedly. The Bancrofts had, despite their largely liberal leanings, defended the *Journal's* deeply conservative editorial board, whose philosophy, "free markets, free people," and its flame-throwing editorials made it the vanguard of the conservative movement. That summer, however, Murdoch had presented a $600 million decision: turn down his offer, and they could watch the shares continue to founder at around $35, where they had been trading before he came on the scene. (There was the strong possibility that the shares would plummet, too, leaving the family stuck with their dwindling prize.) Or, they could accept Murdoch's offer, which boosted the value of their Dow Jones stake by more than half a billion dollars, and leave Dow Jones, once and for all, "to the professionals."

The Hudson glimmered in the sun as Diller's party of fourteen guests surveyed his new $100 million building, which would mystify passersby and was home to IAC's holdings such as the Home Shopping Network, Ticketmaster, and LendingTree. Diller's decision to include Murdoch—his old boss, friend, and occasional tormenter—had been spur-of-the-moment. He had called Rupert that morning to congratulate him and found himself issuing an invitation. The two had a history.

Diller had been instrumental in the creation of Murdoch's wildly successful Fox television network, which had taken on what seemed at the time the ironclad dominance of the big three networks. After nearly a decade of devotion to all things Murdoch, Diller left unexpectedly after Murdoch refused to give him partnership in the business he had helped build. Even then, Murdoch had an instinct for self-preservation through family control, though his own clan had weathered its difficulties, beginning in a predictable fashion when Murdoch became attracted to a younger woman.

As he was falling in love in the 1990s with the opportunity that was China, he was simultaneously diverted by a young Chinese employee at Star TV. Wendi Deng, the daughter of a factory manager, was almost forty years Murdoch's junior. Unlike his second wife, Anna, Wendi didn't urge him to work less or spend more time at home.

Romance blossomed—one that to this day Murdoch denies having begun until separating from Anna. Even his children—he had three with Anna and one with his first wife, Patricia Booker—doubted his version of events. "Absolutely it was going on. I know from his friends," one confessed. "He'll deny it to his dying day."

On the night of the Diller fete, Wendi was traveling, unable to join the festivities. Anna Murdoch had held a spot on the News Corp. board, occupied an office in the headquarters, and had her own assistant. But in her position at the company she rarely ventured far afield from organizing social events for executives and their wives and protecting her children's future stake in the empire. Unlike Anna, Wendi launched herself, however peripherally, into News Corp.'s business, consulting on the company's MySpace online social network site in China. She was also planning to start up a production company with film star Ziyi Zhang. (Wendi had introduced her countrywoman, on Murdoch's own yacht, to Vivi Nevo, the Israeli venture capitalist and single largest shareholder in the Time Warner company. The two became a couple.)

Lately, despite the efforts of his young wife, who was pushing Murdoch into the twenty-first century and into trendy black shirts, his age had begun to show. His eyes sagged. He meandered even more than usual in conversation and appeared, on occasion, more grandfather than rapacious mogul. Some of his executives saw his soft spot for the *Wall Street Journal* as evidence of his decline.

When Diller reached Murdoch on the phone that morning, he had congratulated him and quipped, "I know you have nothing else going on, but I'm having some people on the boat tonight and wanted to see if you'd join me." Many empire builders would have had their own victory party planned, but Diller knew that Murdoch was neither a social animal nor a seeker of publicity. Murdoch had uncorked a bottle of Shiraz the previous afternoon with a few of his executives, but he had no wide group of friends to tap that night.

"Well," Murdoch replied, "I'd love to come."

Diller never liked his waters too calm. Releasing Sulzberger and Murdoch in the same room on this particular night added an interesting undercurrent. It was a worthy dramatic effort for Diller, a former Paramount chieftain whose social life seemed about as recreational as open-heart surgery. The other guests would enjoy sizing up the competitors.

In the early-evening sun, Murdoch had slipped on board quietly and made his way with his uneven gait to New York City mayor Michael Bloomberg, the succinct former businessman whom he greeted with what appeared to be genuine warmth. Practical and pragmatic, Murdoch preferred politicians to Hollywood types, and Bloomberg's business background and higher ambition made him a friend who would almost certainly be useful. Bloomberg could talk engagingly about Murdoch's true loves: media and politics. The mayor's date and longtime companion, Diana Taylor, the city's regal and unofficial first lady, chatted with Anna Wintour of *Vogue*, who had admired Taylor's style enough to feature her in a five-page spread in the magazine several years earlier.

Film director Mike Nichols and his wife, Diane Sawyer, talked nearby, pleasant fixtures when Diller held court. *Vanity Fair* editor Graydon Carter had become a Diller devotee after the mogul helped Carter establish *Vanity Fair*'s legendary post-Oscars fete in Hollywood. On the yacht, Carter chatted with John Huey, editor in chief of Time Inc., and Lally Weymouth, whose family controlled the Washington Post Company. Weymouth's daughter Katharine would soon take over as publisher of the *Post*. Steve Rattner, a former *Times* reporter who had become a powerful media financier and confidant of the Sulzbergers, talked with Carter's wife, Anna.

As Murdoch moved on to greet the other guests, Sulzberger and Diller chatted with Bloomberg, whose company had not long ago completed construction on a gleaming monumental headquarters building of its own. All three men had, in fact, braved the difficulties of construction. Sulzberger had just overseen the completion of the new *Times* headquarters on Eighth Avenue, a creation of architect Renzo Piano that resembled a minimum-security prison. Critics noted that the building reflected that part of the *Times*'s ethos that tried too hard to show its import. Still, that special kind of ambition had produced the paper's thirty-five bureaus around the world and its global perspective. The *Times* had always been committed to giving its readers the world beyond our shores and our Brangelinas. The creation of an American publication comparable to the *Times* or the *Journal* seemed unimaginable now. Some at the party wondered, Could Murdoch have built such an institution, or was it his role to just buy one?

On the boat, Sulzberger pulled Murdoch aside. "I don't really feel that we can have dinner together without my telling you that we have an editorial about your takeover of the *Journal* in tomorrow morning's paper. And I have read it, and I can assure you I don't feel it's faintly anti-Murdoch." Murdoch thanked Sulzberger for the heads-up. The two continued chatting, sharing their thoughts on the state of their business. Despite their differences and the tussles still to come, they were united in a special way, for there were probably no other two men on the face of the Earth more committed to the future of newspapers. Murdoch, straightforward as always, talked about what he hoped to do with the *Journal* and did not conceal his irritation at the *Times*'s coverage of the Dow Jones deal. Despite the tension, their conversation was friendly, almost playful.

As the boat neared the Statue of Liberty, the guests gathered around a large rectangular table for dinner, exchanged pleasantries, and avoided the potentially awkward topic of Murdoch's latest purchase. They returned to Diller's building for a quick tour, dutifully praising the plump, cavernous structure. As the evening came to its close, the Sulzbergers walked out onto the street. All the other guests, the moguls, editors, and moviemakers, had cars and drivers waiting in expertly chosen locations to whisk them off to their splendid sheets. The Sulzbergers found themselves contemplating the near impossibility of finding a cab on the piers on the far West Side of Manhattan at that hour. Taking pity, a fellow partygoer offered them a ride in his car, which they accepted. As they clambered into the car, Arthur laughed like a kid, very much unlike the media titan he was. "Wow," he said. The star-studded evening had left its impression.

The next morning, Murdoch was in his office working on his next potential acquisition, swapping his once coveted but now stagnating social networking site MySpace for a stake in Yahoo!, and fuming. Under a spare headline—"Notes About Competition"—there was the editorial Sulzberger had warned him about. Far from an innocuous mention, the *Times* had, Murdoch felt, fired a shot across town to let him know the newspaper was watching him. "If we were in any other business, a risky takeover of a powerful competitor might lead to celebration," the editorial began. "Not in our business. Good journalism, which is an essential part of American democracy, thrives on competition."

The piece did some predictable tut-tutting about the cutbacks in national and foreign coverage at the *Times*'s impoverished competition, "such formerly formidable competitors as *The Los Angeles Times*," before praising the pre-Murdoch version of the *Journal*. Then, as Murdoch read on, the tone of the piece changed and he became the center of its attack: "The *Times* and the *Journal* have reported extensively about Mr. Murdoch's meddling in his media properties: How he reneged on his promise of editorial independence for the *Times* of London and how, to curry favor with China's leaders, his satellite broadcaster, Star TV, stopped carrying news from the BBC." The editorial concluded by suggesting, "The best way for Mr. Murdoch to protect his $5 billion investment is to protect the *Journal*'s editorial quality and integrity." Doing so would "be good news for all Americans."

Murdoch, who prided himself on being direct, stewed at Sulzberger's false assurances the night before. Here it was again, a piece attacking him in all the most predictable ways, dredging up examples he had long tired of answering for. "If that editorial wasn't anti-Murdoch," he thought, "I'd hate to see his version of what is." Murdoch dashed off a letter, beginning a new game of jousting with his crosstown enemy.

"It was a pleasure seeing you again last night, although I don't agree with your characterization of today's editorial," he wrote. Then he stridently denied the *Times*'s accusations point by point: "I don't know how many times I have to state that I did not take the BBC off Star TV for political reasons, nor have I ever given any sort of political instructions, or even guidance, to one editor of the *Times* or the *Sunday Times*." Toward the end of the letter, he penned a sentence that played to Sulzberger's vanity—as a scrupulous owner who never interfered in coverage—but that Murdoch meant as a dig. "On a broader basis," he continued, "I promise you that I will treat you as an example in my relationship with editors." It was a fitting ambiguity, similar to Sulzberger's "don't feel it's faintly anti-Murdoch." What type of example would Sulzberger be when Murdoch spoke to his editors?

Murdoch couldn't resist a final dig. The last line of the letter stood alone in simple type.

"Let the battle begin!"

1

The Fix

DOW JONES SEEMED destined for Rupert Murdoch long before the official dealing had begun. For decades, Murdoch had coveted the *Wall Street Journal*. His children couldn't remember a time when he wasn't talking about it. His most trusted colleagues called it a "preoccupation" for him (even more than the *Financial Times,* which he had tried and failed to buy, or the *New York Times,* which he also eyed). He was open about his admiration, and among Wall Street's bankers, brokering a deal between the Bancroft family and a deep-pocketed media mogul such as Murdoch was a tantalizing opportunity.

So in the summer of 2002 when James Bainbridge Lee Jr. stood in his dark-wood-paneled office on the executive eighth floor of JPMorgan Chase & Company's midtown Manhattan headquarters, he prepared carefully for his upcoming call. He was contemplating how to break into one of the most difficult-to-crack media families in the country, the Bancrofts of Dow Jones & Company and the *Journal*.

As Jimmy checked the market movements and news on the five computer screens on his desk, his image stared back at him from the framed *Forbes* cover on his bookshelf. Under the headline "The New Power on Wall Street," the photo displayed a slightly younger version of the Wall Street banker in his cufflinks and suspenders, his graying hair slicked back and curling slightly below the ears. The piece invited readers to "Meet the New Michael Milken." Jimmy, as he was known on Wall Street, could have served as the model for "investment banker" if the Museum of Natural History mounted a diorama of the species, but his thoughts that day were not on his appearance.

Jimmy had made his reputation more than a decade earlier as a young banker making big loans to clients who wanted to make even bigger deals. His Rolodex was the source of his power, and he used it. He was sometimes derided as a glorified matchmaker. Every day, he started a new page on his yellow legal pad, jotting down in his all-caps scrawl a list of names to contact. By evening, after his usual frenetic day of jokes and ingratiating storytelling, the names were crossed off with his thin royal blue marker.

That midsummer day in 2002, he had already scribbled through one page and had moved on to the next when he dialed Richard F. Zannino's number. Zannino had just been named the chief operating officer at Dow Jones & Company, an elevation that put him a single step away from the spot where Jimmy wanted him for the match he had in mind. Dow Jones, while a storied media firm, seemed increasingly small and outpaced alongside entertainment conglomerates such as Viacom Inc., Time Warner Inc., and News Corp. Even pure news outlets such as Bloomberg LP and Reuters PLC now dwarfed the parent of the *Wall Street Journal*, which had been struggling since the implosion of the Internet bubble in the spring of 2000 had dried up much technology and financial advertising. The *Journal* was in the process of losing more than $300 million in advertising revenue, and the paper would spend the next three years losing money. The company's stock had peaked near $78 a share in the summer of 2000. Currently it was trading in the low $40s.

That Zannino would pick up the phone at all to chat with a banker like Jimmy represented a change at Dow Jones. Zannino's boss, Dow Jones CEO Peter Kann, would never have thought to befriend someone like Jimmy, much less talk on the phone with him on a summer afternoon. For Kann, even speaking to a rogue banker about company strategy was a step outside the bounds of Bancroft-approved isolationism. Kann, who often spoke slowly, his hand rubbing the top of his balding head, which pitched ever so slightly forward when he addressed a group, had served as the company's CEO since 1991 and was a *Wall Street Journal* journalist who had risen through the ranks.

At another publication, the ascent would seem unusual. But at Dow Jones, the best journalists wound up running the company, and so it had been with Kann. He was awkward in front of crowds; his presence was unassuming until he started to write. Then his prose enchanted, something his performance as an executive had never managed to do. More than any living Bancroft, Peter Kann embodied the understated spirit of Dow Jones. He once wrote in a letter to *Journal* readers: "We believe facts are facts and that they are ascertainable through honest, open-minded and diligent reporting. We thus believe that truth is attainable by laying fact upon fact, much like the construction of a cathedral. News, in short, is not merely a matter of views. And truth is not merely in the eye of the beholder." As CEO, he had assembled a management team of polite Ivy League executives. He had also promoted his wife, Karen Elliott House, to publisher of the *Journal*. Her proud Texan twang announced her as a standout in the otherwise meek crowd. The journalists called him "Uncle Peter," sometimes affectionately, sometimes with derision.

Kann knew Dow Jones only as a Bancroft-owned institution. He had grown close to the elders in the family and often praised their support of Dow Jones and the *Journal*. He fostered the notion that Dow Jones was a "quasi-public trust"—as was once stated in the company's proxy—and that the family was a worthy defender of one of the finest journalistic institutions in the country. He believed fervently that family ownership at Dow Jones was what gave the institution the independence to pursue its stellar brand of journalism. The best papers in the country—the *Washington Post*, the *New York Times*, and the *Journal*—were all owned by old families with a legacy to protect. During his tenure, he had assiduously established the relationships he needed to keep the company independent.

Kann's tenure as CEO was marred by serious management missteps, capital misallocations, and a foundering stock price, but he waved off critiques of these problems. He had managed something far greater in his mind: the journalistic integrity of the *Wall Street Journal*. And even though he didn't think they were the brightest bunch, he had the Bancroft family to thank for that.

Zannino didn't blend in at the company, where he'd arrived from the rag trade, the son of an Italian Catholic longshoreman who took occasional work at the local bar in Everett, Massachusetts, and an Irish Catholic stay-at-home mom. Married right out of Bentley College, where sometimes it seemed he'd majored in financial aid, he started a family, worked two jobs, and slaved at night for an MBA. At forty-three, he still hadn't shaken Boston's rougher precincts from his voice. Though comfortable at Dow Jones, he had never taken on the company-wide aversion to selling the place. One of his big critiques of the *Journal,* which he kept mostly to himself, was that it lacked positive stories about successful CEOs and their companies. He was a businessman. Take it or leave it.

Jimmy and Zannino had worked together before. When Jimmy was an investment banker at Chemical Bank, Zannino was chief financial officer of Saks Fifth Avenue and later Liz Claiborne. They became Connecticut neighbors when Zannino moved to Greenwich (Jimmy lived in nearby Darien), home to hedge fund managers, CEOs, and their bankers. There he coexisted peacefully with all the other executives, and his son, Joey Zannino, played on the same ice hockey team as Jimmy's son, Jamie Lee—the Brunswick Bruins. As parents often do, Zannino and Jimmy chatted at games and bonded over their kids.

Zannino, with thick dark hair and square-jawed good looks, carried himself with sporty, casual ease. He had often talked to Jimmy about how he couldn't do big enough deals. Dow Jones was small and shackled to the *Journal,* which howled at the tiniest budget cut that diminished its reporting resources or staff. "I can't roll the dice," he told Jimmy. Zannino, with his Pace MBA and blue-collar bite, was greeted with some suspicion by the Ivy Leaguers of Dow Jones. But, despite their frosty attitudes, these naysayers hoped that he would be able to figure out what to do about the company's dire business prospects.

In the year before Jimmy's call to Zannino, the *Journal* had been tested. The terrorist attacks of September 11, 2001, had decimated the company's headquarters. As the World Trade Center towers fell, the impact shattered the windows of Dow Jones, blowing heavy debris across desks, blanketing the *Journal* newsroom with white ash. The *Journal*'s long-serving managing editor, Paul Steiger, led reporters and editors across the river to Dow Jones's offices in New Jersey, where a skeleton staff produced a paper that appeared—remarkably—on doorsteps the morning of September 12, complete with a harrowing eyewitness account of the towers' fall. The paper won the Pulitzer Prize for breaking news for its coverage of that day, which was, the Pulitzer committee said, "executed under the most difficult circumstances." It was a defining moment for the paper. As if the decimated offices weren't enough, just months after the attacks talented feature writer Daniel Pearl, South Asia bureau chief, was abducted and brutally murdered while investigating Al Qaeda links to the "shoe bomber," Richard Reid.

The *Journal* and Dow Jones felt under siege. In a normally skeptical newsroom, there was suddenly shared purpose with everyone from the Bancrofts to Peter Kann. All rallied to support the institution, and Steiger, already beloved, became something of a saint. The Dow Jones "family," as Kann called it, drew together. The newsroom, always aware of its status as belonging to one of a chosen few elite papers in the country, was newly devoted to its mission and the family who allowed them to pursue their craft without the meddling of a more business-minded corporate parent. But such sentiment couldn't beat back the business pressures plaguing the company. The steep drop in advertising revenue that plagued the *Journal* following September 11 was dragging down the entire newspaper industry.

Zannino arrived at Dow Jones in February 2001 as chief financial officer. Seventeen months later, he was on the phone with Jimmy Lee, who loved to chide his pal. "You're too small," he would say about Dow Jones. "You can't take a gamble." But it was all just fun: Jimmy knew he was dealing with a guy who understood the world as he did, through stock prices, profits, and fees. Zannino, he knew, wanted to make his company a place where good journalists practiced journalism and good businesspeople took care of the business. Jimmy thought, "Maybe this is the guy who provides the bridge. And I know someone who can cross it." The person he was thinking of? Rupert Murdoch. Of course.

As Jimmy stood in his office on that morning in July 2002, pen poised, waiting for Zannino to pick up the phone, he thought, "I can deliver this." After congratulating Zannino on his new appointment as chief operating officer, which had been announced earlier that month, and making the requisite small talk, Jimmy launched into the purpose of the call.

"So, isn't it time for you guys to do a deal?" Jimmy asked.

"The Bancroft family holds all the cards," Zannino replied, in what would become a standard refrain.

Jimmy took his pen and wrote down his notes from the conversation.

The words stared back at Jimmy, their bright blue lettering discouraging and predictable: "BANCROFT FAMILY HOLDS ALL CARDS."

The Bancrofts controlled 64 percent of Dow Jones through a class of super-voting stock that gave them ten votes per share on any issue that came before shareholders, namely, takeovers. Jimmy knew this; it was stated plainly in the company's public filings. But that protected stance was something Jimmy viewed as his job—his *duty*—to circumvent. He wanted Zannino's help.

"Well, how do I get to them?" Jimmy asked. "I guess it's like anybody else, you've got to make a compelling pitch with some value to get their attention."

"Sure," Zannino said. "Make a compelling pitch. Value always gets people's attention."

"Should I call Peter?" Jimmy asked.

"If you call Peter—" Zannino paused. "I mean, nobody has put a number to them, so it's easy to say it's not for sale."

It was true. The family's stance remained untested. They had been carefully shielded, it seemed. Later, some in the family would describe what they termed the "unholy alliance" between Peter Kann and Bancroft trustee and Hemenway & Barnes lawyer Roy Hammer.

Hemenway & Barnes, one of the oldest law firms in Boston and a specialist in managing the city's old, private money, relied heavily on the Bancroft account, which was its main source of business. The firm's relationship with the family dated back to World War II, when "Grandpa" Barron's daughter Jane, left alone after her husband's suicide—he was a depressive who some in the family say was driven mad by his father-in-law's abuses—hired the firm to protect the family fortune. Since then, the thirty-lawyer practice—with the motto "A Wealth of Experience"—had grown in power within the family with each successive generation. As family trustees died, Hemenway lawyers typically replaced them. The trusts paid Hemenway 6 percent of any income generated, which meant that the generous dividends from Dow Jones's stock produced a reliable stream of money for the law firm—all for keeping things exactly as they were.

Hammer had sold some of the family's stock and bought other investments, an effort to diversify their wealth. Now, Dow Jones stock made up less than half of their assets. But the company was still the greatest single asset the family held in common, and the structure of the trusts automatically divided the generations. Jessie's, Jane's, and Hugh Jr.'s children, known as the "upper generation," received automatic disbursements from the trusts, which came mainly in the form of annual dividends from Dow Jones's stock. They decided how much cash their children received. Mostly, however, the kids could get to the fortune only after their parents' death.

For years, Kann and Hammer successfully rebuffed overtures from interested suitors in an effort to protect the *Wall Street Journal* and their position in the constellation of players who derived both prestige and a sense of self-satisfaction that came from proximity to such a national treasure. Anyone who talked to Kann would hear the same response: that the family was not interested in selling. If he needed confirmation, Kann would call Hammer, an imperious man with an aristocratic air, who repeatedly assured Kann the family hadn't changed its mind. Hammer turned down expressions of interest and informed Kann afterward.

Jimmy scribbled:

MAKE COMPELLING PITCH. VALUE TO GET ATTENTION
CALL PETER—NOBODY HAS PUT A NUMBER TO THEM—EASY
TO SAY IT'S NOT FOR SALE

"You'd need to talk to a board member who gets it," Zannino said. "If you go to Peter, he doesn't even report to the board until after the fact," Zannino added. "Go to Roy with a number."

Jimmy's pen busily noted the instructions:

2. BOARD MEMBER WHO GETS IT
3. GO TO PETER—DOESN'T EVEN REPORT
4. GO TO ROY WITH #.

Jimmy had studied Dow Jones for years, but now he had an insider. Zannino had just handed Jimmy a playbook for how to scale the seemingly impenetrable wall that surrounded Dow Jones.

Jimmy continued to press Zannino about the best way to approach the company. Zannino knew enough of the directors to provide some insight into the dynamics on the board.

Jimmy started a new page on his notepad.

Jimmy had to understand, Zannino explained, the family thinks they are protecting the *Journal* by keeping Dow Jones independent. Despite the failing stock price, some in the family thought selling a single share in the company was an act of disloyalty. "That's what they believe and that's what Peter believes," he said. They would sell only if they could have some kind of assurance that the company would remain at least partly independent.

FAMILY WANTS ASSURANCE—COMPANY STAYS INDEPENDENT.

"It's like somebody making an offer for your store; you still want to be able to manage it," Zannino offered. "They care about the independence of the *Journal*."

OFFER FOR YOUR STORE—INDEPENDENCE OF THE JOURNAL

Jimmy understood all that, and it sounded like the typical noises of a family business before it sold. The Bancrofts, he perceived, all wanted assurances and to be dragged across the finish line. What he needed to know was how to make the approach.

"Who else is on the board?" Jimmy wanted to know. "Who might 'get it'?"

Zannino mentioned four board members. Three of them had been nominated in 1997 to bring some outside voices to an insular board: former American Express chief Harvey Golub, former Bankers Trust chairman Frank Newman, and former Pfizer CEO Bill Steere. Former Hallmark CEO Irv Hockaday was a long-serving board member and the company's lead director. Of those four, Harvey, Irv, and Frank were the closest to Peter Kann.

HARVEY NEWMAN HOCKADAY STEERE
OF THEM, HARVEY, IRV & FRANK

After the two hung up, Jimmy filed his notes away in a thin red folder marked "DOW JONES." He called Rupert Murdoch to update him on the conversation. He told Murdoch, again, that Zannino understood the company's strategic dilemma. There were many hurdles yet to clear, but Jimmy sensed, as he put down the phone that day, this time it really could happen.

Peter Kann's love of journalism began early. At age nine, he started publishing the "Jefferson Road Snooper" (with the help of his mother) in his leafy Princeton, New Jersey, neighborhood. In high school, he worked for his local paper, the *Princeton Packet*, owned by Barney Kilgore, who transformed the *Journal* from a narrow investment daily to the nation's business paper. At Harvard, Kann reported for the *Crimson*. After college, he was hired by the *Journal* as a reporter in the Pittsburgh bureau in 1964.

Glynn Mapes, who started at the *Journal* a year before Peter Kann, remembered the young reporter: "He was a really nice guy who didn't give a damn about business stories. The word was he never wrote one, and he never wore a wristwatch. He also rarely had a word changed by any of his editors." From San Francisco, Kann quickly moved to Los Angeles and then abroad to Asia, where, at twenty-four, he became the paper's first resident reporter in Vietnam. (One of his stories told of a nine-nostriled water snake that South Vietnamese villagers feared more than the Vietcong.) By the early seventies, when he won a Pulitzer for his coverage of the 1971 India-Pakistan war, Kann had become something of a romantic figure. For ten years he lived in an antique-filled apartment halfway up Victoria Peak in Hong Kong. He owned a motorized junk and hosted what became legendary poker games.

Kann's worried mother, if she hadn't heard from him for several weeks, would call the paper's Page One editor, Michael Gartner (later of NBC News), to check on her son's whereabouts. The first time she contacted him, Gartner heard her heavy Austrian accent—

she and her husband were refugees of Jewish descent who arrived in the United States during World War II—and answered her question truthfully: he hadn't heard from Kann in weeks. This news upset her greatly, and so the next time Gartner stretched the truth. "I just out-and-out lied to her," he remembered. "I'd say, 'Oh, yes, I just talked to him yesterday.' Or this morning. And she'd say, 'Where is he?' And I'd say, 'He's in a hotel room somewhere.' And then I'd send him a wire: Peter, call your mother."

In 1974, the *Journal* hired Karen Elliott, a tall, outspoken blonde reporter from the Texas panhandle, to work in its DC bureau. She worked her way up through the ranks of the *Journal* with the same intelligence and grit she had developed in the tiny town of Matador, Texas, from her churchgoing parents, who forbade a television or phone in the house and didn't allow her to date. In 1975 she married Art House, a Connecticut-bred power broker in Washington who later served as staff director to Senator Robert Byrd. In 1978 she became the paper's diplomatic correspondent.

It was around this time that Kann revealed his surprising interest in more managerial pursuits. After charming the company's CEO, Warren Phillips, Kann won the task of starting up the Asian *Journal* in 1976. To do it, he conscripted the paper's Tokyo bureau chief, Norman Pearlstine, who would become a close friend. Back then, the business and news sides of the company were divided by almost religious writ. In the *Journal*'s San Francisco bureau, sales executives and reporters played handball together outside the office, but when Monday morning came around, the salesmen were forbidden to step inside the paper's newsroom. In New York, the advertising staff was similarly banned from physically entering the reporters' sphere.

"Peter was the most talented storyteller and writer I've ever met, and I never understood why with that much raw talent would he not want to continue writing," says Pearlstine. "He had the gift, so why didn't he want to be a better Halberstam, or a better Talese? I'm not saying he didn't have to sweat his stories, but I saw that gift as almost supernatural."

By 1980 Kann was the associate publisher of the *Journal* in the United States and widely recognized as the company's likely next CEO of Dow Jones. He and Karen House met at a party in Washington in 1981. They were both still married but separated from their spouses. House was dating a Washington, DC–based television anchor named Charlie Rose at the time. Her relationship with Kann became common knowledge by 1982 among some in the *Journal*'s New York bureau. After telling the paper's executive editor, Fred Taylor, that he and House were together, Kann added that since House didn't report to him, he didn't think it would pose a problem.

Kann's first wife died in July 1983. House and her first husband were divorced in August. Word of their relationship officially emerged when Kann joined House, then the *Journal*'s assistant foreign editor, on a trip to the Middle East in 1984, where she was following Jordan's King Hussein. She had just filed a series of stories on him to Page One and called then–Page One editor Glynn Mapes to complain about his editing. The conversation became heated, and soon House and Mapes were shouting at each other.

"Your stuff reads like a book jacket," Mapes yelled as his editors listened, engrossed. (The lead-in to her first piece was a series of quotes strung together without transition.) And then, after a pause, "Oh, hi, Peter," Mapes said.

Always the conciliator, Kann had picked up the phone. He told Mapes, "You two should cool on this for a while and you can get back together when tempers have mellowed." The series ran days later on the front page of the paper as the gossip surged.

Thanks to the call, what had been insider knowledge among those in New York quickly spread through the newsroom and out to the bureaus. Kann and House married shortly after she won the Pulitzer for her series in the spring of 1984. That same year, House became the *Journal*'s foreign editor. But by the time Kann was named publisher in 1989, House's temper and forthrightness had created enemies throughout Dow Jones's empire. Kann's promotion to CEO of Dow Jones in 1991 left many House haters cringing.

As Kann and House soared, the company declined. While competitors such as Bloomberg, Reuters, and Time Inc. kept growing, Dow Jones struggled to expand beyond its core businesses, the *Journal* and Dow Jones Newswires. A piecemeal purchase of financial data provider Telerate—totaling $1.6 billion—was beginning to fall apart. That same year, just after Kann took the helm, Dow Jones bungled an opportunity to acquire Financial News Network, a business cable channel later picked up by General Electric Company and merged with its existing business channel, CNBC.

Gun-shy from such failures, Dow Jones's management and board of directors became increasingly risk averse. As the company's profits diminished, an increasing proportion of them went to dividend payments largely destined for the Bancrofts.

2

Cousins

ISSURES IN THE Bancrofts' normally united front of the Dow Jones family may have first appeared after Jessie Bancroft Cox dropped dead at the '21' Club in 1982. But the world had no notion of the rifts until another of the family's *grandes dames* met her demise. When Elisabeth Goth's mother—Bettina Bancroft—died of cancer in 1996, Elisabeth (an only child after the tragic death of her younger brother, Michael) became the woman to please. Thanks to the structure of the family's trusts, the thirty-two-year-old heiress was the only member of the family who received the trust's income and, because she had no children, remained a beneficiary.

Elisabeth grew up in the most removed of the Bancrofts' three branches. Of Clarence Barron's three grandchildren, Jessie Cox's restive contingent spent summers at her lush Cohasset estate; Jane Cook's children and grandchildren also gathered in New England. But Hugh Bancroft Jr.'s descendants—among them Bettina Bancroft and her daughter, Elisabeth—traded the East for more pioneering locales out West. Adding to their isolation, Hugh Jr. had divorced Bettina's mother, then remarried and had three more children. Bettina became a stepchild in her own family.

Elisabeth's parents—Bettina and her first husband, Michael Goth Sr.—married young and wandered free. "We moved constantly," Elisabeth later remembered. By the time she was ten, she had been uprooted eight times, moving between bucolic Dutchess County in New

York State to Corona del Mar, California; Greenwich, Connecticut; Riverside, California; Palm Beach, Florida; Amherst, Massachusetts; and finally Los Angeles, where the family settled. All the while, her young parents fought and occasionally lived apart. At one point, Bettina moved back to California to finish her studies; Michael moved away to race cars in England. As a result, Elisabeth and her brother shuttled between coasts to follow their parents and kept up as best they could with the fast pace. As a child, Elisabeth developed a love for horses, where she found a welcome consistency in her otherwise tumultuous world. "The whole environment that my brother and I grew up in wasn't really like, oh, happy family time."

Before L.A., the only sign of her family's wealth and power was that she lived in the biggest house on the block—Elisabeth didn't know her family owned the most powerful business paper in the country. But by the time she was an adolescent and spending much of her time in Bel Air, she was surrounded by the likes of Billy Wilder, Merv Griffin, and the Disney family. When Mel Brooks and Anne Bancroft were playing tennis in her friend's backyard, Elisabeth realized that the Goth residence wasn't any ordinary household.

Soon after the move to Los Angeles, following near-constant arguments and occasional infidelities, Elisabeth's parents divorced. Elisabeth, who was beautiful and blond, with tightly drawn features and quick, almost birdlike movements, started drinking and smoking pot. She was drawn in by the glamour that surrounded her. It was around this time that her mother told her of the family connection to Dow Jones. She occasionally joined Bettina for pilgrimages to New York and the Carlyle Hotel for meetings at the '21' Club, where Jessie Cox presided on the eve of the company's annual meeting each spring. It was the first time Elisabeth had met many of her cousins.

Elisabeth started experimenting with cocaine and heroin as a teenager, and her habit put her in and out of rehabilitation clinics, a source of great pain for her mother, who couldn't quite manage to get her daughter under control. (A friend of her mother's lived with the family in Hollywood for a time and provided Elisabeth with cocaine, which she sometimes sold.) When Elisabeth was twenty-one and relapsing from yet another attempt to get sober, she called both her father and her mother, who were by then long divorced, and begged them to pick her up from the Pasadena psych ward where she was being held after her latest exploit. Convinced, rightly, that she was not mentally ill but an addict, she wanted the right kind of help. But she couldn't avoid a bit of drama. Elisabeth's mother had been dating a good-looking art collector named Andrew Klink. The relationship was serious, and Bettina had hinted at marriage. But Elisabeth saw a problem: Klink's bisexuality.

Bettina willingly overlooked this trait in Klink, but it troubled Elisabeth. And in the car that day on the way to the clinic, she took a stand. She blurted out to her mother that Klink was gay. Her mother flew into a rage. But her protest had little effect; Bettina and Klink were married the following year.

Klink returned Elisabeth's ill will. He remembers her in the least flattering terms. "Heroin, coke, speedballs—she was fucked up all the time," he recalls. "I had to go to the hospital to pick her up after an overdose one night. I got a call from one of her girlfriends saying they thought her heart had stopped.

"She was a problem child from day one—she's a bitch on wheels; spoiled, bright, self-centered, beautiful, but so conniving. She played her mother for everything she had."

At home, Bettina and Klink led typical Hollywood lives: their parties were lavish, they graced only the finest restaurants, and wherever they went, Bettina's fortune guaranteed fawning and the best table in the house. Bettina was a champion rider and "looked like $35 million when she was dressed up," Klink remembers, recalling a particular dress of ostrich plumes. The couple attended cattle barons' balls in Texas for the local ranchers and landowners. In the south of France, they went to parties with Bettina's half brothers, Christopher and Hugh Bancroft III, known as "Wink," who split his time between Switzerland and Monaco with his first wife, a Dutch-Brazilian model, working on a prototype for a racecar. Elisabeth saw the darker side of her mother and Klink's life together: "I knew she was unhappy with him. I have all her diaries."

The Bancrofts' ownership in Dow Jones was funneled through an overlapping web of trusts. Many of the trusts were generation-skipping, which meant that the trustees (Bettina's generation) received income from the shares in the trusts, typically through Dow Jones's

quarterly dividends, and their offspring (Elisabeth) were the beneficiaries, dependent on the value of Dow Jones's stock. With Bettina's
death, Elisabeth had become, for the purposes of family wealth, a
member of two successive Bancroft generations. She inherited most
of the roughly seven hundred thousand shares her mother owned in
Dow Jones—worth about $23 million at the time. But most of her
fortune and influence stemmed from her position as one of four
beneficiaries of the family's largest trust—Article III, worth about
$350 million. The problem with that wealth was that it was invested
in Dow Jones, and the proceeds wouldn't be distributed to the beneficiaries of the trust until the last member of Bettina's generation died.
With some in their fifties, they had a long way to go. Elisabeth met
with family friend and financial adviser Brian McNally, who painted
her a grim picture of the company and its prospects. Thanks to the
performance of the Telerate business, Dow Jones had become the
worst-performing stock in the S&P 500 publishing index the year of
Bettina's death.

Elisabeth, less sentimental than her forebears, faced a choice
about how to deal with the legacy—and fortune—she had inherited.
Would she continue to politely ignore the performance of her family's company? Or would she, in an unprecedented manner, challenge
the status quo that her mother had accepted? Even though she knew
about the company's lagging performance, when she looked at the effect of it on her inheritance, she was shocked. Dow Jones was in a deep
slide and her fortune was in peril. Her horses, the leisurely life in California, all of a sudden seemed more precarious. Since her mother's
death, she had battled for what was rightfully hers. She fought Klink
over Bettina's will. (A particularly memorable battle broke out over
who would walk away with the Hermès beach towels. Klink, desperate for money, held a garage sale at Bettina's home.) Then she took
on the family's lawyers, who had been omnipresent since the funeral.
Accustomed to acquiescence, the attorneys seemed to be attempting
to use her lack of experience to exert even more control over how she
dealt with her Dow Jones stock.

Roy Hammer had been the Bancrofts' most powerful representative at Hemenway & Barnes since he took over the lead trustee role
for the family in the 1970s, a quarter of a century before Bettina's

death. Tall and slim, with expressive white eyebrows, Hammer was careful with his words—the pauses between his sentences could seem interminable. He guarded the relationship with the family fiercely in his laconic, high-handed way. Years before, Hammer had feuded with the elder Bancrofts—Jessie Cox and Jane Cook, "the old ladies," as they were known at Dow Jones—after he sold shares in the company in the 1980s. It was an act of disloyalty they wouldn't abide. The relationship healed, but the younger Bancrofts often felt dismissed by him.

"Roy Hammer was like the don and all the rest were really the henchmen that were sort of carrying out his orders," complained Elisabeth's third cousin Billy Cox III, who, when he wasn't voicing displeasure with Hemenway & Barnes, was often heard deriding the company's management—Peter Kann in particular—and his father's loyalty to both. By the time Elisabeth's mother died, he was itching for a fight.

Hammer and his younger partners, Michael Puzo and Michael Elefante, knew of Elisabeth's reputation within the family: she was a dilettante, and then there were the well-known drug problems. (Hammer had personally helped her out of a few jams.) She wasn't what anyone in Boston envisioned as the most reliable of stewards. Elisabeth, who detected their unarticulated disapproval, put her foot down. She was sick of Hemenway's attitude. She saw them in cahoots with Peter Kann in diminishing her fortune through neglect.

Billy Cox III was one of the few family members ever to have actually worked for the company, most recently as managing director of Dow Jones Global Indexes. He shared Elisabeth's lack of sentimentality, her disdain for the frosty lawyers, and her aversion to losing money. He was more than willing to help Elisabeth exert her new-found influence. He looked up to his grandmother Jessie Cox, and felt that his father, Bill Cox Jr., who also worked for the company in a middle-management role, hadn't stepped into the role of patriarch that Billy wished for him. Billy had met Elisabeth as a child, on her occasional trips to join his family in Nantucket for summer vacation. The two had always been friendly. Now, with Bettina's death and Elisabeth's new inheritance, he found his opportunity. He approached her at the Hotel Bel-Air reception Elisabeth was hosting after the funeral. He wanted to commiserate over mismanagement at the company.

Billy, who considered himself more of a businessman than anyone else in his clan, had weeks before been reading through Warren Buffett's 1993 letter to shareholders, when he came upon a paragraph that mentioned Dow Jones. Buffett, the legendarily wise Omaha investor who regularly doled out advice to worthy listeners, had mentioned the firm and its uninvolved owners. Billy was intrigued. He asked a friend if he could help set up a meeting. Then came Bettina's funeral, and Elisabeth. Billy thought his cousin, with her newfound power over the family fortune, might be just the right person to come with him to see Buffett.

Bancrofts—proper, unemotional, reticent in all ways—rarely discussed money or business. ("My mother would rather discuss pornography," one said.) Amid all the drama of the funeral and the inheritance, Elisabeth wasn't quite prepared for Billy's approach—but she wasn't surprised. She knew him well enough to expect some rabble-rousing from this like-minded soul. When Billy asked the young heiress if she would come to Omaha, Elisabeth looked past her grief and agreed to accompany Billy to the meeting. The times, quite suddenly, were changing.

The following year provided a whirlwind education for Elisabeth and her cousin in the subtleties of family control. A few weeks after her mother's funeral, Elisabeth was on a plane to meet Buffett. Awed by the prospect of meeting such an esteemed investment mind, Elisabeth dressed up in her favorite white Chloé suit. She prepared herself to hear what kind of advice the mentor to the Washington Post Company's Kay Graham might have. Elisabeth was a newspaper heiress of a new generation and of a different ilk from Mrs. Graham. She didn't want to run the company; she just wanted it to make money for her. With Billy at her side, she approached Buffett's legendarily modest Berkshire Hathaway headquarters and explained their situation to him. They were frustrated with Dow Jones's management and their inability to break through with Hemenway & Barnes. Billy's frustration showed, and he appeared petulant in front of Buffett. Elisabeth, the more savvy and self-aware of the two, made a better impression.

They thought Dow Jones's management was doing a poor job of running the company, but they couldn't find anyone in a position of power to give them a serious hearing. At the time, Billy's father, William Cox Jr., and Elisabeth's uncle Chris Bancroft, who had taken over Bettina's seat at her request, both served on the board. But even their relatives, or rather, especially their relatives on the board, wouldn't hear of any complaints about the company. Chris Bancroft lived in suburban Dallas with his wife, an accomplished bassoonist and arts philanthropist whom George W. Bush named to the Texas Commission on the Arts while he was governor. Tall and athletic and an avid sportsman, Chris ran a small investment company where he mainly managed his own fortune. He was a disappointment to many in the family, who had expected him to take a more active leadership role, perhaps even as a patriarch. He felt more comfortable on the sidelines. Yes, the performance was disappointing, but the "professionals" were taking care of it. Certainly neither Billy nor Elisabeth had the expertise to judge the company's management, they were told time and again. Elisabeth met Buffett alone several times after that first meeting and spoke with him regularly.

Buffett told them something different: they had standing at the company, especially Elisabeth in her new role as an income beneficiary of the huge Article III trust. They should use it to prod management, Buffett advised. "Act like owners," he said. He suggested they contact Tom Murphy, who ran Capital Cities/ABC with Buffett as his largest shareholder, to sound him out about taking on a role at Dow Jones.

Elisabeth went about hiring a team of advisers better equipped to mount a company takeover than to advise a young thirty-two-year-old woman on her inheritance. Her financial adviser McNally was a friend of Nancy Peretsman of the boutique media investment bank Allen & Company, whose yearly summer Sun Valley conference was a breeding ground for stratospheric media networking that sometimes led to very lucrative deals. (The seeds of Disney's acquisition of Capital Cities/ABC began there when Michael Eisner sat down with Buffett and Murphy and proposed buying the firm.) Elisabeth and Billy went to see Peretsman, who listened carefully to their complaints. She then laid out the dismal prospects of Dow Jones. The stock was trading at around $36 a share in 1996, down from its then high of $56.25 in 1987 (missing one of the great bull markets in history). Profits had been roughly flat for the past ten years, at about $185 million. When Peretsman compared the company to its peers, she offered a stark picture: ten years before, Dow Jones and Reuters had the same market capitalization of $3.5 billion. In 1996, Reuters's market capitalization was more than $20 billion, while Dow Jones's stayed stuck at $3.5 billion. The only number that had continued to rise consistently over the past decade, Peretsman noted, was the amount the company had paid out in dividends, much of which went to the Bancroft family elders. In 1986, dividends totaled $53.6 million and were the primary source of income to the trusts. Ten years later, the number had climbed to more than $90 million, about 50 percent of Dow Jones's net income. To the untrained eye, it looked as if Dow Jones was paying off the Bancroft elders to keep them out of company affairs.

Nancy Peretsman became Elisabeth's close confidante in the ensuing months. (Stan Shuman, Allen & Company's managing director, was Rupert Murdoch's banker, a connection that was, at the time, unspoken and unnoticed, at least by Elisabeth.) Peretsman introduced Elisabeth to Ira Millstein, the influential corporate governance sage of Weil, Gotshal & Manges, who quickly took on the cousins' case. Elisabeth soon had some of the most powerful names in Corporate America on her side battling the entrenched lawyers at Hemenway & Barnes.

Early on, she wanted to confide in her new group of advisers. "I had been arrested for drugs. I had a felony charge. I wanted them all to know right up front because I knew it would come out," she remembers. Buffett, in particular, didn't care. He encouraged her to seek a seat on the board. "Warren did say, 'Well, who are they comparing you with, Jesus Christ? Everybody's got skeletons in the closet. That's ridiculous.'"

The confession—and absolution—emboldened Elisabeth. She and Billy called on cousins of their generation who might be sympathetic to their cause, and family elders who were not. Whenever she doubted her path, there was an army of her advisers cheering her on, unlike her family, who seemed only to withhold and judge.

Billy could not contain his enthusiasm for the progress they seemed to be making. "Finally," he thought, "we'll get the company to where it needs to be." As he and Elisabeth continued their crusade, word eventually trickled out—"It was very orchestrated," Billy remembers—about the dissatisfaction within the family. "Disgruntled Heiress Leads Revolt at Dow Jones" appeared in the February 3, 1997, issue of *Fortune* magazine, publicizing the cousins' attempt to challenge Peter Kann and the lawyers at Hemenway & Barnes. The piece laid out all the company's ugly numbers and talked about family rifts.

Even the elders who wanted to gloss over the troubles couldn't deny them: "I think Lizzie is very much behind the company," Martha Robes, a family board member and one of Jane Cook's New England daughters, told *Fortune* at the time. Robes was particularly close to Kann and lived in Etna, New Hampshire. She was a member of the older generation and had inherited her mother's blind loyalty. "But she's listening to a lot of outsiders . . . who are getting her all wound up." Later that year, Robes resigned from Dow Jones's board from her sailboat, where she and her furniture-maker husband had begun a six-and-a-half-year circumnavigation of the globe.

Though there had been tension before, airing the dirty laundry in the press was a step too far. Elisabeth's uncle Chris barely spoke to her. Billy left his job at Dow Jones just before the article appeared. (He wrote a resignation fax and left a voice mail for his boss; he packed his office over the weekend.) After the story appeared, Hemenway & Barnes called an emergency meeting of the family, extracting loyalty oaths from each of the attendees. The four family members on the board—(Elisabeth's uncle) Christopher Bancroft; (Billy's father) William Cox Jr.; his sister Jane MacElree, the Hill family matriarch; and Martha Robes—decided to make their own public statement, which they did to the *Wall Street Journal* and *Fortune*. The outrage under the surface was hard to detect in the tight-jawed statement:

We are members of the Bancroft family and directors of Dow Jones & Co. On behalf of the family, which has controlled the company for nearly a century, we want to respond to your recent articles so that there can be no misunderstanding about our family's long-term commitment to Dow Jones.

The Bancroft family met this past weekend at one of our regular meetings. At that meeting family members representing all parts of our family unanimously reaffirmed their commitment to Dow Jones's remaining an independent public company and the world's premier business news and information company. The family has absolutely no interest in relinquishing control of this important and unique enterprise. At the same time, as owners, we, along with the rest of the board of directors and management, want to see increasing shareholder value over the long term.

A sound system of corporate oversight is critical to the success of the company. Dow Jones has a long history of strong and capable independent directors. We all believe that this tradition should be continued.

The family is confident about the future of this great company and fully intends to be part of it.

The cozy relationship between Dow Jones and its ruling family was never the same. Billy and Elisabeth were thrown together by the circumstances of their rebellion and grew closer. But their actions catapulted Dow Jones & Company into a most unwelcome spotlight and put Elisabeth and Billy at bitter odds with the elder generation of Bancrofts. They forever cemented their joint reputation as Bancroft family rogues.

The articles heightened Murdoch's interest in Dow Jones, and he lined up with the other circling CEOs—among them Don Graham of the Washington Post Company, Arthur Sulzberger of the New York Times Company, and Marjorie Scardino of Pearson PLC—to see Kann. Murdoch, obviously not the most prized suitor on this occasion, eventually got a meeting. He had heard about Kann—the Pulitzer Prize–winning CEO with the close relationship to the Bancroft family. Murdoch told Kann he'd love to own Dow Jones; Kann told him it wasn't for sale. He might as well have added the words "especially not to you."

Though he had a global empire of cable networks, movie studios, and satellite businesses, Murdoch loved to think of himself as a newspaperman at heart. The identity, inherited from his father, Keith, was as important to him as the trappings that came along with his wealth and held far more appeal than the other entertainment holdings Murdoch had acquired. The *Wall Street Journal* and the *New York Times* were the best newspapers in the United States, Murdoch's adopted home. Owning either paper would be the epitome of being a newspaperman. (Owing to its conservative editorial page and its devoted coverage of the business world, Murdoch had always preferred the *Journal*. He had once joked in front of a crowd of admiring CEOs, "I'd love to buy the *New York Times* one day. And the next day shut it down as a public service.") And he always enjoyed owning a hometown paper. "From 1988 to 1993 were probably the unhappiest years of his life," notes his longtime former general counsel Arthur Siskind. "It was the only time in his adult life that he lived in a city [where] he didn't own a newspaper."

Despite the pressure, Kann survived, though even his most loyal supporters had begun to doubt his skill as a CEO. The nepotism factor, too, troubled the Bancrofts. In an age when modern boardrooms were bowing to shareholder pressure and demanding CEO performance, a husband-and-wife team atop a publicly traded company was difficult to defend. To appease the family, Dow Jones appointed some new independent directors to its board in 1997, ones who were meant to increase the professional quotient on the board and keep management in check. The family, eager for a more forceful presence on the board, pushed for Hammer to take a seat as a director.

Murdoch would remember his meeting with Kann for years to come. Kann dismissed the meeting so entirely that ten years later, he couldn't be sure it had even happened.

After the *Fortune* piece surfaced, Jimmy Lee called Roy Hammer and asked him, "What do we need to do?" There was a motive, of course, in this method: he thought the financial stress of the Telerate debacle—Dow Jones had to take a nearly $1 billion write-down in its investment in the firm the year after Bettina died—might help move the Bancrofts toward selling. But Hammer, loyal to the family elders and mindful of his 6 percent fee derived from the company's generous dividends, was characteristically standoffish and gave Jimmy little hope.

Jimmy had continued to think about ways the mogul Murdoch might move on his prey, and he broke through personally with him at Herbert Allen's Sun Valley conference in 1998, nearly a year and a half after the world learned of Elisabeth's revolt. Jimmy was pleased to be attending the conference; he was the only investment banker allowed inside the exclusive gathering of the world's most powerful media executives and their families. He had been coming since 1994, and every year he plotted his movements carefully. Ever since the meeting here between Buffett, Michael Eisner, and Tom Murphy in 1995 sparked the merger between Disney and Capital Cities/ABC, the demand to attend the gathering had exploded. The guest list expanded, and the relaxed cocktail parties, hayrides, and white-water rafting outings promised billions of dollars in business to attendees who made the most of their visit.

One by one, the gleaming Cessnas, Falcons, and Gulfstream jets filed into the small Hailey airport, on the edge of the Sawtooth Forest, their passengers transferring to SUVs that whisked them to the green oasis that was the Sun Valley resort in the shadow of Dollar Mountain, transformed every year into a high-powered playground for media barons. The conference took over the entire town that week. Herbert Allen was one of the most powerful bankers in the entertainment and communications business, and he drew his pick of influential and rich moguls each year to the resort where Ernest Hemingway had started to write *For Whom the Bell Tolls*. The conference had grown considerably to four hundred or so attendees and now included tech geeks such as Microsoft's Bill Gates and Intel Corp.'s Andy Grove—but Allen still reached for the old Hollywood glamour that had initially defined the gathering. Everything was studiously casual, and Allen wrote a personal note to every conference goer that was waiting in his or her suite or cottage upon arrival, often perched on the fleece jackets Allen doled out each year for chilly nights. Jimmy kept close tabs on who would be invited to the chalet-style resort, and once in his room, he carefully looked through the meticulous conference agenda and list of attendees.

He had come that year to Sun Valley troubled by the fact that while JPMorgan had a leading relationship with almost every big media firm in the world, there was a glaring hole: News Corporation. As he looked through the conference schedule of speakers and their topics, he noted the mix of mogul and celebrity—Barry Diller, Edgar Bronfman Jr., Harvey Weinstein, Diane Sawyer, Tom Brokaw—and his eyes stopped and lingered on three names: Lachlan Murdoch, Rupert Murdoch, James Murdoch.

His opening to introduce himself to this dynasty came at the cocktail party by the resort pool Friday night, where Jimmy had arrived early. He grabbed himself a beer and amid the quietly gathering crowd, he noticed the three Murdochs, off by themselves, seemingly unaware of any alternative purpose to the night other than enjoying a beer in the evening sun. Murdoch was tanned from time on his yacht, the *Morning Glory,* where he worked as obsessively as he did in his office in midtown Manhattan. The only difference was that on the yacht Murdoch traded pinstripes for casual slacks and open-necked shirts.

The Murdoch sons were conspicuously young—in their late twenties and vulnerable after the shock of their father's separation from their mother a few months before, which they still thought might just be temporary. All their lives, the younger men had alternately sought or shunned their father's approval, but on that night, as the CEOs and founders hovered, the three Murdochs appeared relaxed and supremely comfortable with one another, despite the marital discord. Surrounded by his sons and his fellow robber barons, Murdoch was in his element.

As Jimmy Lee approached this triumvirate of casual ease and staggering wealth, he saw generations of business before him. Happy-go-lucky Lachlan was the deputy chief operating officer of News Corporation, running the company's thirty-five TV stations, its Australian newspapers, the *New York Post,* and HarperCollins. As the elder son, he was the heir apparent (temporarily, as it played out) to all his father had created. Murdoch said at the time that the children had reached a "consensus" that Lachlan would take over for him. "The children selected him," he said. "It was their vote." James was fifteen months younger than Lachlan. He had yet to rise to the role of his brother's challenger. Lachlan was still seen as the Murdoch most like his father. He had started out working as an apprentice with the printers in the pressroom of Murdoch's Adelaide paper, the one from which Murdoch had grown his empire. He was also, at least at this time, the least rebellious of the children. James had dropped out of college but quickly came back into the fold, joining News Corp. in 1996, and was at the time working, with only limited success, on scouting out digital investments for News Corp. Their sister, Elisabeth, almost thirty, was at the time of the conference running digital operations for Murdoch's SkyTV satellite operator. She had given birth the previous year to her second child with Vassar classmate Elkin Pianim, the son of a once imprisoned opposition figure in Ghana. More recently, Elisabeth had begun an affair with public relations impresario Matthew Freud, great-grandson of Sigmund, much to the delight of the British tabloid press. She and Pianim divorced, and her father hadn't approved of any of it. Prudence, Murdoch's eldest daughter and only child of his first marriage, lived in Australia and stayed out of the succession race.

At the time of Jimmy's approach, the sons and their father were in the middle of talking about a subject near and dear to their hearts: their workouts. James was slim, a black belt in karate; Lachlan, a hunkier-looking athletic type with spiked hair and a tribal tattoo. The men compared notes and swapped stories. "Do you lift?" Jimmy asked. "Do you run?" It was a comfortable, manly conversation between a banker and moguls, and Lachlan asked Jimmy if he would like to work out the following day.

"Geez, I'd love to. No sweat," Jimmy replied. "What time?"

"Oh, around five," Lachlan said.

"Great, but doesn't dinner start then?" Jimmy asked.

"No," Lachlan corrected. "We meant five in the morning." Jimmy got up early to make the appointment.

Murdoch, always seeking to guarantee his longevity, was accompanied by the former captain of the Australian Rugby team, who was traveling with him. The men worked out together and discussed, among other things, Dow Jones. After Jimmy flew back to New York, he drew up a "book"—a financial brief—outlining how Dow Jones could fit into News Corp.

Soon after, back in New York at a Fox News party, Jimmy sought out Murdoch to tell him, "I've done a lot of work on Dow Jones." He presented the book to Murdoch and his loyal chief financial officer,

Dave DeVoe, with whom he discussed the logistics of how such an offer might work, such as whether to offer News Corp. stock to buy the
company or just cash, or a combination of the two. Jimmy was determined that JPMorgan would land some News Corp. business, and so
he stayed in touch, always looking for ways to be useful to Murdoch.
With Hammer and Kann still in place at Dow Jones, however, no
one could make much progress. "The art of the possible wasn't possible while we had guys who wouldn't have the conversation," Jimmy
remembered.

3

The Unraveling

O N THE COLD MORNING of November 12, 2005, Mike Elefante arrived in New York with an unlikely ally for an unprecedented task. He was joining with one of his most persistent critics in the Bancroft family—Leslie Hill—to drive Peter Kann, Dow Jones's most powerful executive, from his chair.

Elefante had earlier that spring taken over Roy Hammer's seat on Dow Jones's board. Elefante, the son of a New Jersey hairdresser, grew up far from the country estates inhabited by his clients. He had been working for Hemenway & Barnes since 1970, a year out of Harvard Law School, and had grown to know the New England Bancroft sisters after working for years as a lawyer on their account. Elefante now served as a trustee on almost half of the family's trusts.

Like his imperious predecessor, he had long held the view that Dow Jones was best as an independent company under the control of the Bancroft family. Unlike his predecessor, however, he was open and friendly. Tall, with salt-and-pepper hair, he kept a mustache long after it was out of fashion.

In the spring of 2005, Elefante was facing an increasingly restless Bancroft family. Throughout Elisabeth's campaign, one group of cousins had watched her travails with particular interest. The Hill family—rooted in Philadelphia but spread now to Hawaii, California, and up and down the East Coast from Washington, DC, to Boston's quiet suburbs—were by far the least glamorous of the Bancrofts. They were argumentative, a trait the more docile factions of the Bancroft clan blamed on their upbringing. The Hill matriarch, Jane MacElree—married to Louis Hill, an ambitious, hard-working Pennsylvania lawyer and state senator who left her in 1975 for the campaign manager of his unsuccessful Philadelphia mayoral campaign—had encouraged her children to discuss the events of the day, and disagree, at the dinner table. With seven children, the family couldn't help but be a touch cacophonous, an unusual trait in the broader family tree and one that made MacElree and her children particularly irritating to Roy Hammer and Peter Kann. Unlike their cousins, they held down unglamorous jobs and seemed the unlikeliest of newspaper scions. MacElree's oldest son, Crawford, was a high school biology teacher; his youngest brother, Michael, worked as an environmental scientist; their oldest sister, Leslie, was a retired airline pilot. They didn't keep horses the way their cousins did, race cars, or throw elegant dinner parties. They lived in relatively modest houses with threadbare furniture and came to their lawyers' offices carrying documents in tattered bags.

They did, however, take great interest in the business of Dow Jones. Growing up, the Hill family visited Jessie Cox's rambling mansion on Cohasset Harbor. The Hill kids played with their Cox cousins—Billy Cox III among them—and dug through Clarence Barron's old trunks full of his canes and hats that their grandmother kept in the attic, using the paraphernalia as props for plays.

Leslie Hill was the Hills' representative on the Dow Jones board of directors. Her decidedly demanding profession suited her perfectly. She was the picture of WASPy practicality. She wore no makeup, and her brown hair ran chin length and showed streaks of gray. Her husband, whom she met at a flight school on Cape Cod, loved her willful manner. Like her siblings and cousins, she didn't advertise the family's connection to the paper. Her house, on a leafy block in suburban Washington, DC, was filled with modest sofas and armchairs that had been clawed by the family cat. Many of her neighbors knew her only as a pilot, not as a member of the Bancroft dynasty.

Inside her family, she was well known for her stubbornness. She tended to disagree with whoever was speaking or whatever proposal was on the table at that moment. She loved Dow Jones, but she was tired of what she saw as the company's inept management. If some-body came along to save the company, she would support him or her. Unless she decided she wouldn't.

Even beyond the Hills, the goodwill that had extended to Kann im-mediately following the attacks of September 11 was dwindling. The dot-com bubble had deflated, and the flight of advertisers from news-papers hit the *Journal* harder than most; the paper had lost money for the past three years. Kann, ever unflappable, had come up with a reassuring refrain for investors, employees, and Bancrofts: these were cyclical problems, just part of the ups and downs of the eco-nomic cycle. The Internet had come and gone, he reasoned, and this scare, too, would pass. But this explanation was losing credibility.

The company was desperately trying to dig itself out of the print medium's decline and move the paper itself beyond the technology and financial advertising on which it relied so heavily. In January of that year, at the urging of Zannino and Gordon Crovitz, president of Dow Jones's electronic publishing division, Dow Jones had bought the financial news site MarketWatch.com, to expose the company to what executives hoped would be a boom in online advertising. The *Journal* was planning to launch a weekend edition of the paper, cov-ering "soft" topics such as food, fashion, and what Karen House called "the business of life," to attract a wider range of advertisers to the pa-per. The company was in need of rescue. Revenues at the *Journal* had fallen nearly 9 percent in the first quarter of the year.

Michael Hill, the Hill clan's youngest brother, was a grown man living outside Boston. He was close to his older brothers Crawford, the high school teacher, and Tom, a documentary filmmaker and cor-porate videographer, and seemed the mildest and most patient of the bunch. The Cohasset house had served as a daycare center of sorts for him when his older siblings followed their parents on vacation out West, hiking the Sierra Mountains and the Grand Tetons. Mike, too young to hike, stayed home for many of these trips and amused himself on a small sand patch his grandmother Jessie had hauled in and dumped on the corner of her property for him. He spent so much time there the family called it "Michael's beach."

With his high-pitched voice, Mike was often drowned out in con-versations with his brothers, who talked over him and cut in when he seemed to meander in his explanations, which happened frequently. None of the Hills had worked for Dow Jones (save a brief stint for Leslie at Dow Jones's library and at one of the company's Ottaway community papers on Cape Cod). Mike seemed to regret his lack of involvement. With soft eyes and a round face topped with feathery brown hair, Mike thought his family should have been more caught up in Dow Jones's business, and was frustrated by the role Hemenway & Barnes played in keeping his family away from the company they owned.

Kann was sixty-two at the time, and as his retirement age approached, Mike, his brothers, and their sister Leslie asked Hammer, and later Elefante, at every opportunity, "What is being done about Peter Kann's succession plan?" Their mother, who served as trustee for a large number of family trusts, asked the same thing. But Hemenway & Barnes seemed to barely listen and quickly dismissed the Hills.

Leslie and her brother Mike were talking frequently in 2005 about the company. As a director bound by the confidentiality of the boardroom, Leslie knew a great deal she couldn't repeat to her brother. That frustrated Mike, who thought that if only the family could have more insight into the company, they could help improve it. One late-spring day that year, in one of their many conversations, Mike, after another failed attempt to get some information out of his sister, said, "You know what? A great Christmas present would be some change before the end of the year." He had no idea that the change was already under way.

The momentum had started early in the year, when James H. Lowell 2nd, a money manager and professional trustee hired by Hemenway & Barnes to advise on the Bancrofts' investments, grew frustrated with what he saw as Hemenway's neglect of its client. Lowell, an outspoken Boston native, was spurred by a combination of chivalry and anger. In one of the family's regular meetings earlier that year at Hemenway & Barnes's antiseptic offices in downtown Boston, Lowell had watched as Hammer dismissed MacElree's questions. "He's treating her like shit," he thought. He had decided to take action.

Lowell's job was to advise Hemenway & Barnes, not to deal directly with the Bancrofts outside of quarterly trustee meetings. But he had been talking to Hammer for years about how the family should take on more of a role at Dow Jones. Hammer ignored him, too. Lowell decided to go straight to the people he thought Hemenway was mistreating. The Bancrofts had to figure out what the hell they were going to do with the company. And Lowell wanted to help them. The first step was getting the Hemenway lawyers out of the way.

Lowell wrote to Jane MacElree in February. "Dear Jane," he began, "I am asking for your help in trying to build a family consensus . . . Why start with you? Simply because your family has perhaps been most critical (deservedly), yet individual complaints are easily dismissed by an arrogant Board of Directors." Lowell went on to say that Kann needed desperately to reduce the company's debt and explain in detail to the family how he planned to fix Dow Jones. He closed by writing that he was making this unusual overture to her not because he wanted to be paid—"I am not looking for any compensation for my efforts"—but because his legacy, as well as the Bancrofts' legacy, was on the line.

Lowell sent a copy of the letter in March to MacElree's brother, William Cox Jr., who was as close a thing as the family had to a patriarch but who, as his son Billy frequently pointed out, couldn't rally the family. Cox, ever loyal to Dow Jones, didn't respond to Lowell. All the while, Lowell kept talking to Mike Hill, who seemed one of the most receptive of the Bancrofts.

Mike, whose nagging tone had begun to irritate Kann, Hammer, and his second cousins in the Cook branch of the family, thought he had found a soul mate in Lowell. "So I'm not crazy," he thought, as he listened to Lowell's ideas about reducing the company's debt and installing the Bancrofts as more active stewards of Dow Jones. Getting more involved in the company seemed appealing; he thought it could be a new life passion.

Mike sat down in April and penned a letter of his own, this one to Peter Kann himself: "When I was growing up," he began, "Dow Jones was one of the most admired companies in the world . . . Unfortunately, the experience for the sixth generation of my family . . . is the opposite." He asked for the family, the company's management, and shareholders to "move from being bystanders to 'upstanders'" and take a more active role at Dow Jones. He asked (echoing Lowell's request) that Dow Jones disclose its three-year business plan to all the members of the Bancroft family and allow them to participate in its revision.

Kann wasn't about to allow a younger member of the Bancroft family to force Dow Jones into revealing its business plan; the request seemed naive. Kann knew from his rounds with Elisabeth and Billy that the family had its weak links, and he knew the Hills had been campaigning against him. He did what he could to keep the family informed about the great journalism they were protecting at Dow Jones, but Dow Jones's business was a different matter. Over the years, Kann had grown close to several members of the family, namely, William Cox Jr., shy Jane Cook, and her three daughters in New England—Martha Robes, Jean Stevenson, and Lisa Steele. He praised and courted the Bancrofts, invited them to his home, and socialized occasionally at their summer houses. He introduced them to the paper's Pulitzer Prize winners every year at the company's annual meeting and talked about how a company could have "values *and* value." He made them feel proud of the paper they controlled and told them that what they were doing—keeping the *Journal* safe from outside encroachments—was important.

Deflecting complaints from the younger generation of Bancrofts was something Kann had grown accustomed to with Elisabeth and Billy. He answered questions with hypothetical responses and never responded to the family's concerns in writing. After he received Mike Hill's letter, he invited him in to meet with two members of Dow Jones's board of directors, Irv Hockaday and Frank Newman. Kann knew they would shoot down what Mike Hill was asking—opening up the company's strategic plan to a thirty-five-member family with a history of talking to the press. He never discussed the letter with Mike but cordially set up the meeting and promised not to attend, to allow a free and frank discussion between this young heir and two distinguished company directors.

Hockaday's wise and steady demeanor had helped persuade many of those whom he encountered of his sagacity and professionalism. A native midwesterner with a flat plains twang, he had previously been CEO of Hallmark, the long-successful family greeting-card company founded by J. C. Hall in 1910. Hockaday also served on the boards of the Estée Lauder Company and the Ford Motor Company, also family controlled and grappling with the modern-day tensions attendant to those situations. Compared to the Fords and the Lauders, the Bancrofts' much discussed "hands-off" approach was notable. Hockaday, who had taken in and learned from the situations and difficulties in all the corporations where he had served, almost certainly considered their distance—dissatisfied as it was—counterproductive. But he was a Princeton man, well bred and disciplined in the patriarchal fashion of old-school companies with familial constituencies. He was effective but rarely ruffled feathers. Frank Newman, the former president and CEO of Bankers Trust and the deputy treasury secretary under President Clinton, had been named to Dow Jones's board to appease the architects of Elisabeth Goth's rebellion eight years before. His résumé was unparalleled, and he was one of the heaviest hitters on the company's board.

Mike Hill came to town that April for the company's annual shareholder meeting, which was open to any and all Dow Jones shareholders and attended by many of the Bancroft cousins. Mike sat in the audience in the World Financial Center tower adjacent to Dow Jones headquarters, where the meeting was held in the American Express Company's auditorium. He watched as Roy Hammer, who had reached the mandatory retirement age of seventy, relinquished his position on Dow Jones's board to the younger Michael B. Elefante, a transition Mike welcomed. He watched as the shareholders approved a measure that would allow his family to sell more Dow Jones stock—thereby raising cash—and still maintain control of the company. Under the previous bylaws, once the family's holdings of super-voting Class B shares fell under 12 million, all of their shares would convert to the regular common stock, and the family would lose control of the company. Under the new measure, officially proposed by the company but actually proposed months earlier by Hammer, in need of a measure to keep the Bancrofts happy, the level down to which the Bancrofts could sell their shares fell to 7.5 million. Such a move flew in the face of modern shareholder democracy, but for the moment, everyone was willing to overlook it in order to keep the Bancroft family happy and in charge.

After the meeting, Mike walked through the breezeway with Hockaday and Newman to Dow Jones's headquarters, and the men made their way up to the company's executive eleventh floor, where the beige carpets were plusher than the soiled blue ones in the newsroom a floor below. In one of the small conference rooms, Mike sat down nervously with Hockaday and Newman. He was looking forward to his audience and felt the weight of his family responsibility. "Maybe we're finally making progress," he thought.

Hockaday and Newman were friendly but standoffish. They didn't reveal anything to Mike. Hockaday led the conversation; through his many years on Dow Jones's board he had become the de facto lead director. "It was our impression that the Bancroft family was happy with the way things have been going at Dow Jones," Hockaday said. "That's not the case," Mike Hill responded. "We're very concerned about succession," he continued. "It will be difficult for the family to go through another twenty-year period of poor stock performance." Hockaday and Newman assured him that they were dealing with the issue of succession; in fact, the two of them were on a subcommittee of the board to select the company's next CEO, a tidbit they didn't share with Mike, who left the meeting that day disappointed.

Not long after the meeting, Roy Hammer gave a short interview to *Fortune* magazine. In defense of the family's decision to sell down stock and still remain in control of the company (a privilege denied the rest of the company's common shareholders), he said it wasn't such a good deal for the Bancrofts to sell their Dow Jones stock at the measly price of $33 a share, down 44 percent from five years earlier. "We'd rather sell at $60 a share," he quipped. "If you know any buyers, send them my way." By then, even Hammer was caving a bit under the pressure of the Bancrofts' dissatisfaction. (Murdoch noted the piece and had begun making renewed inquiries into the Bancrofts' stance toward the company.)

Despite his rebuff from Kann and the board, Mike Hill didn't give up. He continued talking regularly with Lowell, who, aggravated by what he saw as Hemenway's inert stewardship, decided to write a letter directly to the Bancrofts to shake them out of their torpor. Weeks after Mike Hill's letter to Kann, Lowell addressed the following to the Hemenway lawyers and the Bancroft family:

It is our belief that your company is hemorrhaging and will not survive the onslaught of Google and Yahoo. If the family wishes to save the company, it must unite and make some drastically painful decisions.

For some time, we believe the Bancroft family has taken an apathetic stance towards the direction of the company. They have allowed the firm's moral compass to wander as their financial interests have diverged from those of the talented staff. They have become absentee landlords, looking to diversify their holdings into more promising opportunities.

To save the company under its current ownership, we believe the family needs to begin acting like owners again in order to counteract the destructive image fostered at the company's recent annual meeting. We advocate the creation of an Oversight Committee that will begin to set a new agenda—an ethical, ownership agenda—for Dow Jones. The Committee would be made up of Lowell, Elefante, and eight (8) family members representing the two classes at interest—the current senior members and the remaindermen. Only family members would vote on issues.

If the family is serious, the following issues must be resolved:

- No further sale of Class B shares over the next two years except for unusual circumstances.
- Cut the B Stock dividend by at least 50 percent with that savings used to cover over half of the annual interest on the debt. (Interest savings to go to reward staff.)
- Earmark half of cash flow to debt reduction.

All of the above implemented by the end of July.

Well, in the Bancroft family, people just didn't talk that way.

"It's time to stop pointing the finger and making comments that inflame and hurt Dow Jones board members, management and family members," Martha Robes wrote to Hill, in an e-mail copied to the entire family. Robes and her sisters were soft-spoken and cringed at the direct Hills. "Your approach is so negative and divisive that it's almost impossible to get beyond the venom to come up with something we can all support," she said.

Mike's oldest brother, Crawford, the high school biology teacher, outspoken and opinionated, came to his defense: "How dare anyone accuse Mike Hill of being divisive," he wrote in a response to Martha. "Being blind to reality is divisive—how could it not be?"

Elefante didn't appreciate the turmoil the Hills were stirring up; he was furious with Lowell. It was suddenly very clear that the dissatisfaction in the Bancroft family was no longer limited to Billy and Elisabeth. Even the Cook branch needed to free up funds for their philanthropic efforts that relied on gifting Dow Jones stock; the declining stock price had made it difficult to keep up with their commitments. Mike knew Hemenway & Barnes was going to have to make some kind of move to keep the family happy, and the most obvious problem was Peter Kann.

Unlike at News Corporation, the issue of succession would not be decided by the imperial CEO. The board had, in typical Dow Jones fashion, formed a committee to study the situation. The board was looking at its options and had been discussing the situation ad nauseam. The committee, made up of Bill Steere, James Ottaway Jr., Hockaday, Newman, Harvey Golub, and Elefante, had identified the three obvious internal candidates: Rich Zannino, who was chief operating officer, and two of his direct reports, Gordon Crovitz, who ran the company's electronic publishing division, and Karen Elliott House, the publisher of the *Journal* and Peter Kann's wife.

Dow Jones's board committee had started interviewing the potential CEO candidates early in 2005, and Zannino was offended that he was competing for the job with two people who worked for him. Hockaday, who knew how perilous CEO searches could be, had pulled Zannino aside to assure him that he had the edge in the three-way horserace. Hockaday didn't want Zannino becoming so frustrated that he started looking for other jobs or, worse, left the company out of impatience with the process.

Hockaday knew Zannino was ambitious; he had left his previous job at Liz Claiborne after just a year and a half as chief financial officer at the apparel maker. Hired at Dow Jones as chief financial officer in February 2001, by early 2002 Zannino had been met with passive aggression by some veteran Dow Jones executives, who bristled at Zannino's presence and simply ignored his requests. He was, at the time, one of many executives reporting to Peter Kann. Zannino wanted the other executives to report to him, and then he, in turn, would report to Kann. He had ideas for how the business side of the company could run better, and he thought he was smarter than he was getting credit for. The media world was getting under his skin and he wanted to be a part of it.

One afternoon in the winter of 2002, he told Kann he wanted to go out to dinner to talk about his future at the company. The two left Dow Jones's soulless New Jersey campus and drove to Lorenzo's, an Italian restaurant Kann frequented. Not long after they sat down, Zannino launched into the purpose of the dinner: "I don't think things are working out," he said. "I'm not happy." He explained he wanted a bigger job and more authority within the company. Kann listened patiently to his request, smiling and nodding when appropriate. It was a perfect Peter Kann moment. When he was faced with a dissatisfied employee, his job was to defuse the situation and make Zannino, who seemed smart and savvy and who had been helpful in his first year at the company, stay on board. Kann praised Zannino's performance and enlisted him in trying to figure out a job that would make Zannino happy. Given that Zannino was already the chief financial officer of the company, there was only one promotion Kann could really offer him without relinquishing the chairman or CEO title. "We could make you the chief operating officer of the company," Kann said. Top executives at the company would then report to Zannino, who in turn would report to Kann. Zannino breathed a sigh of relief. This was what he wanted. He would stay.

Then the two continued to talk about how that appointment would change things at the company. After talking in circles for a minute or two, Kann came up with a suggestion: "We could make Karen publisher," he offered. House had been running the company's international division for almost a decade and would welcome the change. Zannino jumped at the idea, ready to sew up the details. It barely occurred to him at the moment that he was agreeing to an impossible situation: he was overseeing Karen Elliott House and reporting to her husband. He quickly found out what the dynamic was going to be. His first week in his new job, House told him, "I can't be the publisher of the *Journal* on the days you don't want to be," a warning that Zannino should stay out of House's affairs.

By the fall of 2005, the arrangement had become almost unbearable. Zannino was House's boss, but if he gave an order she disagreed with, she would talk to Kann about it at home, or at least that's what Zannino believed. (House and Kann both adamantly denied they talked shop at home. "I don't think Rich ever believed that, but it was true," House said.) Zannino felt constantly in the middle of their relationship, making his job a political minefield and, on bad days, downright miserable. Zannino felt Kann was blind to the flaws of his wife, who had run roughshod over many executives and editors throughout the company. House thought Zannino was a micromanager. Worse, she thought he didn't respect the *Journal*'s journalism the way she did. "Fundamentally Rich did not care about the *Wall Street Journal*," House later remembered. "He wasn't interested in the product we produced and the integrity. He didn't drink the Kool-Aid."

During the year-long process of interviewing Zannino, House, and Crovitz for the CEO job, Zannino had grown impatient, despite Hockaday's assurances. So had Leslie Hill, who had been asking about the succession plan for months. She felt, once again, that the directors were stonewalling her. Even Hockaday could be dismissive, and she was tiring of the treatment. She was on the board of directors, so she heard regular updates on succession, but progress seemed virtually nonexistent. And even though she had been assured numerous times that Karen House would not be the next CEO, she remained in the running for the job, which was worrisome. What would prevent Kann from replacing himself with his wife, much as he had done for the publisher position three years earlier? Leslie wondered. She wanted the company to look outside for a CEO candidate, and she had told Mike Elefante as much. Elefante raised the issue in the search committee, but it went nowhere. Hiring a search firm to look outside the company was risky. The news, if it leaked, would shine an unwelcome spotlight on the company, which was unaccustomed to management turmoil. At sleepy Dow Jones, better to not attract attention. For Elefante's part, replacing Peter Kann was something he wanted to do sooner rather than later.

So it was united against a common enemy that Elefante and Leslie found themselves in the fall of 2005, when they walked into the November board meeting. The CEO search was on the agenda that day, and the fourteen directors gathered around the wood-paneled boardroom filled with a long oblong table facing south toward the Statue of Liberty. After Peter Kann was excused from the boardroom, as was common during the discussions about his successor, the board discussed the candidates. Former Pfizer CEO Bill Steere was heading the succession committee, and he went over the "360" reviews for each candidate. House's was a disaster. Her colleagues said she was undermining and could be abusive. In her earlier presentations to the board, she seemed aloof to many of the directors. Crovitz was a Rhodes scholar with law degrees from both Oxford and Yale. He started as an editorial writer for the *Journal* and then had become editor and publisher of the *Far Eastern Economic Review* before joining the corporate ranks in New York. He fit the old mold of Dow Jones CEOs, but the times called for someone more business-minded. Crovitz, soft-spoken and cerebral, didn't seem decisive enough to the board. He seemed to avoid confrontation. Furthermore, directors felt he would stay on at the company even if he didn't get the top job. If Zannino was passed over, he was certain to leave.

"Are we going to go outside to look for other candidates?" Leslie asked. "We already went outside," interjected Harvey Golub, the former American Express chief, who with his curmudgeonly manner and far-right politics was a frequent commenter in the boardroom. The company had hired a search firm to find Zannino as a new chief financial officer. Steere concurred. Going outside to look for a new CEO would just destabilize the company. Leslie was visibly frustrated, shaking her head, talking under her breath. It was clear to her that if she didn't speak up, the search would continue at a glacial pace. Kann would hang on and give himself more time to position House as the next CEO. (House had, in fact, taken herself out of the running months before when she spoke to the board's subcommittee. "I have the job I want," she told the committee. "I wasn't campaigning for the job twenty-four seven like Rich was," she later said.) Leslie and Mike looked at each other, and then Leslie spoke up. "If we're not going to go outside, then we seem to know who the candidate is," she said. "And I think he should take over sooner rather than later." Mike concurred. The directors around the table looked at one another, shocked. Vernon Jordan started to object, as did Lewis

Campbell, CEO of the aeronautics firm Textron Incorporated, but they swallowed their words, knowing it wouldn't make a difference. "The horse is out of the barn," Jordan muttered. Kann wasn't supposed to retire for another year and a half, and here, after years of acquiescence, the Bancrofts were pushing for the ouster of the CEO most on the board thought the family adored. Steere knew any protest was useless; he also knew Zannino was the right choice. Rarely did the Bancrofts speak up in such a forceful way. Now that they had, the directors couldn't ignore them. Nor did many of them want to. It was time for Kann to go.

Steere walked down the hallway to Zannino's office to deliver the news: "We've made the decision," Steere said. "Congratulations. You're the guy." Zannino was the next CEO and would take over in February 2006. The board had decided to push up the date of Kann's planned retirement as CEO a full year earlier than expected. Kann would retain the chairman title until his retirement the following year in April 2007. After Steere left, Kann came into Zannino's office and offered him heartfelt congratulations. And just like that, Peter Kann's reign was over. Zannino had no idea that the Bancrofts had hastened his appointment. He barely knew a single member of the family.

Zannino soon started making changes. He told Hockaday immediately after the meeting that he didn't want Kann to stay on as chairman. "I don't see how I can make the changes necessary with Peter still chairman," Zannino said. "Plus, I think the market will see it as a vote of no confidence from the board." Even if the board didn't feel comfortable giving him both jobs, Zannino continued, they should pick an independent chairman. The board discussed the matter but was unmoved. Zannino wasn't a journalist. He clearly valued stock prices over scoops and had a limited understanding of what journalism was for. With *Journal* managing editor Paul Steiger's retirement looming, the board wanted the continuity of Kann's presence as chairman. Zannino would be in charge of the company, Hockaday assured him. To have Zannino, the first non-journalist in the modern era, run the company was a big enough step. Kann would stay on as chairman for another year and a half until his mandatory retirement age.

Zannino noticed that Kann cooled to him after he objected to

Kann's continued presence as chairman. Things got worse on Friday, December 30, 2005, the day before the New Year's holiday break, when Zannino walked into Kann's office in the company's South Brunswick, New Jersey, campus and said: "So I've decided to make some management changes. I'm going to combine the print and online responsibilities for the *Journal*. I'm going to have Gordon run it. Unfortunately I don't have a place for Karen in the new structure." Up until that point, the two sides had been split. Gordon Crovitz was responsible for the online operations of the company and House ran the business side of the print *Journal*. Such divisions, Zannino rightly realized, were out of date in a world where the online and paper versions of the *Journal* needed to operate seamlessly. Sitting in Kann's office, surrounded by bookshelves filled with snapshots of Kann's children and *Journal* paraphernalia, he delivered the news bluntly. Kann barely registered a response. He had become expert at cloaking his feelings for House in front of other Dow Jones managers. He referred to her by her first and last names in meetings and kept public interactions with her distant. He maintained that House would have risen faster in the organization had he not been the company's CEO, a notion many other Dow Jones executives rejected. The two continued talking for two hours about company structure. "Peter, can you think of any role for her?" Zannino asked, suggesting that perhaps there was a place for her writing for the *Journal*'s editorial page.

"Gee," Kann said, "I don't think you go from being publisher back to being a reporter or writer."

"Would you like me to speak with Karen today or would you like me to wait until after the New Year?" Zannino asked.

"I think you should tell her now," Kann said. He had been urging Zannino to tell both House and Crovitz what his plan was for the company before the end of the year. He knew House had been nervously anticipating Zannino's decision.

Zannino went quickly to House's office, which was a few doors down, and told her almost verbatim what he had told Kann. "I'm going to reorganize, but unfortunately I don't have a place for you in the new organization structure."

"Really?" House questioned, showing what appeared to be genuine surprise.

"Really," Zannino responded. "So we're going to move on and I'm willing to make all the communication be about you so this can be as graceful an exit as possible."

"Well," House said, clearly emotional, "it really can't go on the way it's been going on. And I have no interest in being anything other than publisher." Unlike the other executives who reported to him, she talked back.

Over the weekend, Zannino, House, and Kann worked out the details of the press announcement. House consulted Paul Steiger on how best to announce her departure; he suggested getting all the news out at once: Zannino's new job, House's retirement, and Kann's chairmanship. The announcement of the changes came on Tuesday, January 3. Dow Jones's stock rose 10 percent on the news. Already, coverage of the event questioned whether Zannino was angling to sell the company. "I'm firmly committed to the independence of the company, but it's ultimately not my decision," he told the *Journal* the day of the announcement. By the time he was done with his executive changes, seven out of the nine people reporting to Zannino were new to their jobs. And with that, the old Dow Jones was swept aside.

Over at News Corporation, the news elicited great interest. Murdoch had seen Hammer step aside; now Kann was gone. Almost immediately Jimmy Lee was on the phone, chirping in Murdoch's ear about setting up a meeting with Zannino. Murdoch made it clear that he wanted any and all intelligence on Dow Jones. One of his top aides, Gary Ginsberg, who had worked in the Clinton administration and then as counsel to John Kennedy Jr.'s short-lived magazine, *George,* came to News Corporation in 1999 and had become close to Murdoch's own chief operating officer, Peter Chernin, who ran the company's entertainment business from Los Angeles. Ginsberg and Chernin were lonely liberals at News Corporation, and one of Ginsberg's great hopes, as the company's top communications executive, was to distance News Corporation's image from Fox News, which Ginsberg felt provided an unfortunate caricature for the company's entire reputation. Ginsberg didn't know many people over at Dow Jones, but he had gotten to know Nikhil Deogun, one of the *Journal*'s most powerful and connected editors, when Deogun was editing the *Journal*'s coverage of the media industry, shortly after the *Journal* had written an amazing thirty-five-hundred-word story in 2000 about Wendi Deng Murdoch, Murdoch's then new wife.

The story had been explosive. Following a tip that Wendi, who didn't work for the company at the time, was showing up at events in China with her own News Corp. business card, the reporters uncovered a story about how the wife of the News Corp. chairman had come to the United States twelve years before as a nineteen-year-old and broken up the marriage of the couple sponsoring her in the United States. After her host mother and father split, she married her host father for two years and seven months, "seven months longer than what was required for Ms. Deng to obtain a 'green card,'" which allowed her to stay in the United States, the article said. The story outlined her apparent liaison with another man closer to her age whom she called her "husband" even when she was married to her host father. The article portrayed her as wildly ambitious and ready to sleep her way out of her modest background in China (her father was a factory manager in Guangzhou) into a power position at one of the world's largest media conglomerates. As the story was going to press, Ginsberg became almost apoplectic in his efforts to keep the *Journal* from publishing. Murdoch called managing editor Paul Steiger to ask him to grant his wife privacy. The *Journal* published anyway; the story was a bombshell. It was picked up by scores of other papers and to this day is the most detailed account of Wendi Murdoch's path to News Corporation.

Deogun, who came to the media job after the story had run, had the job of fixing the relationship between News Corp. and the *Journal*. He cultivated Ginsberg and the two became close. Deogun had just moved from his position as the paper's main mergers-and-acquisitions reporter; his was the prestige beat at the paper. A native of India, he had moved to the United States for university and joined the *Journal* as a young reporter. Now, like many of the paper's employees, he was proud of and loyal to the institution. Deogun's keen reporting instincts and calm decisiveness had won him a wide range of powerful sources in the banking world. He had broken the kind of big, sensitive corporate merger stories that depend on mutual trust between the reporter and the highest echelons of corporate America.

As an editor, he continued to cultivate these influential sources. Ginsberg had become one.

When the Zannino news emerged, Ginsberg called Deogun, now in Washington, to gauge the paper's mood. Celebrated dealmaker Bruce Wasserstein, CEO of Lazard Limited, had been pushing Murdoch to make a preemptive bid for Dow Jones. "Now that Kann is gone, we're thinking of making a bid," Ginsberg said. "Are you crazy?" Deogun replied, his voice rising. He knew that the Bancroft family was eager to give Zannino a chance to turn things around. Now was not the right time for a bid.

Ginsberg reported Deogun's reaction to Murdoch, who was rounding up as much information as he could about the Bancroft family. In any case, he was in the middle of his own battle to maintain control of his company. He was trying to figure out how to get John Malone, a fellow mogul and chairman of Liberty Media, to relinquish his 16 percent stake in News Corp., something Malone had started to accumulate during Murdoch's transfer of his company's domicile from Australia to the United States in 2004. Murdoch didn't want to expand his empire while Malone still had a piece of it. Dow Jones would wait.

4

The Newsroom

RICH ZANNINO TOOK on his CEO job Wednesday, February 1, 2006. Before he could get to running the business of Dow Jones, he had to first face the newsroom. Paul Steiger was nearing his retirement age. He would be sixty-five in 2007, and *Journal* editors had been jockeying to be his successor for years. Zannino knew enough about the paper to understand that more than any other position at the company, the managing editor of the *Wall Street Journal* was perhaps the most public position besides his own. "I know what will happen if we screw up the *Journal*," he told the paper the day of his job announcement.

But Zannino had never banged out a story on deadline in the staid and sterile *Journal* newsroom, whose walls appeared ashy under the glaring fluorescent lights that highlighted the mild stains in the industrial blue carpet. There, the journalists, who sat in neatly divided cubicles, many littered with stacks of notebooks and newspapers, talked quietly into their telephones, whispering comforting words to sources who might unload a detail or two to make the reporter's story stand out from the rest. Zannino called himself "a devoted longtime user of the company's products," but even that statement, referring to the *Wall Street Journal* as something akin to after-shave, didn't endear him to the newsroom. The journalists mistrusted him, and he returned the feeling.

Though the Dow Jones offices had been spruced up after the devastation of September 11, the newsroom seemed threadbare. The windows had been replaced and the building thoroughly cleaned to remove the white dust and debris that covered the headquarters following the attacks, but the building, which sat in a nondescript collection of office towers in the always removed Battery Park City development, attracted little affection from its inhabitants. In the four-plus years since the World Trade Center towers fell, the journalists had trudged past the dust and paralysis of the giant hole of a construction site that was the monument to the attacks. Zannino, who took a car to work, as had Kann and House before him, was largely spared the grimy spectacle.

By the time Zannino was named CEO, the newsroom had taken on the quality of Spartan neglect. The low-ceilinged conference rooms contained nonworking speakerphones, the paint was chipping, pieces of cubicle dividers lay detached on the floor. On the executive eleventh floor, sandwiched between the three newsroom floors on levels nine, ten, and twelve, however, the walls were lined with wood paneling and the carpets were a plush beige. Sharing those civilized corridors was the editorial staff of the *Journal*, a signal perhaps that the conservative bent of those writers made them safer office companions than what executives viewed as disaffected news types.

The disrepair of the news floors was indicative of the slow deterioration that had begun years before, as the pretenders to Steiger's throne had tired of their place in his court and left. Years before his retirement, Steiger's deputies had begun auditioning to replace him. Their stage was often the daily morning news meeting, which took place every weekday at 10:30 a.m., when the top editors of the most influential business paper in the world gathered together in a conference room overlooking the Statue of Liberty.

Steiger, an understated and affable manager, quick to laugh and slow to anger, was facing a looming deadline. He and Peter Kann, Dow Jones's chairman and chief executive, had acknowledged years earlier they would retire together. The board had cut short Kann's CEO tenure. With Steiger's own retirement approaching, the meeting became a regularly choreographed exercise of preening and intellectual one-upmanship for the paper's top editors. Beneath the civility, it was a roiling cauldron of office politics.

Following the *Journal's* tradition, the editors wouldn't talk about the biggest news of the day. Unlike every other newspaper in every jurisdiction of every country in the world, the *Wall Street Journal* didn't put news on its front page. The paper relegated the biggest news stories to the inside of the paper, on page A3. Epic features and investigations for Page One were mapped out weeks if not months in advance. Because of this *Journal* peculiarity, the morning news meeting was not a frenetic debate about the most disastrous or dramatic news events, but rather a mannered recitation of the day's "sked" of stories. In a business of attention-grabbing headlines and color photos, the paper treated its front page like a quiet haven for reflective storytelling. Breaking news was important, and the paper did plenty of it, but the craft of feature writing was the center of the paper's identity. Such a tempo left plenty of time for the auditions.

Bureau chiefs, news editors, and page editors would file into the conference room or log on to the conference call. Steiger supervised this discussion. He would indulge his entourage and listen patiently to the story lineup. Mid- and lower-level editors hoped to be noticed for their clear-sighted news judgment or a lucid explanation of an arcane story. The less ambitious kept their heads down and hoped not to be put on the spot. The participants were well aware of the importance of their decisions: they were helping shape the agenda for the nation's business paper, regarded by the country's corporate executives with a combination of admiration and fear. CEOs often asked themselves, "How would this look if it appeared on the front page of the *Journal*?" The paper held sway simply by existing.

Those gunning for the top job could exhibit how much they deserved to run the most powerful business paper in the world. They tortured their underlings with probing questions. Some of the interrogations were sincere attempts to delve into an important topic; others were merely the kind of showmanship that played well when positioning oneself for advancement. Like any live show, wardrobe played a role: once, a deputy managing editor and candidate for the top job performed a 360-degree turn at Steiger's behest to show off her snazzy suit before taking her seat at the meeting.

In his later years, his detractors in the newsroom whispered, Steiger had started showing interest in the latest celebrity gossip and fashion trends. He was reading *Women's Wear Daily* magazine and paying attention to the vogue in women's shoes. His editors attributed these attractions to his third wife, Wendy Brandes, a striking young jewelry designer and fashion blogger twenty-five years his junior who looked like a modern-day Snow White with a high-fashion wardrobe and a sleek bob. As his retirement approached, Steiger joked that Brandes had threatened him: "The first day she finds me in the apartment in sweatpants after 10:00 a.m., it's not divorce; it's murder." He hadn't yet determined what he would pursue after retirement, but he didn't plan to be idle.

A year before Steiger's retirement, New York's media world was scattered with the erstwhile candidates: Larry Ingrassia, the former *Journal* money and investing editor (and brother of Paul Ingrassia, president of Dow Jones Newswires), had left to become the business editor of the *New York Times;* Steve Adler, the top investigative editor at the *Journal,* was now the editor in chief of *BusinessWeek;* Joanne Lipman, the steward of the paper's lifestyle sections, had just left for Condé Nast's new glossy monthly business magazine, *Condé Nast Portfolio.* Daniel Hertzberg, long Paul Steiger's main deputy in the newsroom, was still at the *Journal,* but he was too close in age to Steiger to be considered a successor. Of the original pool of *Journal* candidates to succeed Steiger, only Marcus Brauchli, the youngest of the group at forty-four, remained at the paper.

A journalism enthusiast, Brauchli had spent virtually his entire career at the *Journal,* minus a requisite year and a half as a copy boy at the *New York Times,* a stamp for any and all aspiring journalists of a certain generation. He was among the last of that old breed, yet despite his youthful demeanor he affected a world-weariness that made him seem a seasoned member of the club. Slim and good-looking, with a broad nose and a boyish face, he had a hairline that had receded to the point where he had adopted the closely shorn haircut of many middle-aged men hoping to look less aged. His suits, many of which he brought back from his years as a correspondent in China, were bespoke; he bought them from the cut-rate De-Luxe Tailor Shop in Hong Kong.

Brauchli spent twelve years in Asia with Dow Jones and a year and a half in Europe (with a short break for a prestigious Nieman fellowship at Harvard). As a foreign correspondent, he wrote creative, probing stories and seemed to model himself as a swashbuckling reporter much like Peter Kann.

But he occasionally grew frustrated with taking orders from New York; Brauchli wanted to try his hand at delivering the orders. In 1999, he got his chance and was offered the position of national editor at the *Journal*. Brauchli planned the move back to New York and thought of it as an experiment. As he traveled through Mongolia the summer before he returned, Brauchli promised himself that if he was good at navigating officialdom, and enjoyed it, he'd stay. But if not, he'd be right back out on the road.

He took easily to the series of managerial projects that awaited him upon his return. These propelled him up the ladder of the newsroom so quickly that he became known as "the Rocket." Brauchli just laughed at such monikers and kept moving ahead. Often, however, he would think back wistfully to his years as an Asia correspondent as he suffered (and thrived) through bureaucratic newsroom meetings. Despite these yearnings, he became known to most reporters in the *Journal* newsroom as a master manipulator of newsroom politics. His roles expanded, and he began to take on more business-oriented projects. In 2005, he helped redesign the paper's small and struggling European and Asian editions, turning them into smaller tabloid formats, which sold better on newsstands in Europe and saved the company money in production costs. By the end of that year, he had started to work on a redesign of the paper's U.S. edition.

When Zannino was appointed CEO, Brauchli saw the move as favorable to his chances at the managing editor slot; he and Zannino had gotten to know each other through Dow Jones's Senior Leadership Team events, meetings for the company's executives to brainstorm about strategy. Brauchli sensed that Zannino liked him.

The redesign of the U.S. paper was gaining momentum just as Zannino took on the CEO role. To save money, Kann and Zannino and House had agreed on one thing: to shrink the size of the *Journal* by three inches to save on newsprint and production costs. The old size of the paper, an expansive fifteen-inch width, made it unique, but such grandiosity was no longer possible in a world of dramatic budget constraints. The paper would shrink to become a foot wide.

Now, the project was Crovitz and Brauchli's to implement. The *Journal*, like every other newspaper in the country, was suffering from an identity crisis. Not only was advertising down, but the paper was competing with online news sources and twenty-four-hour cable news. The immediate reason for the redesign was the adoption of a narrower-size paper that would allow the *Journal* to be printed on presses across the country that weren't owned by Dow Jones. The move would save $18 million a year. Crovitz refused to blame the change on the tough times. Instead, in an Orwellian twist, he would take this literal shrinking of the paper and sell it to readers as a sign of a strong future.

Crovitz decided he would call the new iteration of the newspaper "*Journal* 3.0." He arrived at the name—never popular in the *Journal's* newsroom or executive floor—by taking particular note of the *Journal's* lead front-page story the day after Japan attacked Pearl Harbor: "War with Japan Means Industrial Revolution in the United States" read the headline. The story outlined the implications of the attack on the country's economy, industry, and financial markets. For Crovitz, it also marked the end of the first phase of the *Journal*— "*Journal* 1.0," the time between the paper's founding in 1889 and December 5, 1941. During that period, the *Journal* reported the news like any other outlet. After that headline and under Bernard Kilgore, who became the paper's managing editor the year of the Pearl Harbor attack, the *Journal* started adding more analysis to its stories and expanded its coverage beyond business and finance. Crovitz defined "*Journal* 2.0" as starting on December 8, 1941. He planned for it to end on December 31, 2006, when he would usher in the paper's third phase. To compete against the immediacy of the Web, Crovitz wanted the paper, instead of running stories that rehashed what people had learned the day before on their BlackBerrys, to become more analytical. *Journal* reporters would break news on the Web site and then examine it in the next day's paper.

Though Brauchli appeared largely unchallenged inside the *Journal* newsroom, another candidate from another Dow Jones division, Paul Ingrassia, was a leading contender for the managing editor post. Ingrassia, who had served as the *Journal's* Detroit bureau chief in the 1990s, had won a Pulitzer Prize in 1993 for his coverage of the automobile industry. For the past ten years, however, since 1996, he had served as president of the company's storied "ticker," which was one of Dow Jones's largest and most profitable divisions, and one that *Journal* reporters had always dismissed as a journalistic stepchild. Newswires wrote bare-bones stories for investors. They had no pretensions to craft a gripping narrative; their job was to report on the corporate news of the moment, updating the investors who subscribed to their service. Newswires reporters were judged on how many seconds their stories appeared before competitors' at rival newswire services Reuters and Bloomberg. During Ingrassia's tenure as the head of Newswires, he had maintained its profitability and built up its journalistic credibility, though the division still lagged in reputation behind Reuters and the ever dominant Bloomberg. Still, Ingrassia had done good work. The ticker hadn't won a single award for its journalism in the 115 years prior to Ingrassia's arrival but then accumulated thirty during his time in the job. The position gave him what Crovitz called "management maturity."

Ingrassia had been talking to Crovitz about a strategy for all of Dow Jones & Company, one that included gradually merging the reporting bureaus of the *Journal* and Newswires. It was, in some ways, an obvious step. The wire had a huge reporting staff of 700; the *Journal*, 250. On any given day, the two newsrooms often covered the same story, be it an earnings release from a company or the market's movements for the day. The newspaper industry was facing an increasingly demanding shareholder base. Given the mounting financial pressures on the business, it only made sense for the two units to coordinate. But such a combination was anathema to the proud staff of the *Wall Street Journal*, where many reporters saw themselves as storytellers with a powerful audience, not stenographers for the broker set. Indeed, cooperation between the two staffs had been attempted before, never with much success. Each time, after a few months of halfhearted coordination, the two staffs would retreat to their spheres of comfort, where *Journal* reporters would file their stories on a 5:00 p.m. deadline for the paper, long after it was of much use to the Newswires staff, who had to feed investors during the stock market's open hours between 9:30 a.m. and 4:00 p.m.

Under Zannino and Crovitz, the idea was gaining new momentum yet again. Ingrassia found himself in a horserace with Brauchli, and surprisingly, at least for observers in the *Journal* newsroom, which backed Brauchli, Ingrassia had the early lead. In fact, one could say he had already won the race in early 2006. In the first few weeks after Zannino officially took over the CEO spot in February, Crovitz had been talking regularly with Ingrassia and assured him "there's no one else" for the job. It was over a year before Steiger would reach retirement age, but Zannino and Crovitz were ready to make a move. They agreed that Ingrassia, with his experience, his attention to the bottom line, and his position somewhat outside the *Journal* newsroom, was the right choice.

They made that choice without consulting Steiger, a practice that would seem perfectly acceptable in any other company, where typically a sitting executive doesn't pick his successor. But Paul Steiger had been shaping the *Wall Street Journal* and its journalism for fifteen years as managing editor, encouraging his reporters to dig out "the definitive story" on their beats and pursue stories with "moral force." He had learned to court and when necessary deflect the powerful executives who had been an almost continuous presence on the job, at cocktail parties or editorial lunches, or in an angry telephone call after an unflattering *Journal* story. The proximity to such power and his comfort with it had lent Steiger an air of gravitas. He showed the subjects of the *Journal*'s stories respect and deference, but he landed careful blows when he had to. Through this measured approach, he had become one of the great newspaper editors in the country.

Under the plan Zannino and Crovitz had in mind, Ingrassia would take over for Steiger, who would, for the last year before his retirement, take on a senior editing role overseeing both Dow Jones Newswires and the *Wall Street Journal*. It amounted to a proverbial kick upstairs for Steiger. For Zannino and Crovitz, it kept Steiger's name and reputation attached to the *Journal*, helpful for this brand-new executive team. Steiger's new position atop both the *Journal* and Newswires would bless the Ingrassia-outlined revolution.

Zannino and Crovitz discussed their choice of managing editor with Dow Jones's directors. Lewis Campbell, the Textron CEO who had worked at General Motors when Ingrassia served as the *Journal*'s Detroit bureau chief, had lobbied for him with fellow board members. Peter Kann personally blessed the pick. A press release was drawn up to announce the move as part of Zannino's other executive appointments. Only then did Zannino and Crovitz approach Paul Steiger with their decision. Crovitz took Steiger to lunch at City Hall restaurant, a Tribeca establishment blocks away from the *Journal*'s offices, to lay out the plan. Steiger listened patiently. But he had something else in mind. He calmly explained that he felt the new scenario would give him no authority. Ingrassia would be designated heir apparent, rendering Steiger a lame duck.

"I've had this job for fifteen years, longer than anyone else," Steiger told Crovitz. "If you think I've had it too long, I'm happy to step out of the way," he added, in the same calm, soft-spoken, and halting tone that neutralized irate CEOs and staved off complaints from embittered editors and reporters. "But if you want me to stay, I want to be the managing editor of the *Wall Street Journal*."

Crovitz asked Steiger to come talk to him and Zannino together, which he did, and he repeated his arguments. A job that lacked real authority was not a job Steiger wanted. "Why make a decision before you have to?" he said. To rush the selection of managing editor, Steiger reasoned, seemed ill-advised. The editors were busy working on the planned redesign of *Journal* 3.0. "Why don't you put off the decision until the redesign is complete?" he said. The launch of the new paper was still nearly a year away. When Zannino pressed Steiger, he voiced some reservations about Ingrassia, saying he had been out of the *Journal* newsroom a long time and didn't have an easy relationship with his former colleagues. But he reserved his harshest criticism for later.

Zannino and Crovitz, brand-new to their jobs, had underestimated a seasoned corporate operator like Paul Steiger. They both respected Steiger and knew they needed him. They were about to learn how little power they wielded within the company. Until Zannino, Dow

Jones had been run by journalists. Now, even though there wasn't a reporter in the corner office, the newsroom maintained its sway over the company.

Zannino now had to deal with the veiled threat that if he went ahead with his existing plan, Steiger would leave. He, the non-journalist CEO, the guy who had come from Liz Claiborne, didn't want to be responsible for that. This battle between the *Journal* and the business side would go to the newsroom. Zannino and Crovitz put off the decision on the managing editor by placing Ingrassia in charge of a "news strategy" committee that would spend the next year exploring ways to get the *Journal* and Newswires to cooperate. It would give Ingrassia something to do for the year until they made a final decision.

That spring, Zannino was mounting another project as CEO: meet the other chiefs in the media business and take Dow Jones out of its isolation. During his three months in the chief executive's office, Zannino had been making the rounds with his counterparts at other, larger, more dynamic media companies. He was warming to his role. He had gone to breakfast and lunch with media players such as IAC's Barry Diller and Reuters's Tom Glocer, and after a concerted effort by Jimmy Lee, he was going to have dinner with Rupert Murdoch. Jimmy had been trying to get Zannino to attend his annual JPMorgan Leadership Conference earlier that spring in Deer Valley—where Murdoch had been—but Zannino demurred, telling Jimmy the venue was too public for such an introduction.

That Thursday evening of May 18, Jimmy Lee was the first to arrive in the Oak Room at the Links Club on East 62nd Street, where the banker often entertained JPMorgan's most favored CEOs. Tonight he believed his guests could accomplish something quite advantageous for all involved. The dark paneling and the hushed greetings at the club were the perfect atmosphere for Jimmy, though both his guests would find the surroundings staid and stuffy. This was unfortunate, as Jimmy had hoped for a casual effect that signaled ease and a not-too-aggressive approach. He didn't even plan to raise the topic—"the thing," as he often said—that was behind the occasion. To him, bringing up the deal at this point was like going on a first date and talking about when to have children—it was a turnoff.

Rupert Murdoch arrived later than Zannino, as planned. Jimmy didn't want them to be seen entering the building at the same time. The perfect host, Jimmy ushered each man, upon arrival, to the small Oak Room, where they opened a bottle of expensive Australian wine. Jimmy had been busy making the match for months, telling both men they'd really like the other. He saw them both as "guys' guys"— the same way he saw himself.

Murdoch arrived at the dinner facing myriad threats to his kingdom, but he was, as ever, moving forward. John Malone, the cable magnate, had bought up his stake in News Corp. The stake was threatening because it wasn't much smaller than the Murdoch family's own 30 percent share, and Malone was just wily enough and opportunistic enough to never be trusted. The previous summer, Murdoch's elder son, Lachlan, who had been groomed his whole life to take over from his father, had left his post as deputy chief operating officer of News Corporation. Lachlan had suffered from what some called a "corporate conspiracy to undermine him" at the hands of Roger Ailes, the programming genius behind Fox News, and Peter Chernin, the company's chief operating officer. But it was more than just a corporate defeat. The move was a "tragedy" for the family, in the words of one of the kids. The problem was that Lachlan's father had allowed it to happen. Murdoch had prepared Lachlan to be the heir apparent, but when Lachlan started to falter, Murdoch allowed him to fall. "It wasn't the most emotionally intelligent way for Dad to handle it," said Elisabeth, Lachlan's older sister. "He doesn't really have the tools to express that he's sorry."

Lachlan's defection in 2005, unthinkable until it happened, had been hastened by another threat to the old Murdoch family: Murdoch's third wife. Murdoch had long been separated from his second wife, Anna, with whom he had Lachlan, his older sister, Elisabeth, and his younger brother, James. Anna, an elegant woman, knew her husband well. She could almost have anticipated his affair with Wendi, whom Murdoch met on a trip to China in 1997. During the divorce in 1999, Anna's children watched bemusedly as she focused single-mindedly on cementing her children's control over the family trust that gave the Murdochs control of News Corporation. "I told her to stop being so paranoid," one of the children said, as Anna warned them that their father would start a new family and have more children and supplant the existing kids' total control over the trust. "He's not going to have more kids at his age," they said, shrugging off their mother's concerns, the way children often do.

Anna could have walked away with half of Murdoch's empire. The Murdochs were residents of California, and after a thirty-one-year marriage, Anna was likely due half the estate, worth nearly $8 billion at the time. But to blow apart the family, after all the work she had put into it, seemed foolish. She had gotten her children up in the morning early to see their father before he went to work. She had nurtured a feeling of Murdoch loyalty. "Growing up, we moved around a lot, and it always seemed that if everything else went wrong, we still had each other," says Elisabeth of her family. Even if Rupert Murdoch was going to throw that away, Anna wasn't going to let the divorce threaten the dynasty. She took a relatively modest $200 million in exchange for a guarantee of her children's future control of the company.

When the news came that Wendi was pregnant, Anna's wounds were salved just a bit by the knowledge that she saw this coming. When Wendi's second daughter, Chloe, was born less than two years after the first, Anna braced for the next step. It came as she predicted.

When the little girls were just babies, Murdoch strove to assure Wendi that she was truly part of the family and that all his children were equal in his eyes. Murdoch told his older children he needed to split the trust. "We'll split the family if you don't get in line," he said. For months, they haggled over the outline of the trust with their father. It fell to Elisabeth to tell her mother the children's decision to give in to their father's wish to split the trust. The four older children retained voting power but agreed that all the children—Grace and Chloe included—would receive a $150 million distribution from the trust. It was a grueling ordeal, and it seemed, for a time, that the dynasty might falter. (Lachlan left for Australia in the midst of the dispute.) But the grown children stood by their father in the end and made peace, however uneasy, with his new life, and their new siblings. By then, Anna was remarried to a man who finally would take

her to the opera and spend afternoons at home. She described her recovery from the divorce as "coming out of a deep mental illness."

Zannino had pretended to agree to this dinner reluctantly. He knew
Murdoch was interested in Dow Jones and how their meeting might
appear if discovered. The early awkward moments of the meeting
past, Zannino breathed a sigh of relief. Someone brought up the show
American Idol, which aired on Murdoch's Fox network. (Murdoch's
daughter Elisabeth had urged him to buy the program years earlier.)
Then the talk segued into the price of newsprint. Murdoch knew
how to play this part of the game and maneuvered adeptly, seeming
neither too eager nor too distant. For his part, Zannino was equally
adept. Just over three months into his first CEO job and there he
was, already in the shark tank with one of the most determined and
skilled dealmakers in media, trying to avoid the subject that brought
them together while, at the same time, making an impression. They
all knew the purpose of the gathering but it was never mentioned.
"To get a big deal done, that's how it works," Jimmy says, recalling the
evening. "You don't just invite everybody into a room and say, 'Hey,
wanna sell Dow Jones for $60 a share? Yeah, sure!' You need to get
to know people, to introduce them." Murdoch left the meeting feeling comfortable that Zannino was different from Kann, in a way that
would certainly be advantageous.

Meanwhile, Zannino and Crovitz were trying to contain the disaster brewing in the newsroom. The "news strategy" position they had
created for Ingrassia clearly wasn't working. It was an inflated title
with very little real responsibility that bought them time before Ingrassia would take a permanent position. Crovitz had presented the
interim job to him as a mere delay in the appointment, but the delay
threatened to become indefinite. Marcus Brauchli's star was rising,
and Ingrassia, with Steiger against him, seemed to retreat. Suddenly
rumors coursed through the newsroom that Ingrassia would cut 20
percent of the *Journal* staff (a claim Ingrassia denied he ever made).
Brauchli's allies were vicious about Ingrassia, who believed, despite
the barbs, that the job was safely his.

5

Billy

I N THE TEN YEARS of family fireworks that followed Billy Cox's coming together with Elisabeth Goth for the express purpose of saving, and perhaps advancing, their fortunes, the disaster of Dow Jones remained a regular topic of conversation for Cox. Now fifty-one years old in the fall of 2006, his light brown hair thinning, his skin showing age spots, he had moved on to a second marriage and a career as an independent investor, far from the frustrations of his family and Dow Jones.

A few days prior to the publication of the *Fortune* article, Billy had left his job as managing director of Dow Jones Global Indexes. A few days later, he was on a plane to see Buffett again, who was interested in exploring a possible combination of Dow Jones and the Washington Post Company, in which Buffett owned a significant stake and where he served on the board. Billy continued to monitor Dow Jones's situation closely, sending off pointed missives to his family members, disputing Peter Kann's claims that all was well at the company. He continued to criticize the company in the press, much to the annoyance of his father, William Cox Jr. Billy talked to any reporter who managed to get him on the phone. He defended his indiscretion by saying he had no other choice: "There is no mechanism within the family to discuss openly the business issues surrounding Dow Jones," he told *Fortune* in 1998, in a follow-up story on his and Elisabeth's

campaign. "I didn't see any other alternative." His Christmas card in
1997 lamented his "divorce" from "my . . . mistress: Dow Jones."

If they were included in family meetings, he and Elisabeth were
sternly warned not to talk to the press. Elisabeth eventually obliged;
Cox never did. Because of his public critiques, bankers and private
equity executives frequently contacted him, hoping for a sliver of insight into his family and Dow Jones and who might be willing to sell
the company. He readily shared what he knew of his family dynamics. He had divorced his first wife, with whom he had four children,
and remarried in 1998. With his new wife, Beatrice, who was French
American, and his young son, Clarence, who was six years old, he
moved to Barcelona to give Clarence a European education. Still, he
returned often to Princeton, where his four children from his first
marriage resided, and never missed an opportunity to launch into a
litany of Dow Jones errors.

The New England sisters, he told them, were "clueless." His own
siblings seemed woefully uninterested in Dow Jones. His father had
stood with Dow Jones management against him, something he hadn't
forgotten but tried to gloss over. "We agreed to disagree," he told his
cousins. Still, he had felt abandoned ever since and took every opportunity to try to return the slight, rolling his eyes at his father's comments in meetings and mentioning how his dad didn't measure up to
Jessie Bancroft Cox as a leader the family desperately needed. While
Billy moved around Europe, his father had retired to Palm Beach and
split his time between his airy home there and his summer place on
Nantucket, playing golf and enjoying a quiet life.

At the time of the family forum in mid-October, five months after
Zannino and Murdoch's first meeting, Billy had moved to Rome and
had recovered from his second hip surgery. (He had sustained a nasty
ice hockey injury a few years earlier.) As he approached the offices of
Hemenway & Barnes, which occupied two floors of a red-brick building in downtown Boston, he felt the familiar bile rise in the back of
his throat, but he wasn't going to let this opportunity pass. Today was
the day he would deliver another message to his family.

Elisabeth wasn't attending the meeting that day. Frustrated by her
failure years before, she had sold her personal holdings of Dow Jones
stock (she remained a beneficiary of the largest trust, Article III) and

backed away from the fight. She was preoccupied at the time with her new marriage to Robert Chelberg, an American software entrepreneur who lived in Prague. Just the week before the meeting Elisabeth had flown from Prague to the East Coast for Robert's grandfather's eightieth birthday party. Just before the party, she had met with the Hemenway & Barnes trustees. Elefante told her he was concerned about the company's ability to increase its stock price, given all the negative factors facing the newspaper industry. Rather than feel alarmed, Elisabeth was relieved. Finally, she thought, they are being honest with me. Maybe it was that Hammer was gone; maybe it was because the news had gotten so bad that it could no longer be ignored. Regardless, Elisabeth welcomed the candor. After the meeting at Hemenway, she checked in with Mike Hill, and the two commiserated about their frustrations with the company.

Since he left Dow Jones's employ, Billy had nurtured his disrespect for the factions of the family loyal to Peter Kann—namely, the New England branch of the Bancrofts who had descended from Jane Cook, the meek sister to Billy's boisterous grandmother Jessie Cox. Jane's daughters—Lisa Steele and her two sisters—were among those who saw selling their stock as heresy.

Lisa Steele, a member of Dow Jones's board, typically took Mike Elefante's advice, as she had Roy Hammer's before him. She was often busy with her real estate company, which promoted responsible development in the remote town of Shelburne, Vermont, and didn't have the time or inclination, unlike her cousin Leslie, to do a lot of her own research outside the official channels. It seemed like a waste of time to her. Moreover, the family's advisers had always seemed honest and forthright. Robes, when she wasn't on her boat, spent time at her house in Maine and was probably the family member closest to Peter Kann. Stevenson and her husband occasionally hosted family meetings, hoping to lessen the tension.

Billy's contempt for his family was returned. Some of his relatives said his ill temper had to be the result of a chemical imbalance. It wasn't. He was just almost perpetually annoyed at his relatives. Discreet where Billy was outspoken, understated where Billy showed off, Lisa and her New England sisters saw Billy as possibly dangerous to the family and someone who couldn't be trusted. Even the cousins in his own branch—the Hills—thought Billy too reckless. His problem in a secretive family may have simply been that he talked too much.

The occasion where Billy was headed on that October day was a Bancroft family forum, one of the family's regular meetings to discuss the state of Dow Jones. The New England sisters arrived and, after politely greeting Billy, sat far away from him in the large conference room upstairs from the law firm. Billy sat with Mike Hill and his wife. (Hemenway & Barnes didn't have a large enough conference room to comfortably seat the two dozen family members who showed up.) Also in attendance were the Hill siblings, who were increasingly dissatisfied with Hemenway & Barnes. Mike had gotten nowhere with all his letter writing, and the entire family was contemplating pulling their funds out of the firm, believing as they did that Hemenway had squandered the family's money.

Mike Elefante stood before the even more restive Bancroft clan that day. He took note of Billy's distracted expression across the conference table but didn't pay much attention. Billy was a regular at such meetings and always a bit of a troublemaker.

The meeting had an anxious but ultimately hopeful feel. From the perspective of Elefante and some of the Bancrofts assembled, Dow Jones's prospects seemed to be improving slightly. Rich Zannino had been in the CEO chair for roughly nine months and had begun a reorganization of Dow Jones. Many were relieved that Kann was finally gone from the CEO spot.

Elefante had broached the topic of forming a more ironclad trust—something like what the Sulzberger family had at the New York Times Company—that would allow the family to vote as a bloc instead of through the dozens of overlapping trusts that currently governed the family's money. But the conversation stalled, mired in the logistical hurdles of refiguring the trusts, not to mention the aimless dissatisfaction in the family that made any progress nearly impossible.

After a time, Billy forced himself to the front of the room to deliver his message: "Rupert Murdoch is going to make a bid for the company," he told his relatives gathered in the conference room above Hemenway & Barnes's office that crisp fall day. "I've been talking to some guys about it," he continued. "I think it could be $50 a share." No one took him seriously. Billy's history—always name-dropping, not entirely reliable—obscured his message. He had talked in the past about how bids were going to come in for Dow Jones. They never did. But this time, he *had* been talking to someone about a deal. An old acquaintance of his, Andrew Steginsky, a money manager who had served on the board of the Princeton Symphony Orchestra with him years before, had been telling him Murdoch wanted to buy Dow Jones.

The family had grown weary of his refrain. "It's coming," he said, pausing. He heard—he could barely believe it—laughter. "We've got to figure this out," he continued, his face flushing.

"Oh, he's got helicopters, eh?" Buzzy Stevenson, Jean's husband, replied, joking about how Murdoch would swoop in to take over the company.

"You guys aren't even gonna know what hit you," Billy sputtered, too exasperated to care anymore about what he saw as the family's complacency. He left the meeting, went back to Rome, and called his friend Andrew Steginsky.

Rupert Murdoch would talk to anybody who had a good piece of information for him. He was democratic in that way. And he could certainly keep more than one game going at once and spent most days on the phone, like the thousands of reporters he employed, gossiping. He talked to Jimmy Lee about Rich Zannino and Dow Jones's board, and he talked to Andrew Steginsky about the Bancroft family.

Steginsky, currently running his own investment firm, Steginsky Capital LLC, in Princeton, New Jersey, had started investing in News Corp. in the mid-1980s, when News Corp. already owned the *New York Post* and 20th Century Fox and later launched the Fox Broadcasting network. Still, the company was based in Australia and didn't have many American investors. Steginsky, then a fund manager at Schroders bank in New York, had good access to Murdoch, who always returned Steginsky's calls and occasionally invited him to News Corp.'s offices when both men were in Manhattan. Balding and slightly overweight, Steginsky didn't cut an inspiring figure. Perhaps this was the reason he was drawn to forceful entrepreneurs. He counted Rupert Murdoch as one such man.

Steginsky's opportunity to be truly helpful to Murdoch came in early 2005, when he was sitting with the mogul in Murdoch's mid-town Manhattan headquarters. To make conversation, he asked Murdoch what he thought of the *Wall Street Journal,* a copy of which was sitting on Murdoch's desk. "I'd love to own it someday but the Bancrofts will never sell," Murdoch replied. Steginsky, reflexively ingratiating himself, responded that he knew one of the Bancrofts. He had once served on a board with Billy Cox III.

Steginsky's relationship with Rupert had deepened when Lachlan Murdoch arrived from Andover to attend Princeton University in the 1990s. Wary and perhaps too aware of the world and the way wealthy young men could be used and often hurt, Murdoch sometimes mentioned his son to Steginsky, who lived just minutes away from campus. Steginsky, who had a casual and obsequious manner, told Rupert he could at least have Lachlan over for dinner to make sure he was eating right. And so Lachlan came over, Steginsky cooked him meals, and the two got along. Steginsky was a fan of opera and would invite Lachlan to hear the arias using tickets from Schroders, which were happily doled out to Steginsky whenever he told his superiors he was entertaining Lachlan Murdoch.

Steginsky spent months trying to dig up a contact number for Billy, eventually tracking him down in April of 2005 when Billy was living in Rome. Steginsky had called and told Billy of Murdoch's interest. Billy was delighted. Murdoch's desire to own the *Journal* was always assumed in the Bancroft family, but it wasn't clear he was ever going to make the move. Now, this seemed concrete. Steginsky had a way of talking about Murdoch as if he were a dear friend, something Billy often did himself when he was talking about business deals. He mentioned the director Ron Howard and McGraw-Hill CEO Terry McGraw as if they were his brothers. Billy said he would set up a family meeting to discuss Murdoch's interest. Then came the Bancroft family forum in October 2006 when he finally delivered the message.

Afterward, he told Steginsky about the meeting and how the message was received. Steginsky realized he needed to delve deeper. He mentioned to Murdoch that it might be helpful to visit Billy in Rome, and Murdoch agreed. It was then that Steginsky, sensing genuine interest, suggested that such a trip and such a project might require a significant amount of time and money. Murdoch quickly said he'd give him some money up front for the time and travel and would compensate him generously if anything came of his work. Murdoch saw Steginsky as a small-time money manager who was eager to curry favor, but he sensed the sycophant might be useful.

As Murdoch was hearing from Steginsky about the Bancroft meeting, Jimmy Lee was busy arranging another meeting—this one a lunch—for Murdoch and Zannino. Four days before their meeting, on October 25, 2006, Murdoch got a call from Jimmy. Murdoch and Jimmy knew what they wanted to accomplish, and they spoke straightforwardly about Murdoch's next move. He wouldn't make an offer that day but would further gauge Zannino's stance. Both Murdoch and Jimmy knew about the Bancrofts' big family meeting in Boston and Billy's announcement of Murdoch's interest.

After they hung up, Jimmy called Zannino. Here, the conversation was much more complex. Zannino was careful and, as was frequently the case with an acquiree, not entirely ready to give up the reins. But Zannino was more aware than ever of the limitations of Dow Jones. The environment for newspapers continued to worsen. He had spent his first several months replacing his management team, reorganizing the company into two divisions, and cutting costs. But Dow Jones's stock price had barely budged, and the competitors were in nose-dives. Newspaper company profit margins were rapidly dwindling. In Chicago, the Tribune Company was desperately trying to sell itself at the urging of the Chandler family, which retained a large stake. The future of the industry was undoubtedly bleaker than its storied past, and even the optimists—who kept hoping that the masses of readers who had turned away from traditional newspapers would turn back to them in their digital form—were getting nervous. Zannino knew his company was up against it. When Jimmy called Zannino, the two started up the easy banter they often did, and the topic was Dow Jones. As usual, Jimmy took notes.

This second meeting would be more serious than the first. The men were meeting at Jimmy's offices, and he would reserve one of the executive dining rooms looking out over the Chrysler and Empire State buildings, a majestic setting for the cause. Five months had passed since their last rendezvous. Murdoch made no secret of his interest in Dow Jones, though he had spoken out a few months earlier to express his displeasure with the redesign of the paper. Even then, Murdoch's comments betrayed an interest well beyond that of an enthusiastic subscriber.

Zannino had been watching the dire developments in Chicago at the Tribune Company. He and Dow Jones's publisher, Gordon Crovitz, had just explored an acquisition of Business Wire, an idea that was rebuffed by the independent directors of Dow Jones and the Bancroft family directors. Much to Zannino's and Crovitz's chagrin, Warren Buffett snapped up the company shortly thereafter for 20 percent more than what Dow Jones had offered.

When he got on the phone with Jimmy, he shared his thoughts. Zannino had been working on a three-year plan for Dow Jones and had presented it to the board at the last meeting. "I got us up to $47 a share in two years," Zannino said proudly. But even with his aggressive plan, he saw that there were limitations. "In the hands of a bigger company, we wouldn't have to think twice about spending money," Zannino said. Dow Jones had been planning to spend $12 million on a branding campaign but now could not, given the dire state of the industry and the dwindling advertising revenues, he lamented.

Jimmy told Zannino about the Bancroft family's gathering earlier in the month. Zannino, who barely knew the family, hadn't heard the news. Given everything, Zannino said, "It's not a bad time to say something." Jimmy let the words hang there as he contemplated them. He scribbled down in his notes:

NOT A BAD TIME TO SAY SOMETHING.

Zannino sounded frustrated on the call and shared with Jimmy his feelings about the board's earlier decision to keep Kann on as chairman of Dow Jones. Jimmy made a mental note to talk to Rupert about the chairman role. Maybe that was something they could discuss at lunch.

SAY SOMETHING ABOUT CHAIRMAN. MAYBE RICH MAYBE NOT MAYBE YES. PETER KANN?

Then Rich talked to Jimmy about how the board was about to change. At the company's annual meeting in April, when Peter Kann would retire as chairman, Dieter von Holtzbrinck, Irvine Hockaday, and William Steere would all step down from the board, Rich said. Jimmy scribbled:

DIETER VAN—OFF BOARD

IRV—OFF BOARD

STEERE—OFF BOARD

Jimmy remembered from his conversation years ago with Zannino that Hockaday and Steere were two of the influential board members Zannino had flagged as Kann loyalists. Having them gone might be an advantage, Jimmy thought. If a hedge fund started stirring the pot, Jimmy mused to himself, this would be a golden opportunity.

With that, the two wound up their chat, planning to meet that coming Friday at JPMorgan. Murdoch would arrive at noon and Zannino would come slightly later, at twelve thirty.

The lunch, interrupted by a drop-in by JPMorgan CEO Jamie Dimon (orchestrated by Jimmy to make both his guests feel special), was uneventful. But by showing up at the second lunch, Zannino had sent the message. "He may have just been vaguely interested in meeting with us the first time," Murdoch says, recalling the meetings. "The second time, he would have realized what was in my mind, that I had made up my mind." There was no direct discussion of the takeover, but all the participants knew the purpose. "I think that was sort of unsaid," Murdoch remembered. "You know?"

One morning in November, after the Bancrofts had gathered in Boston and Zannino and Murdoch had dined together for the second time, Steginsky called Billy to gently press him about meeting face-to-face. Finally, Billy casually offered what Steginsky had waited months to hear: "If you come to Rome, I'll help you." Steginsky was still in his pajamas, but as soon as he hung up the phone, he dialed a limousine service and ordered a car to Newark airport. He dressed quickly, throwing clothes into a small bag, and only when he was halfway to the airport did he realize he hadn't booked a flight. He called

Continental, the only airline he could remember with a direct flight from Newark to Europe, and asked to get a seat on the next flight to Rome. The next available flight wasn't until five thirty, and it was just after noon. Shaking his head, he chastised himself. He was too early and would have four hours to kill at the airport.

When he arrived in Rome, he headed straight to his hotel, the Hotel de Russie, between the Spanish Steps and the Piazza del Popolo, near Billy's apartment. It was before 7:00 a.m., and too early to call, so Steginsky, who had waited all these months, waited some more. Finally, midmorning, he dialed Billy's number.

"Boy, it must be early in New Jersey," Billy said, confused by the call that was coming so soon after their last chat. Typically they talked every few weeks or months. "What's up?"

"I'm in Rome," Steginsky replied excitedly. "At the hotel across the street." Billy paused for a moment before he could answer. He recovered quickly, amused by the eagerness with which Steginsky was courting him. The two set up a lunch meeting for that day.

Billy, his wife, Beatrice, and their son, Clarence, arrived at the café. Steginsky sat at an outdoor table. To avoid the sun, still strong at this time of year in Rome, they moved inside for lunch. Steginsky tried not to bring up the Bancrofts or Dow Jones. He knew casual conversation might make Billy feel more comfortable and make him more likely to hand over important information about his family. He was there to ignite a Bancroft family blowup and had picked the right powder keg. A schism was what Murdoch needed for Clarence Barron's heirs to finally part ways with the company they had protected for the past century.

The next night, Billy and Steginsky went to dinner alone. After a few glasses of wine and the slightest of prodding, Billy started talking. Steginsky took notes, and by the end of the night (and the end of a few bottles) he had about twenty-five names and phone numbers of Billy's siblings, cousins, aunts, and uncles. Steginsky went back to his hotel happy. He sent an update to Murdoch and slept soundly, knowing he was getting somewhere.

The following morning, Steginsky and Billy met for breakfast at the Hotel de Russie, by now with the rapport of college drinking buddies after a bender. Billy was nursing a hangover from the night before. "What did I do last night?" Billy asked Steginsky, with a laugh.

"You gave me about twenty-five names in your family," Steginsky replied.

"Oh, no," Billy groaned.

"You're a friend," Steginsky said quickly, fearing he was losing his target to regret. "I won't do anything with these until you tell me to." Billy visibly relaxed and took a breath.

"Well," he said slowly, "if you are going to contact people, you should start with Elisabeth."

"Well, let's call her!" Steginsky said, handing his cell phone to Billy.

Billy dialed his cousin. "Hi, Elisabeth," Billy said. "So I'm sitting here with a friend of mine who is working on behalf of Rupert Murdoch and he wants to know if you'd be open to meeting with him."

That an emissary of Rupert Murdoch's would be interested in talking to Elisabeth was neither surprising nor alarming. She was accustomed to these kinds of approaches. She wasn't entirely certain if Billy's friend was really working with Murdoch. But she knew that Murdoch, with his stable of newspapers, was a natural buyer for Dow Jones.

"Sure," she said, carefully. "Have him come meet us."

Before Billy and Elisabeth had hung up from that conversation, Steginsky was on his way to talk to the concierge at his hotel about arranging a flight to Prague to see Elisabeth.

The VIP lounge of the Prague airport, outfitted with pleather chairs and surly waiters, reminded the forty-two-year-old Elisabeth Goth Chelberg, older now and a bit battle-weary after her tussles with her family, of all the imperfections of her partially adopted home. Elisabeth had been married about a year to her second husband, Robert Chelberg, and she was spending roughly half of the year in this cold city and the other half of the year in Springfield, Kentucky. There, in the center of the state's famous horse country that lay halfway between Lexington and Louisville, off the Bourbon trail and close to the stables where she kept her horses, she resided in a rambling stone mansion with her two Jack Russell terriers and a basset hound. Elisabeth had lived alone long enough as the center of her own universe to have grown accustomed to her own rhythms and schedules. When she and Robert met, she became infatuated with him and her world changed immediately, but fitting herself into his ready-made life in Prague, where his first wife and child lived nearby and where business dictated his schedule, had been difficult. Prague was Robert's place and she tried to tolerate it, sometimes successfully.

Elisabeth had become active in the local community of recovering addicts. Once she became completely clean, she had gotten an elaborate new-age tattoo, but she still sported pearls and Yves Saint Laurent rhinestone-studded jeans with her riding boots. In her small town in Kentucky she was well known among the locals who shared her passion for equestrian pursuits. Because of her move abroad, she had dramatically scaled back her riding from the days when she won the Three-Gaited World's Grand Championship, but she still maintained several horses at a nearby stable. The horses, as they had been after the deaths of her brother and mother, were a comfort. Her scarred relationship with her uncle Chris was healing. She had refurbished the garage behind her house into a stylish, cozy apartment for her assistant, Philip, who provided real companionship with his witty quips and big-city irony. She socialized with a supportive group of women whom she had, over the years, collected. After the difficult childhood, the years alone, the battles with her stepfather and her broader family, she had emerged on the other side of it all intact and felt quietly triumphant. The only remaining disappointment was Dow Jones.

Waiting for her mysterious visitor that cold November afternoon in 2006, Elisabeth remembered all the suitors who had come since the death of Bettina. With carefully tended honey-blond hair that framed her sculpted, delicate features, Elisabeth had grown accustomed to being doted on by billionaires. The Bass family had sent their intermediaries, as had George Soros. For hours she'd entertained the entreaties of value investor Michael Price. This time, as always, she knew her admirer was interested in her not for her looks or her money. He came for the family jewel—the *Wall Street Journal*.

Elisabeth looked up brightly as Steginsky approached her. The day of his breakfast with Billy, a uniformed security guard ushered Steginsky off the plane in Prague and led him down the tarmac to a private car that drove him to the VIP lounge, where Elisabeth and her husband were waiting. Elisabeth was, as was customary in her first meetings, wary and reticent to blurt out the kind of specifics Billy seemed ready to produce. Elisabeth saw through Steginsky's self-deprecation and obsequious nature. He seemed to be trying very hard to appear very friendly. Steginsky, eager to find Bancrofts sympathetic to his cause, asked Elisabeth what she thought of someone like Rupert Murdoch buying Dow Jones.

Elisabeth knew that it would fall to her to help facilitate this purported interest in her family's company. The elders in her family and their lawyers couldn't be trusted to respond responsibly to acquisition offers for Dow Jones. Elisabeth remembered that back in 2003 she had learned that Arthur Sulzberger Jr. of the New York Times Company had met with Roy Hammer, the haughty Bancroft family trustee, and proposed that the Times Company buy Dow Jones. Hammer rejected the notion. Hammer informed Kann but told the board only after he had rebuffed the offer. Elisabeth learned the news only later from an investment banker friend of hers at an opera fundraiser. She wasn't going to let something like that happen again.

"Because of what has happened in the past, if you want to get some kind of an adequate response, you'll have to put something in writing," she advised Steginsky.

"I'm worried that the trustees might turn down the offer out of hand, without even talking to the board or the family," he said.

"Then send it to the trustees *and* the board," she replied.

Without having left the airport and without even having had his passport stamped, Steginsky boarded a return flight to Rome, single-minded. He returned to New York the following day, bearing useful news for his Australian patron.

6

The Chase

RICH ZANNINO WAS on vacation at the elegant Ocean Club resort in the Bahamas with his wife and four children in February 2007 when he received an e-mail from his assistant that, at least temporarily, ended his interlude of fun and frivolity. Rupert Murdoch had called and asked for a call back, even though Zannino was on vacation. It seemed odd, but Zannino had already been interrupted once by Dow Jones's incoming board chairman, M. Peter McPherson, president of the National Association of State Universities and Land-Grant Colleges. McPherson had served on the board for several years and often sat in meetings with an unlit cigar in the corner of his mouth, cheerily whiling away the hours. Though not a veteran of corporate boardrooms, he had extensive political experience as a special assistant to President Ford and as deputy treasury secretary under Reagan. McPherson was calling to talk to Zannino about the ongoing search for the *Journal*'s next managing editor. Some board members wanted to get an update on the decision making, McPherson had said. Zannino agreed to loop them in when he returned. No rest for a young CEO the first year on the job, he thought. He knew his time to improve his company's performance was limited. Zannino, a student of traditional business rules and time frames, knew that new CEOs had about eighteen months to show the fruits of their work. He was a year into his job and the stock price hadn't budged from the mid-thirties.

Once Murdoch called, the clock was ticking. To the mogul, "vacation" simply meant the relocation of his office to his 184-foot Perini Navi yacht, the *Rosehearty,* designed by Christian Liaigre (a Wendi Murdoch favorite) and comprising six minimalist suites, a gym, six flat-screen televisions, always-on wireless Internet, and two small dinghies, named *Grace* and *Chloe.* There, his children and grandchildren played together and he spent most of his time, as he always did, reading the papers and talking on the phone. He didn't consider interrupting someone else's holiday an imposition. As his staff well knew, he was used to immediate responses and he got them. (Murdoch's employees were openly thankful that he had not yet adopted a Black-Berry, though he made ample use of Wendi's.) Zannino didn't work for Murdoch, but of course he knew what was required when summoned by a figure at such lofty heights in the financial hierarchy.

The phone conversation that followed on that sunny evening in the Bahamas was short and deceptively mundane. With Murdoch, there were no jokes, flourishes, attempts to charm. He was a blunt instrument with a busy day ahead. "Will you have breakfast with me?" Murdoch asked. "Sure," Zannino replied. "I thought we could do it at my offices," Murdoch stated flatly. Their assistants set up a date.

After Zannino and his family returned to the United States, the new CEO actually felt somewhat refreshed—a lucky respite given that his life wasn't about to get easier. The world of newspapers was collapsing as if felled by some zealous natural disaster. A brief review of the communications industry revealed fear, havoc, and stockholders who seemed to be taking on the personalities of bloodthirsty warriors. Since Zannino had taken the reins at Dow, he had watched the McClatchy Company, owner of the *Sacramento Bee,* buy Knight Ridder Incorporated, the nation's second-largest newspaper chain and a storied name in the business. McClatchy had then turned around and sold off Knight Ridder's weaker papers, showing that even a newspaper empire that had turned itself inside out to please its investors was not immune to being attacked by one. (Knight Ridder CEO Tony Ridder, who resolutely cut his papers' staffs for the sake of his shareholders, had tried to assuage the aggressive newspaper investor Bruce Sherman's complaints, before being forced by Sherman to sell himself.) Elsewhere, the Tribune Company, which owned the *Los Angeles Times,* the *Chicago Tribune, Newsday,* and the *Baltimore Sun,* among other once great titles, was battling with its own ruling family, the Chandlers, while desperately seeking a way to goose the stock price. Then there was the virtually unknown Morgan Stanley money manager in London, Hassan Elmasry, who was challenging the New York Times Company. Elmasry had, politely but persistently, attempted to engage Arthur Sulzberger Jr. in a letter exchange about the latter man's business decisions. The scion brushed off Elmasry's entreaties, delayed meeting with him personally, and as a result stoked his anger and invited a proxy war. Sulzberger was, by tradition, both chairman of the Times company and publisher of its flagship paper. The dogged investor wanted someone else to hold at least one of the positions; he thought the heir to the Sulzberger family wasn't up to the task. Elmasry received substantial support from the Times company's common shareholders, but it didn't matter. The Sulzbergers, the same as and yet very different from the Bancrofts, controlled the votes. The episode was an embarrassment from a shareholder rights perspective, Zannino thought, and he wasn't going to allow anything like that to happen on his watch at Dow Jones.

He knew that sooner or later his company was going to find itself "in play," Wall Street's term for being up for sale. Obviously, he had to start playing the game—planning and strategizing. So he talked it over with his board of directors and talked to several investment banks, including Goldman Sachs, the best there was at financial parrying, so he could be prepared.

As Zannino made his way to News Corp.'s headquarters in midtown Manhattan a few minutes before seven thirty on a Thursday morning in late March, his cell phone made its usual annoying noise.

"Hey, how you doing, buddy?" Jimmy Lee said, a little too cheerily given the hour and Zannino's slightly anxious mood. The two friendly conspirators hadn't spoken in months, but they slipped easily into idle banter. Jimmy knew this was the moment in the scenario where their interests might diverge. Whatever happened, each knew that they would, almost certainly, have to unite again. So they entertained each other. Zannino couldn't be absolutely positive that Jimmy Lee knew his destination that morning. Murdoch wasn't gabby or a man too likely to trust even his allies. So Zannino made no mention of his business.

As his car pulled up in front of News Corporation, Zannino, who was not going to be late for his appointment with Murdoch, started his rather abrupt attempt to extricate himself from the call. "OK, I gotta hop," he said.

Without missing a beat, Jimmy replied, "Have a good breakfast."

Of course Zannino realized the significance of Jimmy's comment, which revealed, in fact, that Jimmy knew it all, all along. Murdoch wasn't quite the lone wolf he had envisioned. He had to have talked to Jimmy about the meeting. After all, Jimmy was Murdoch's Zannino expert. He would have been consulted.

Upstairs in one of Murdoch's executive dining rooms, Zannino sat down for what would probably go down as one of his life's least leisurely repasts. His sixth sense told him something, and to an observer he might have called to mind an eager young athlete from the second string waiting to be ordered off the bench. But Zannino wasn't entirely certain that Murdoch was about to put him in the game. He had told his general counsel, Joseph Stern, about his breakfast, but no one else. The meeting with Murdoch, he reasoned, willfully ignoring the obvious, was just like any other CEO chitchat. He knew it could appear the way it obviously appeared—as if he was flirting with a verboten suitor—but he wasn't going to let that kind of thinking deter him. He was a media CEO, and it was perfectly reasonable for him to sit down with any other media CEO for breakfast, he thought, in preemptive defense against his critics who thought Murdoch a dangerous presence, best kept far away from Dow Jones. Plus, Zannino wouldn't mind getting Murdoch's advice on the business. He sensed what might be coming. A guy like Rupert wasn't about to waste time on a seduction act if he wasn't going to make a move.

Seemingly at ease, Murdoch steered the conversation from vacation spots to—again—*American Idol* to the tribulations of the newspaper business and the likely outcome for the Tribune Company, which would be sold days later to Chicago real estate mogul Sam Zell, a deal Jimmy had helped arrange and finance. Zannino was impressed by Murdoch, and at one point in the conversation he acknowledged the mogul's experience in the industry with a deference that, given the rapidly changing circumstances and Murdoch's purpose, would seem like the most perfect of invitations: "What would *you* do with Dow Jones?" Zannino asked. Murdoch didn't answer the question directly. Conversations in the big leagues were, surprisingly, punctuated with fumbling throat clearing and semi-awkward silences. One such moment of quiet followed Zannino's question, but Murdoch didn't dive in immediately. The minutes crawled by and the wait seemed increasingly endless. Finally, as the plates were about to be cleared, the action kicked in. Maybe Murdoch followed some sort of old-fashioned dictate that forbade actual business discussion until after the food had been eaten.

"I'm thinking about making an offer for the company," Murdoch said. "I think it's the right time."

"Rupert, you know as well as I do that it's not my call, that it's the family's call," Zannino said. "Just at our last board meeting it came up and they said they didn't want to sell."

The response was part reflexive and part ploy; first approaches are always met with lack of interest or lists of difficulties impossible to overcome. But the sentiments to which Zannino referred were not merely fabricated to serve the needs of the negotiating table. He offered an informed reply. Whatever modifications had occurred among the Bancrofts, whatever shifts had been seen in their attitudes toward reducing their Dow stock holdings, a sale of the company by the increasingly divided family was still very hard to envision. At the company's February board meeting, the topic of selling the company had, indeed, come up.

That February meeting was one of the first in the newly renovated conference room Zannino had ordered up as soon as he won the top job. Down the hall from the smaller, wood-paneled arena where Kann and his predecessors had presided, Zannino wanted something lighter, airier, more contemporary. The new spot had glass doors and updated leather chairs. It was all a part of the overhaul of the executive quarters he had ordered when he took the job. These details, it turned out, were the easiest things for Zannino to change. The rest of the company was proving more stubborn. The meeting was well attended. Almost all of the sixteen directors were present, including Kann, Hockaday, Steere, McPherson, all three Bancroft directors, and Mike Elefante.

Zannino, CEO for about a year at this point, presented the board with his plans for the company. It was a typical three-year strategic plan, set out in bullet points and slides and full of numbers and profit estimates, far more detailed than the type of dutiful yet meandering picture Kann would have shown the directors. Zannino wanted his regime to be entirely different. One of the side topics of conversation was the decision to start selling advertisements on the front page of the *Journal*. The rest of the conversation was typical for him: he was, as he had shown with championing acquisitions such as MarketWatch.com and Factiva.com, going to move Dow Jones away from its newspaper roots and into the digital world. At the end of the three-year plan in 2009, the company would generate more than 50 percent of its revenue from digital businesses, he told the directors. The company still generated well over half its revenues from print newspapers. Some in the *Journal* newsroom joked that he could get there simply by waiting for his flagship paper to shrink. The plan was, importantly, measured in the end by how Wall Street would reward that performance, and he told them that in three years, the company's shares would be worth $47 apiece, a respectable boost from where they were currently stalled. At the close of the presentation, the directors started giving their feedback. Someone said that everyone seemed happy with the plans.

"Well," said Hockaday, haltingly, "not everybody might be happy."

And then Hockaday opened up a conversation about the company's future and whether the Bancrofts would ever want to sell Dow Jones. It was a topic that despite its implications for Dow Jones's existence was almost never discussed, certainly not in this room, wood-paneled or not. Zannino had not disclosed his meetings with Murdoch to the Bancrofts or the board, although he had informed Dow's general counsel so as to avoid any accusations of subterfuge. The three Bancroft family members in the room—Leslie Hill, Lisa

Steele, and Chris Bancroft—were surprised at the turn in the conversation. Mike Elefante looked as if he had been sucker-punched. The board almost never asked for the Bancrofts' input. And the family had, in its restrained manner, stayed in what it had seemingly been trained to consider its proper place. Then, all of a sudden, with no preparation or transition, came the question of questions, just like that. The elephant had crawled into the room and lain down for all to see. Elefante, new to this game and the eccentricities and conflicts of all factions involved, must have felt as if the board was whispering, "Let's see if he can hit this one. Let's see if he can run with a changing game."

Elefante remembered the family meeting at Hemenway & Barnes, the deafening silence that had followed the errant and occasionally obstreperous Billy Cox's offputting suggestion that Rupert Murdoch was going to be coming in with an offer. In a move indicative of the way the board and family had traditionally communicated and cooperated, Elefante and the Bancrofts hadn't actually shared this news with the rest of the directors. (No one really thought that Billy was completely sane or especially serious. It was just another instance of the troublemaker making trouble.) The relationship between family and non-family directors was superficially cordial but extremely reticent. In 2003, Vernon Jordan had blown up when he heard—after the fact—about Arthur Sulzberger Jr.'s acquisition overture to Hammer. "What the hell" were people like him doing on the board if the family was going to keep that kind of news private? Jordan had thundered.

For their part the many directors did not entirely follow the party line that credited the Bancrofts with being the great protectors of Dow Jones's journalistic standards. Kann was the man for that. The Bancrofts, most of the board members believed, were merely slightly strange and somewhat ineffectual rich people who managed to allow Peter Kann to do his job. At best, they had shown themselves loyal even under the most abysmal of business circumstances. They were to be endured. Sitting on the board of the company that controlled the *Wall Street Journal* brought prestige, and most of the non-family board members believed that this was the Bancrofts' main interest.

As the discussion continued, Zannino took the floor. He, more than anyone else around the table, knew what a dismal atmosphere the company was facing. Goldman had already done some financial modeling for him to show which companies could afford to buy Dow Jones. The most likely candidate according to the results of their work was News Corp. If the family was seriously going to consider a sale, Zannino had thought to himself that day at the meeting, they really needed to seriously consider who the buyer was likely to be.

"I'm not sure where you guys are going with this conversation," Zannino began, taking up the subject of the sale, "but if you go down that road, you're not going to like the buyer who's going to be the most likely winner of the auction. When you go down the list, the most likely buyer is going to be Murdoch."

Lisa, Leslie, and Chris eyed each other as the rest of the directors eyed them, watching for some significant reaction.

"Maybe we should sell the company," Leslie said, in the throw-up-her-hands way she had when frustrated by the discussion. With that, she entered a realm of consideration that had been as strongly and strictly forbidden among the elder members of her family as habitual adultery or nudity at Thanksgiving. It was suddenly a different day, one in which the unmentionable had been invited out of the dark and into the discussion. Lisa lapsed into amazed silence.

Then Christopher Bancroft leaned forward and spoke up: "Mike, when this used to happen, Roy Hammer would pound on the table and say, 'The company's not for sale.' What are you saying, Mike?"

Elefante paused briefly, looking slightly pained before rousing himself to exclaim, with as much certainty as he could muster, "No, the company's not for sale." Elefante's power over the family was more than a historical and symbolic deference to Hemenway & Barnes. He and various partners at the firm held two out of three trustee positions on well over half of the family's trusts. The other slot was typically held by a family member, but no single Bancroft had as much voting power as Mike Elefante. He, like any other trustee, could be removed from his position only through the courts, a lesson some in the family would learn, somewhat painfully, in the coming months.

The Bancrofts weren't ready to throw in the towel, they told Hockaday. All agreed that Dow Jones would continue as an independent company. It would not become another of those papers ruined by dull corporations without taste or integrity. The *Journal* would continue as the *Journal*, their *Journal*, their family's pride and their great-grandfather's legacy. As far as the board was concerned, Zannino was busy working on his plan for the company, and the family was happy.

Something was shifting inside him. Sitting at the breakfast table with Murdoch that morning, Zannino felt his adrenaline begin to flow. "Yeah, I know the family says they don't want to sell," Murdoch said. "But the family has never had a number before. I have a number this time, and the number I'm thinking of is $60."

"Holy shit," Zannino thought. For a split second, he wanted to excuse himself to go to the men's room and call his general counsel, Joe Stern. Stunned by the enormity of the offer, and the automatic weight and responsibility it thrust upon him as the CEO of a publicly traded company beholden to his shareholders, he took a moment to reply. "It's not my call. It's the family's call."

"I'm not going to the family; I'm going to the board," Murdoch said, pausing. "So whom should I approach? McPherson?" he asked. "He's an academic and a new chairman. Hockaday? Nah, he'll go straight to the lawyers. What about Harvey? He's a savvy deal guy. I'm gonna go to Golub," Murdoch said. It was as if Zannino didn't even need to be in the room. Rupert had one last question, just to make sure they were on the same page: "So did I make you an offer?" he asked coyly.

"Please, Rupert. No, you didn't make me an offer. You said you were thinking of making an offer, and you were thinking of $60 a share," Zannino replied, smiling. He didn't want the offer to come in to him at a private breakfast. Everyone would believe that he had invited this. Given that the family didn't want to sell, Zannino found himself in the cross hairs.

"Fine," said Rupert.

On the way back to the office, Rich called Joseph Stern. "You'll never believe what happened," he said. He told Stern the news but wouldn't repeat the number over the phone, within earshot of the driver. "I can't tell you now. It's nuclear. I'll tell you when I get back to the office," he said. Before Zannino got back, Murdoch had called Golub and left him a message.

Back at the office, Zannino and Stern started making calls of their own. They alerted Art Fleischer at Fried, Frank, Harris, Shriver & Jacobson, Dow Jones's outside counsel. They called the Bancrofts' lead trustee, Michael Elefante. Zannino told Elefante the news. "I just had breakfast with Rupert Murdoch and he said he's thinking of making an offer for Dow Jones for $60 a share," Zannino said.

"Wow, that's a big number," Elefante replied.

"What do you want me to say?" Zannino asked.

"I don't know. I have to poll the family," Elefante said.

The two hung up.

"That's it, we're sold," said Stern, who was standing by Zannino for each of the calls. If Elefante couldn't say no right away, the deal was done. It was as if someone asks to buy your child, Stern later joked. If you say you have to think about it, that's a bad sign.

When Peter Kann, the company's outgoing chairman, arrived at work later that day, Zannino and Stern told him the news. "Wow, that's a big number," Kann replied, echoing Elefante. "What did Mike say?"

"He didn't say no," Zannino replied.

Shortly after he got off the phone with Zannino, Elefante called Christopher Bancroft, Leslie Hill, and Lisa Steele. Each was startled by the news, but only one decided to immediately follow up with a call to Zannino. Leslie Hill, one of the most outspoken members of her family, was always a squeaky wheel in the boardroom. She had been eager for Zannino to take the helm and liked his energy and determination to change the company. His was just the kind of new thinking the company needed, she thought.

Elefante told her Murdoch hadn't made a formal offer, but he had verbally floated a price to Zannino—$60 a share—and it seemed as if it was just a matter of time before a formal offer would come before the board. She was thrown. "Just when we were getting going on the right track," she thought. She immediately called Zannino to get the story firsthand. He told her about his breakfast with Murdoch. He talked about the benefits of the deal and mentioned that he was "a total return guy," referring to total shareholder return.

"This is a huge price," he said.

"This is not what I want to hear," Leslie said. "What I want to hear is that you love your new job and you don't want to sell the company. That we could grow the company and find other strategic partners. Convince me you can do something with the company," she pleaded.

7

The Letter

O N A P R I L 4, 2007, the outlook for the U.S. economy was darkening. The real estate industry had peaked the year before, and concerns were mounting about the default rates of subprime borrowers. In the newspaper industry, the Chandler-family-instigated auction of the Tribune Company had turned into not an auction at all, but a desperate fire sale in which Sam Zell had agreed to buy the storied newspaper firm for $8.2 billion, far less than any of the bankers involved in the deal had originally thought it would be worth. Worse for the industry's outlook, Zell had barely been willing to put any of his own money into the deal, instead borrowing vast funds from friendly banks such as Citigroup and JPMorgan. Still, even as the world's financiers were losing faith in the newspaper industry, Rupert Murdoch was undeterred in his drive for Dow Jones. His shareholders in News Corp. had just the day before voted to approve a deal to swap the company's DirecTV unit for Liberty Media's John Malone's 16 percent stake in News Corp., which had threatened Murdoch's family control. Now, with that interloper out of the way, Murdoch was free to make his move. The CFO, David DeVoe, had been working on the structure with his deputy, John Nallen.

The day after the shareholder vote he flew with Gary Ginsberg and their families off the coast of St. Barts to spend a few days on his boat, the *Rosehearty*. Murdoch, who seemed to have put any discouraging details he had picked up about the Bancrofts' desire to sell in some unreachable compartment in his consciousness, moved forward with zeal and what seemed to be utter lack of doubt about the ultimate outcome of this transaction. Fresh from the breakfast with Zannino, he had instructed his CFO and others to prepare the formal bid for Dow Jones, a fact he had yet to share with Ginsberg, whose constant contact with the outside press and politicians made him, at that early stage, a risky confidant.

The weekend on the boat was an unusual scene of domesticity for Murdoch. His two young daughters, Grace and Chloe, saw him more than his older children had, but he only had so much time. The girls were more accustomed to life with four nannies (two from Australia and two from China), piano lessons, and shuttles between the Episcopal School and the rented penthouse on Park Avenue. The Murdochs were renting the Trump Park Avenue apartment until their $50.8 million purchase, the late Laurance S. Rockefeller's Fifth Avenue penthouse, was ready. Rupert had been eyeing the Rockefeller apartment at 834 Fifth Avenue his entire adult life. Back in the 1970s and early 1980s Murdoch had lived in a $350,000 duplex in the same building. Then, Murdoch was new to New York and Rockefeller was the chairman of the co-op board. Murdoch had attended a few shareholder meetings in the twenty-room, eight-thousand-square-foot triplex with a broad terrace. For Murdoch, the penthouse would be completely renovated by famed French designer Christian Liaigre, who had done Rupert and Wendi's previous apartment. For a few years, the Murdochs had lived in SoHo, when Lachlan and James were still in New York and Wendi was new to the city. In the SoHo apartment, Liaigre had installed a fully outfitted gym and a large screening room and turned the attached water tower into a dollhouse for the girls. Once Lachlan and James left, Murdoch felt the neighborhood was inappropriate for children and planned the move uptown.

The renovation project was taking longer than expected. Wendi would complain to the other mothers at the Episcopal School, who mocked the heavy Chinese accent of the nouvelle arriviste. "Rockefeller apartment, fifty-point-eight million," they would say, replacing the *L*s with *R*s to mimic Wendi's staccato speech. "But we had to put twenty million into it. Gut renovation." They whispered more, in front of the school, as the chauffeur and the nanny climbed out of the black SUV with tinted windows and dropped the girls off. "Those poor things. They never see their parents." The self-appointed minders of Grace's and Chloe's well-being worried especially on fathers' day at school, a Wednesday every year when devoted dads took the afternoon off to pick up the kids and get their photo taken together to be displayed in the school's halls. One year, Grace's photo stood out from the pictures of the other students. She had posed for her portrait arm in arm with the chauffeur, George, not her father. The mothers clucked with amused disapproval. Wendi noticed, and the next year Rupert showed up, but, the story goes, he stayed for only seven minutes and left the moment the flashbulb snapped.

When Ginsberg and Murdoch returned to the office on Monday, April 9, Murdoch, without any ceremony, stood in his office and announced bluntly to Ginsberg that he was about to bid for Dow Jones. Never mind that they had just spent the weekend together and Murdoch spoke not a word of his plan; Murdoch typically had enough going on that he couldn't be completely honest with any single person, much less the executives who had a stake in his action.

Then, with the same deliberation with which he had avoided the topic the weekend before, Murdoch started to talk about it nonstop, mainly to his board members, whom he was preparing for their regularly scheduled board meeting the following week. Murdoch knew a deal like this one at a time when newspapers had utterly lost their appeal as a business had to be seeded carefully with his board. One by one, he called his directors and pitched them. As was typical, none objected—the closest thing Murdoch got to internal resistance was from his chief operating officer, Peter Chernin, who didn't share Murdoch's irrationally exuberant passion for print—and the following Tuesday, the board unanimously approved the offer. Even if one couldn't justify the deal in business terms, the company, with almost sixty thousand employees spread across the globe, seemed to be made up of only one person. His passions had created the business and they would dictate it, for better or worse.

Later that day, the offer letter arrived by messenger at the offices of Dow Jones & Company. Addressed to company chairman Peter McPherson (who was the following day taking up his official post at the company's annual shareholder meeting), it outlined News Corporation's offer for Dow Jones: $60 a share in cash, then a nearly 70 percent premium over Dow Jones's recent share price. The letter praised the company and flattered its management. It invited McPherson and company advisers to a meeting "to discuss all aspects of our proposal, and to answer any questions you or they may have." It requested— "Although we have already completed a thorough due diligence review based solely on publicly available information . . ."—a meeting to begin a more detailed review of Dow Jones's financials. "We aim to promptly conclude a transaction that is enthusiastically supported by you and your Board of Directors, stockholders and employees," the letter said in closing. "We look forward to hearing from you."

When the envelope with the offer arrived, Zannino was expecting it. Murdoch had called Zannino shortly after their breakfast. "I wanted to know when your next board meeting is," he said. Zannino replied, coyly, aware of the sensitivity now of his interactions with Murdoch: "Rupert, I think if you look at the public record, you'll see when we have a board meeting, with the annual meeting, and we posted the date."

"Save me from looking it up. When's your annual meeting? Our meeting is April 17," Murdoch said. Zannino relented and told Murdoch that the board meeting was April 18.

"I'll get to you before the board meeting," Murdoch replied.

So on April 17 when Zannino saw the envelope sitting on his desk —from News Corporation and addressed to the chairman of Dow Jones—he and Joe Stern opened it, knowing what to expect. They read the offer, which contained the same eye-popping price Murdoch had promised to him two and a half weeks earlier. Then they immediately arranged a call for the directors to alert them that the letter had arrived.

April 17, 2007, on the eve of Dow Jones & Company's annual meeting, the forty-five-year-old Marcus Brauchli was in his tiny office on the northwest corner of the *Journal*'s ninth-floor newsroom, an unusual place for the global news editor. Most of the time he wasn't office-bound and could be found moving quickly through the newsroom, engaging his fellow editors in quick conversations or, just as likely, moving out the door to meet with someone more important.

His kinetic presence called to mind a rambunctious child who was perpetually unable to sit still or settle down. He found humor in the frenzy of it all and enjoyed nothing more than the intellectual workout of being in the center of a newspaper in the midst of a newspaper crisis. He often mused aloud about his desire to move back to China, where he had been more of a free agent, unhindered by the day-to-day bureaucracy and monotony his current job entailed. And yet, at each juncture of his career, when presented with a choice that took him off the ambitious track, he chose the very well-traveled road and made fun of it all the way. Whatever his true thoughts, he was smart enough to crack a joke, write a headline, and get to his drinks meeting by six. He had spent the better part of the previous year and a half working on the redesign of the paper, which had allowed him plenty of time to network and engage in a project executives both inside and outside the *Journal* found fascinating. The redesign was, in fact, the main reason he had been such a scant presence in the newsroom.

That afternoon, however, he was sitting at his desk when his phone rang and the name of his colleague and friend money and investing editor Nikhil Deogun popped up in digital font on its small gray screen. Young and ambitious, the two were allies in their plans to shake up the paper. Both were riding high, along with the rest of the *Journal* newsroom, on the back of the two Pulitzer Prizes the paper had won the previous day. The paper had won an International prize for its series on the adverse effects of industrial development in China, and the Public Service award—the most prestigious of all Pulitzers—for its series on business executives who had rewarded themselves with millions of dollars by backdating stock options. The articles led to the federal investigation of more than 130 companies, and at least seventy top executives had lost their jobs. It was the *Journal* at its finest, and all the more meaningful because the paper had been able to hand Steiger the Public Service award just as he was about to retire. A perfect sendoff. Neither would be able to truly anticipate the earthquake that was about to hit them, of course. Brauchli picked up the phone and heard the conspiratorially low voice of Deogun on the other end.

"Can you meet me downstairs by the turnstiles?" Deogun asked. Deogun's tone was steady, much as it was when he was reporting any business deal. Once downstairs in the lobby of the World Financial Center, Deogun pulled Brauchli aside and said, "I just got a call from a source telling me that Murdoch has submitted a bid for Dow Jones." Deogun was in the process of moving from Washington, DC, where he had been a deputy in the *Journal*'s Washington bureau, to New York, where he was taking over the paper's Money & Investing section. He didn't reveal his sources to Brauchli, but Deogun's connectedness had just put him in an uncomfortable position: he had first heard this news earlier in the day from a longtime source who had thought Deogun was still in DC. He told Deogun the news "off the record" and threatened him with legal language when he realized Deogun might actually report it. Deogun liked to be in the game, but he wasn't sure he wanted to be this deep in it. He had told the paper's exiting managing editor, Paul Steiger, but no one else. He was, very uncharacteristically, almost paralyzed by the tip he had just been handed.

Though Murdoch was well known in media circles to covet the *Journal*, an actual bid from him was a shock. Most reporters and editors at the *Journal* couldn't envision what the paper would be like without the Bancrofts; many of them, like Brauchli, had never really worked anywhere else. Brauchli took the news from Deogun calmly, the way one does when in denial of an imminently threatening event. He wasn't certain the offer was for real, or, more important, whether the Bancroft family would even entertain the idea of selling the company. Other offers had come in for the *Journal* in years past, but the paper remained independent, and its journalists remained buffered from the corporate takeover dramas they covered at other institutions with jaded eyes.

Reality set in later that afternoon, when Brauchli's phone rang again, this time with a call from Robert Thomson, the editor of Murdoch's *Times* of London. Thomson suffered from the painful chronic inflammatory joint disease ankylosing spondylitis, which constricted his chest to the point that his posture was perpetually stooped. A native of Australia like his boss, he was known in London for his dry wit, his quiet but winning demeanor, and his idiosyncratic fashions—he seemed perpetually clad in a skinny black suit and skinny black tie.

Brauchli was surprised that Thomson was in New York, but he confirmed the news. "Yes, they just sent it over," Thomson said, when Brauchli asked him about it. "That's why I'm in New York." Thomson's information was more specific than Deogun's—he told Brauchli of the $60 price tag—and he suggested grabbing a drink later. It was clear he had inside knowledge of the bid. Brauchli rushed off the call.

Thomson, who was born thirty years to the day after Murdoch, had become a kind of adopted son to the old man (though one of his own sons claimed it was with his editors that Murdoch had his most successful relationships; his children occasionally rose to the level of being adopted editors). Thomson had strong opinions about the paper. He remembered competing against it half a decade before when he was running the *Financial Times*'s U.S. edition in New York. His team broke stories the *Journal* ignored but then followed days later without recognizing the *FT*'s scoop.

He thought the *Journal*'s focus—long, front-page feature stories that often had very little to do with the day's news—bred complacency and indulgence. And he knew that just a year previously, in what he saw as the misguided retreat dubbed "*Journal* 3.0," the paper was backing even further away from the news. The *Journal* was trying to go in another direction, to emphasize its strong suit and analyze the news in the pages of the paper, not just report it. The effort at analysis, Thomson would later note dismissively, meant starting most articles with the word *how* and filling the paper with clunky analysis. It was, to him, pretending the newspaper wasn't in the business of breaking news. He disapproved of the new approach and had spent years whispering into Murdoch's ear about how he could improve the paper. In 2001, after Thomson had taken over as U.S. editor of the *Financial Times*, he said that the *Journal* was best at covering "midsize companies doing middling deals in the Midwest," while the *FT* was designed for a more sophisticated reader. "It's a Lexus-

Taurus thing." He knew Brauchli from way back when they were both foreign correspondents in Asia, but he didn't like the direction his friend's paper was taking.

A day or two after the bid, Deogun received another call from Ginsberg, bearing the same news. Both Ginsberg and Thomson were calling on Rupert's behalf, gauging the reaction inside the *Journal's* newsroom in order to bring a scrap of information back to their boss and benefactor. Murdoch craved it.

Murdoch and Thomson vacationed together, and their wives, both Chinese and roughly the same age, got along well. Thomson shared Murdoch's Australian puckishness, and both men relished their ability to provoke. Both men were defined by a certain disdain for their backgrounds. Thomson, one of three boys, grew up the son of a typesetter in a small hamlet in Australia. He took a job as a copy boy at age seventeen at the *Herald* in Melbourne.

Thomson had met Murdoch in New York when the former was the U.S. editor of the *Financial Times*. Their bond was cemented when Thomson, in a move that both he and Murdoch saw as a slight from the posh Brits, was passed over to be the top editor of the *Financial Times*. Thomson was deeply wounded by the oversight, and Murdoch, sensing a countryman in distress, scooped Thomson up as his chosen editor for the *Times* of London. With time, the two grew even closer. Thomson's own father having been a complicated presence in his upbringing, Murdoch filled the role.

The same day, April 17, 2007, that Brauchli received the calls alerting him to News Corp.'s offer, he also fielded another call from *Journal* publisher Gordon Crovitz, bearing a different sort of news. Crovitz hadn't yet been notified of the bid (he wouldn't find out until almost two weeks later, when news of it broke on May 1). Brauchli didn't mention the Murdoch bid; he was treating it, for the moment, like an enormously sensitive news story that he wasn't going to spread around.

In Crovitz's mind, the day was significant for a different reason: Dow Jones was going to appoint a new managing editor of the *Journal*, the first such appointment in sixteen years. He had been dreading the day, because it meant he was going to officially have to betray his friend Paul Ingrassia.

After Ingrassia had spent almost a year on his "news strategy committee," his downfall had culminated in a meeting where he presented his committee's results to Zannino, Crovitz, and a few other executives. He, as planned, had proposed combining some of the *Journal* and Newswires bureaus and reported that the combinations would save between $5 million and $7 million in ongoing newsroom costs.

The combinations carried huge political costs for Crovitz and Zannino. If they followed Ingrassia's suggestion, they would finally be taking on what many in the *Journal* newsroom had dreaded for years. The moves would worsen morale and leave Zannino taking the blame for ruining the newsroom—all for a paltry business return. After Ingrassia presented his ideas—to get the Detroit bureau and the Washington bureaus of the *Journal* and Newswires to work together on all stories and plan coverage together—and the relatively small cost savings estimates, Zannino had blown up, visibly agitated at Ingrassia's suggestion and what, to Zannino, seemed like his tin ear.

The managing editor had to be the CEO's cover. If Zannino suggested something that would damage the *Journal,* he wanted someone like Paul Steiger in that role, who had the political skills to navigate the retrenchment without calling attention to it. Ingrassia was too blunt and too insensitive in his handling of the newsroom to be trusted in the spot. Zannino had upbraided Ingrassia in the meeting and stormed out. Ever since then, the choice for managing editor had seemed inevitable—it was Marcus Brauchli. But to be certain, Zannino and Crovitz had created spreadsheets and lists of desirable attributes an ideal managing editor would possess. They ranked both Brauchli and Ingrassia. Even by the spreadsheet, Brauchli won. Zannino was certain of this, but it took Crovitz longer to come to agree with his boss. Crovitz and Ingrassia had known each other for a long time, through Ingrassia's bout with lung cancer and years in the newsroom, though always on opposite sides of the Chinese wall between the news and editorial pages. Besides, he had virtually promised him the managing editor job; backtracking was going to be painful and embarrassing.

Unlike the "news strategy committee," Brauchli's chosen project fared well. He had been the news man behind the *"Journal* 3.0" redesign. The project achieved the aforementioned shrinking of the paper and the placement of an advertisement on its front page. Brauchli and Crovitz had worked together on launching it. Crovitz had written in his publisher's note the day the first smaller paper appeared: "Your print *Journal* will now focus even more on 'what the news means,' beyond simply what happened yesterday."

Crovitz told readers that the paper would "now aim to make eighty per cent of your *Journal* what-it-means journalism." Brauchli had chimed in with his own explanation of the paper's values. "The *Journal* is not really about pack journalism," Brauchli said. "We assume people will get general-interest news not aimed at our audience [elsewhere]. We then step back from the news."

The paper had been operating in its new format for over three months the day Brauchli received Crovitz's call, and even though it had been panned by some—the *Columbia Journalism Review* headlined its story on the redesign "Shrinky-Dink WSJ"—the effort was deemed a success by Zannino and the board. So when Crovitz, entirely unaware of the Murdoch offer that would change all their lives so profoundly, called Brauchli the afternoon of April 17, he asked simply, "Are you planning on going to the annual meeting tomorrow?" Both he and Brauchli knew the new managing editor would be announced the following day after the annual meeting. Both men knew the job was Brauchli's. When Brauchli replied that yes, of course, he was attending the meeting, Crovitz said, "If you'd like I thought we could walk over together." It was the anointing Brauchli had been expecting. Paul Ingrassia wouldn't learn his fate until the following morning.

That evening, after the Murdoch offer had come in and after Brauchli had gotten the signal he would be named the new managing editor, Brauchli and Murdoch's editor Thomson met for a drink that became dinner at the casual bistro French Roast on 11th Street and Sixth Avenue to discuss the day's events.

Thomson had once lived nearby when he was the U.S. editor of the

Financial Times, and the restaurant was one of his favorite haunts. In his signature black suit, Thomson arrived first, and the two sat down to a dinner of Niçoise salads (both men were slender, and Brauchli did not eat red meat) and opened a bottle of Pinot Noir. Thomson was there to gather intelligence for Murdoch, to woo Brauchli and get him on the right side. He wanted to convince Brauchli that Murdoch's ideas were good for the paper. The irony was that many of Murdoch's ideas for the paper had come from Thomson himself, during the many months the two had discussed the *Journal.* While Jimmy Lee gave Murdoch tactical assistance, Thomson was Murdoch's spiritual adviser for the takeover of the paper.

Though Brauchli knew Thomson and Murdoch were close, he couldn't have imagined how much Thomson was reporting back to his boss. Thomson and Brauchli were friends and competitors and intellectual jousting partners. But Thomson's allegiance in this game was to Murdoch. For both Thomson and Murdoch, the *Wall Street Journal* was a vehicle for personal score settling. Murdoch was going up against the Sulzbergers; Thomson was going up against his old colleagues at the *Financial Times,* the ones who had so ill-treated him.

The conversation immediately turned to what Murdoch would do with the paper once he owned it—Thomson seemed certain of that eventuality. Murdoch had his eye on the *New York Times.* Thomson explained to Brauchli how the *Journal* could better attack its crosstown rival. The *Times* was even more complacent than the *Journal,* he felt; its coverage left huge gaps for anyone who wanted to energetically cover the world's events for an American audience.

Brauchli countered that the opportunities were really in digital media, as Bloomberg had demonstrated. News Corp. could consider getting back into the business Dow Jones had abandoned when it sold Telerate, but do it right this time. Their chatter was competitive and witty, as always. Thomson, who knew Brauchli was about to be named managing editor, shared some more personal bits of advice with his friend. He told him to ask for a hefty salary as the new managing editor, reminding him that British editors such as Paul Dacre at the *Daily Mail* made more than $2 million a year. Brauchli laughed and told him he would take it under advisement.

The next morning, the morning of the annual shareholders' meeting, Crovitz stood before the board, dutifully presenting the analysis of both Brauchli and Ingrassia. He praised both men, and in the end, choked up by the betrayal of his friend Ingrassia, Crovitz concluded, "Despite my friendship and long working relationship with Paul, I think Marcus is the best choice for the job."

8

The Wait

A T D O W J O N E S 'S annual meeting, the day after Murdoch's written offer arrived, the company's board members, executives, shareholders, and employees gathered in the low-ceilinged American Express auditorium adjacent to Dow Jones's Battery Park City headquarters. These scripted gatherings were almost aggressively low-key and had in the past provided the occasion for the Bancrofts' dinners at the '21' Club and their lunches with the *Journal*'s Pulitzer Prize winners, but this day was significant for a different reason, and not just because Murdoch's secret offer had been unleashed, finally and irreversibly. Dow Jones was losing its true patriarchs: Paul Steiger and Peter Kann were retiring.

Zannino's relationship with Kann had been frosty for much of the past year; it was almost sixteen months earlier that he had fired House. Now, Kann was stepping down as chairman. Finding his replacement had been a process of elimination. Irv Hockaday had been the most obvious choice, but he (fortunately, he must have thought, given the problems facing the company) was too old to take on the position. Harvey Golub had pleaded that he was too busy. Lewis Campbell, a sitting CEO at defense contractor Textron, was too preoccupied with his day job. Frank Newman was living in Asia, now the CEO of Shenzhen Development Bank. That had left Peter McPherson as the only senior director who wanted the post.

Kann didn't have much time for PowerPoint and flashy presentations. Before the packed crowd in the small auditorium, he sat at the
small folding table the company typically set up onstage, looking as
if he would prefer to be addressing a more intimate event. He didn't
speak like other CEOs. His presentations were halting, his shoulders
hunched, his balding head modestly pitched forward.

When he took the podium at that April meeting to make his last
presentation as a company official, he cleared his throat and offered
"a few final reflections on an institution it has been my privilege to
play various roles in for the past forty-three years." He had stood on
this stage before, but this time he had an explosive secret. (The offer
from News Corp. had been presented to the entire board the night before, and he sensed with uneasiness that his successor, Richard Zannino, would take a decidedly different stance than Kann had when he
was in the CEO spot.)

Kann started off with genuine, albeit mild, praise for the changes
Zannino had made at Dow Jones. "Yet," he continued, "even as Dow
Jones—and the people of Dow Jones—embrace change we also are
committed to a set of core values that should remain constant." To the
executives and board members who knew about the tension that had
grown between him and Zannino over the past year, the message was
a veiled warning to the new chief to respect the institution he had
inherited. To the few who knew about the News Corp. offer, it was a
veiled plea to the Bancroft family not to sell.

A smattering of union protesters usually showed up at the meetings to object to the endless stream of budgetary cuts eroding the employees' pay and benefits. Some of them were Kann's old colleagues
from the newsroom forty years before when he was a young reporter
in the San Francisco bureau of the *Journal,* before he moved to Asia,
to renown as a reporter, and then to the business side. He knew the
shareholder activists who were regulars at shareholder meetings and
smiled every year when they got up to pillory his management. "Peter
Kann should have stuck to journalism!" proclaimed the outspoken
and ancient activist Evelyn Y. Davis at one such gathering.

Kann, in his rambling, self-deprecating, yet oddly winning way,
was at home at these meetings. The $60-a-share offer price would
make a fortune for Dow Jones's shareholders—not instinctually

Kann's first concern—and a boatload for its executives. Selling would be a way out of the numbing spiral of newspaper industry troubles, which had continued to plague the company after a year of Zannino's management. Still, selling to Rupert Murdoch would undoubtedly bring a new era to the *Journal*, one that was decidedly less imbued with the values Kann had defended all his years at the company.

In closing, he said, he wanted to thank the Bancrofts directly. He had known four generations of the family. "Family values and company values have been one and the same," he intoned. "And in that we have been extraordinarily fortunate." He got a standing ovation from the crowd.

Following him onstage was Zannino, who stood out among rumpled journalists with his cufflinks and tailored Italian suits. He was the second non-journalist in the history of the company to run Dow Jones. The only other was Clarence Barron's unfortunate son-in-law Hugh Bancroft, who had committed suicide so many years before. The precedent for someone of Zannino's pedigree was not promising at Dow Jones.

Zannino had been awaiting Kann's retirement day. But now it would also be the day he would face the board to discuss News Corporation's offer. The timing wasn't coincidental. Murdoch knew Kann's reputation. Zannino barely knew the Bancroft family and had tried to make it clear in his meetings with Murdoch that he wasn't cut from the same cloth as Kann. Zannino knew the bid was coming, but still, the letter made it real. Even though he had done everything to invite Murdoch in, he had last-minute regrets. He hadn't yet had very long to right the listing company. "I could still do more," he thought.

But he kept his thoughts to himself. The offer was still a secret, and Zannino knew that if shareholders ever learned of it, nothing he could do as CEO would measure up (except, of course, to sell the company). He could never create the same "shareholder value" through cost cutting or smart management. All told, the value of the offer was over $5 billion. The market thought Dow Jones was worth $3 billion. He knew it was the best offer he was ever going to get for the company, especially in a climate where newspaper stocks had faded from their former glory with very little hope they'd ever rebound. There wasn't a CEO in the newspaper business who looked smart.

As he took the stage, he spoke subtly in contravention to Kann. "While we intend to remain leaders in print, there is no question that we must transform your company," he told the assembled crowd. "We can no longer afford to be as newspaper-centric as we've been in the past. Instead, we must become more brand-centric and content-centric, delivering our offerings wherever, whenever, and however our customers want them." The message was clear. Kann was constancy. The company needed transformation. He closed by saying, "The best is yet to come for Dow Jones—for our customers and our employees and for you, our shareholders." It was true that the best was to come for Zannino, who stood to gain $16 million, and for the Bancrofts, who would reap billions from a deal. But for others involved in this unfolding drama, what was coming was the worst.

As with any takeover tale, at a certain point the advisers—the bankers, the lawyers, the PR specialists—keep the action going forward. The primary players in any deal are temporary, but the deal machinery that keeps an acquisition on track is a network of frequently acquainted and well-paid advisers who meet again and again on the corporate field.

The afternoon of April 19, Richard Beattie, chairman of the white-shoe law firm Simpson Thacher & Bartlett, placed an urgent call to Gary Ginsberg. Beattie, a former Marine fighter pilot with a penetrating pale blue gaze that belied his gravelly, kind voice, was a lion of the mergers-and-acquisitions world and may have been one of the few participants in the summer's deal tango not wowed by Murdoch. He had seen such moguls many times before, and as would be expected of someone of his pedigree and longevity in the deal world, he was personally acquainted with many of this mogul's advisers and the dynamics at Dow Jones. He had worked with Jimmy Lee years before on, among other projects, fashioning a bid for Dow Jones on behalf of Rupert Murdoch. He had also worked with Steve Rattner and Arthur Sulzberger Jr. in 2003 in their unsuccessful bid to buy Dow Jones. His first inkling that something was afoot this time around at Dow Jones had come that morning when Lewis Campbell called. Campbell, who had never lost the twang of his Winchester, Virginia, roots, asked Beattie a hypothetical question: "What are the responsibilities of directors on the board of a family-controlled company if that company has received a really rich offer but the family isn't interested?"

It didn't take Beattie long to figure out what Campbell was talking about. There was only one family-owned company where Campbell served as a director. Beattie recognized this stage of the deal. As in a divorce settlement, the rush for the best representation was on. Dow Jones's independent directors needed a good lawyer.

As directors of a publicly traded company, the board had a legal responsibility to their shareholders to increase the company's stock price as much as possible. By that measure, Murdoch's $60-a-share offer was tough to beat. Yet they were faced with a family (and controlling shareholder) with a duty of their own: never sell the company. Even in their cut-and-dried role as company directors with a "duty" to get the highest price possible—they could face lawsuits from shareholders if they turned down a lucrative offer—many of them still opposed the deal initially, at least intellectually.

Campbell had just taken over as the head of the board's governance committee, and it was his responsibility to make sure the directors handled this offer correctly with respect to their common shareholders, whether or not the Bancrofts decided to sell. Beattie explained that any offer for a publicly traded company could be shot down by the controlling shareholder if that shareholder was decidedly against a sale. In that case, the board of directors did nothing.

The Dow Jones board was divided from the moment the offer arrived. Peter McPherson didn't want the *Journal* to be part of a conglomerate. Harvey Golub feared the deal might compromise his beloved ultraconservative editorial page (Murdoch was, after all, more of a pragmatist than an ideologue). Dieter von Holtzbrinck, himself a scion to the von Holtzbrinck German publishing empire, wanted to preserve the *Journal* as an institution. Even Frank Newman was initially wary of a sale.

The others were more pragmatically minded, and Campbell, in particular, who never missed an opportunity to talk about how he valued his Textron shareholders, saw his reputation in peril if he allowed the deal to fall through. That was why he pushed to get Beattie hired. If one thing could be trusted, it was that, as Murdoch would later note, "as soon as you bring in a banker or a lawyer, they want to see a deal."

Gary Ginsberg had worked for Beattie when Ginsberg was still practicing law. Both were fixtures in Manhattan's Democratic circles. Ginsberg was an assistant counsel to President Clinton, and Beattie had served in the Carter administration and remained a major fundraiser and donor for the party. Theirs was a short conversation that day in April, but it conveyed a clear message.

"This is the last time we're going to speak," Beattie said.

"You mean we're going forward?" asked Ginsberg excitedly.

"I think you know what I mean," Beattie replied.

Ginsberg immediately called Murdoch to share the news. "I don't think they're going to reject it," he said.

Later that day, Peter McPherson responded to Murdoch's offer with an officially bland response of his own. The board wasn't going to reject the offer. It was, based on its legal counsel from Beattie and others, going to punt:

Dear Mr. Murdoch,

I am responding on behalf of the Board of Directors to your letter dated April 17, 2007.

As you know, members and representatives of the Bancroft family, including trustees of family trusts, hold shares representing a majority of the voting power of the outstanding shares in the Company. Accordingly, no transaction opposed by those family members and Trustees can be consummated.

The Board of Directors has asked the Bancroft family representatives to inform the Board of the views of the Bancroft family with respect to the proposed offer. The Bancroft family representatives have advised that family members and trustees will review the offer and will communicate to the Board of Directors their position.

The Board of Directors does not intend to engage in any dialogue or communications respecting the offer until it has received the views of the controlling shareholders and has instructed the management accordingly.

We understand, and trust, that the facts of your offer will be kept confidential.

Sincerely,

Peter McPherson

Now, all eyes were on Bancroft family lawyer Mike Elefante and his clients, the thirty-five adult members of the Bancroft family and their children, whose fortunes hung in the balance.

9

Personal and Confidential

O N FRIDAY, APRIL 20, 2007, at 5:34 p.m., Paul Steiger received an e-mail that would indelibly mar the otherwise impeccable reputation he had worked more than forty years to establish. It came with a simple heading:

PERSONAL AND CONFIDENTIAL FROM RUPERT

In Steiger's world, that meant only one person. As the editor of the *Journal,* he was accustomed to dealing with chief executive officers, so he wasn't intimidated. But as he read the message, Steiger immediately grasped its import: he was now part of News Corporation's takeover strategy.

Paul,

I thought it useful to write you a personal note, given that we are all about to be in the midst of a maelstrom of rumor and speculation. More than anything else, I wanted to assure you that the journalistic principles that you have embodied at The Wall Street Journal will remain sacrosanct. There are many good reasons for buying—or at least attempting to acquire—Dow Jones . . . screwing up the Journal is not one of them.

1. I have absolutely no intention of sending in the bean counters.

I believe in serious investment in serious journalism and that the global need for high quality journalism has never been greater— nor more potentially lucrative.

2. There is no doubt that Marcus Brauchli is a worthy successor, though he has a hard act to follow. Robert Thomson, who has known Marcus for many years, speaks without reservation in his praise of Marcus's editorial ability and his integrity.

3. What is on the Opinion pages will never be allowed to flow into the news pages. The two must be kept distinct and while I sometimes find myself nodding in agreement with the comment and commentators, even I occasionally find the views a little too far to the right.

4. If there are serious concerns among the journalists about "Rupert Murdoch," then we should discuss how best to handle it.

Paul, I look forward to chatting at greater length at a time that is appropriate and convenient, either in New York or in LA.

Rupert

Even before he wrote the e-mail, Murdoch had heard from his intelligence gatherers Thomson and Ginsberg that Steiger knew about the offer, which was now three days old. He had calculated that Steiger wouldn't come out against him. Temperamentally, the recently retired managing editor wasn't hotheaded. He wouldn't throw himself across the tracks to stop a Murdoch deal. Murdoch understood that winning over the Bancroft family meant winning over the leaders of the newsroom. Steiger had more moral weight than anyone else, so it made sense that Murdoch would court him personally.

The letter, like most communication about the offer, passed through Thomson, Ginsberg, DeVoe, News Corp.'s general counsel Lon Jacobs, and others before making its way from Murdoch's computer to its target. It showed self-awareness and savvy, and a willingness to promise what the circumstances required. It also changed the dynamic of Steiger's silence about the offer. Now, Murdoch had approached him directly.

During Steiger's forty-year journalism career, he had seen a generation of businessmen like Rupert Murdoch emerge from anonymity. The e-mail from Murdoch wasn't a complete surprise. Steiger had heard about Murdoch's offer for Dow Jones earlier in the week from Nikhil Deogun. He had approached Joseph Stern and Peter Kann with what he had heard from his editors. When Kann confirmed that an offer had been made, he did so under a promise of confidentiality that was customary for the two men. Steiger had a rigorous policy of not aggressively covering the business of Dow Jones in the pages of the *Journal.* "We don't scoop ourselves," he would explain to successive media editors and reporters eager to dig into the family undercurrents lurking behind the still façade of Dow Jones's ownership. Steiger and Kann had started a year apart from each other as reporters at the *Journal* and had grown up, more or less, as products of the institution.

Steiger's position at Dow Jones had become something of a hybrid in recent years. He was a member of the company's "Senior Leadership Team"—an effort begun several years before to include the company's journalists in discussions of company strategy in a time of increasing business difficulty. Such discussions would have been verboten even ten years earlier. But at all papers, news editors and business executives had begun to take the blurring of the separation between the two halves of the company for granted. Long gone were the days when there was open antagonism between them—there was too little money for that.

But this piece of news was different, and Steiger faced a decision. He could run the story. His own newsroom had gotten the tip. The offer was, under any circumstances, the biggest news story ever affecting Dow Jones. And it involved Rupert Murdoch, mogul of moguls. But Steiger had limited himself in his promise not to pursue the story, and he wasn't going to break the promise, even when the news was so big that it was for the *Wall Street Journal* the story to end all stories.

Almost immediately, the former managing editor of the *Journal* forwarded the e-mail to Zannino and Stern, suggesting the three men talk. He alerted Daniel Hertzberg, his longtime senior deputy, but swore him to secrecy and asked him, as the hour grew late on Friday evening, to be prepared to cover the story in case something changed. By the time Steiger got on the phone with Zannino and Stern, he had made his decision. He was keeping quiet. "I feel this came to me as an executive of Dow Jones," Steiger offered, before either of the other executives had even asked. Many in his newsroom would note that Steiger, who had accumulated a significant chunk of Dow Jones stock during his tenure, stood to make $7 million if the Murdoch offer succeeded.

He then took an additional step, enveloping three editors—Brauchli, Hertzberg, and Deogun—in that same executive cloak. The logic was strained. Brauchli now was a top executive of Dow Jones by dint of his role as managing editor, but he'd been in the role for only thirty-six hours. While Deogun gathered valuable intelligence from non–Dow Jones sources such as Ginsberg, he was first a journalist and hardly a business decision maker. Ditto for Hertzberg. "I made the only decision I could make," Steiger would later say, though he wished, in retrospect, that he hadn't put himself in a position that boxed him in. Once he had, however, he felt there was no choice but to see it through.

Steiger told Zannino and Stern that weekend that he would respond to Murdoch. He waited until Monday morning to do so and sent his own e-mail at 6:34 a.m. It read:

PERSONAL AND CONFIDENTIAL
Rupert,
    Thanks for your email. I very much appreciate your kind words about Marcus and me, and your endorsement of strong, unbiased news coverage. Any sale of DJ would require the approval of people well above me, particularly the Bancroft family, and I wouldn't be involved.
    Sincerely,
    Paul

Over the course of the next several days, a small coterie of editors learned of the bid, including Richard Turner, the editor of the paper's media and marketing group. He conscripted Martin Peers, his deputy and a native of Australia who had worked for the *New York Post* under Murdoch, to prepare a story for whenever the higher-ups decided to pull the trigger. Peers sat in his office for days, hiding his task from the rest of the newsroom. He balanced Harold Evans's book *Good Times, Bad Times* on his lap, typing up the *Journal* story that wouldn't appear until almost two weeks following Murdoch's e-mail to Steiger. Deogun, Brauchli, Hertzberg, Turner, and Peers all waited. But as any good reporter knows, a story as big as this one wouldn't hold forever.

10

Not No

SCARCELY A WEEK after Murdoch made his official written offer for Dow Jones, on April 24, Mike Elefante held a meeting of family members at Hemenway & Barnes's office. Elefante had scheduled bankers from Merrill Lynch, the bank hired to represent the family, to present the deal to the assembled Bancrofts, who numbered at least twenty. Elefante knew he was going to need help navigating through this minefield. His relationship had already begun to fray with the Hill branch of the family over what they saw as Hemenway & Barnes's poor management of their fortune. Elefante wanted some big guns behind him. In addition to the Merrill bankers, he brought in Wachtell, Lipton, Rosen & Katz, home of the legendary mergers-and-acquisitions lawyer Marty Lipton.

Michael Costa, a media banker from Merrill, presented the bank's "book" on the offer. Costa gave an easy presentation, showing the huge chasm between how little the market valued Dow Jones as an independent company and Murdoch's heady valuation. In the world of dry banking "books," the diagram was a blockbuster. None of the advisers had ever seen quite such an overvalued offer.

This deal presented a dramatic change for Costa. He had just recently finished advising the Tribune Company—a newspaper company at war with its own set of unruly family shareholders, the Chandlers—to take itself private in a highly leveraged deal backed by the inexplicably and eternally confident real estate investor Sam Zell.

The attempt to sell Tribune, an effort that had dragged on for almost a year, had been a painful warning sign for would-be newspaper investors. Nobody wanted to buy it. The company's bureaucratic corporate parents had picked away at it for years. The Chandlers, who still owned a large chunk of the company despite selling the *Los Angeles Times* to Tribune seven years earlier, had desperately wanted to sell. To unload the company, they had to agree to heavy debt that threatened Tribune and its newspapers with bankruptcy.

With Dow Jones, the situation was the polar opposite. Rupert Murdoch, an enthusiastic buyer, was offering a mammoth premium for the company. The Bancroft family was reluctant to sell, but younger family dissidents were breaking through the clan's previously united front. All Costa needed was a little family schism to make this deal go through. Then they could all help themselves to Murdoch's money and go home happy.

The schism wasn't difficult to find. In the meeting, Crawford Hill urged his family to consider the deal seriously. "Put aside your emotional reactions to Rupert Murdoch and think of the benefits such a deal might present to the family," he said. He and other members of the family had put their own emotions aside for years, he said. After all, "for some of us it's been very difficult to accept the *Wall Street Journal* editorial page direction. It's antithetical to our beliefs." Just then, his uncle Bill, Bill Cox Jr., who had worked for the company for twenty-five years in its advertising and circulation departments and was known more for his stellar golf game than his business acumen, interrupted his nephew. "It's the best damn paper in the country!" he shouted, in what was a frequent refrain from the man who was the closest thing the family had to a patriarch and remained unfailingly loyal to the institution his mother—the ebullient Jessie Cox—had taught him to love. He slammed his cane on the ground before launching into his defense of the *Journal* and his deep reservations about Rupert Murdoch.

"Uncle Bill's" impassioned defense went beyond his aversion to Murdoch. His nephew had just crossed a sacred line: he had criticized the *Journal*'s content. Doing so violated the family elders' core belief in hands-off ownership. Any discussion of the editorial content or direction of the *Journal* was verboten, seen as a slippery slope to-

ward interfering with the paper's greatness. To Crawford's generation, however, their parents had misconstrued that message to mean
that nobody in the family could criticize the business management of
Dow Jones & Company. Crawford saw the business of Dow Jones as
separate from the management of the *Journal* and resented how Peter Kann always tended to blur the line between the two.

"I'm sorry, but I'm going to finish my point," Crawford said, his
deep voice rising. "You've interrupted me before but this is not even
the main point I'm trying to make. I'm trying to get people to focus
on the facts of this deal, not their emotions." Crawford continued his
plea but didn't sway his uncle.

Crawford's brother Tom asked all the family trustees present—from
Hemenway & Barnes; Northern Trust; U.S. Trust; and Holme Roberts & Owen of Denver—what they thought of the offer. These lawyers
held enormous power over the family's control of Dow Jones. Instead
of providing guidance to the family, the lawyers were silent. Aware of
the tightrope they walked between various family personalities, both
for and against the deal, none felt comfortable giving Tom a view.

After years of slowly building distrust, the Bancrofts communicated uneasily, now mostly in tight-jawed polite exchanges. Most
of the family feared that Billy and Elisabeth would leak the news of
Murdoch's offer to the press; the family hadn't forgotten their dalli-
ance with *Fortune* magazine a decade previously. Neither was invited
to the meeting in Boston, which wasn't much of a loss. Like the many
other meetings the Bancrofts had held over the years to discuss Dow
Jones, very little happened that changed the family's static position
toward the company.

Elisabeth had no desire to restart the hard work she had embarked
upon ten years before. Rupert Murdoch had done quite enough with
his offer. She had a larger circle of allies now. What had been un-
formed dissatisfaction with Dow Jones's management had found a
focal point in the $5 billion bid. The rich offer promised to make
everyone in the three branches of her family much wealthier than
they were before he came along.

Each family member had a different stake in this drama. Because
the three branches had inherited equal parts in the overall fortune,
some Bancrofts, five generations on, stood to get a much smaller pay-

out than others. Elisabeth, for instance, was the only beneficiary of her mother's death and would benefit from the sale of Dow Jones by getting one-ninth of the entire family's fortune. Leslie Hill was one of seven children and therefore stood to inherit only one-forty-second of it. Perhaps those simple numbers explained why two of the family's strongest-willed women stood on opposing sides of the debate over Murdoch's offer.

Leslie's years as a pilot made her sympathetic to labor unions and mistrustful of what she saw as overpaid executives. Elisabeth, a champion horsewoman who had never worked a day in her life, didn't ponder such disparities. She knew that she was incredibly fortunate. Even when it came to horses, she enjoyed the buying and selling of her stallions—unlike some other owners who remained attached even after the best racing years were past. To remain in her fortunate state required some adjustments to her stock portfolio, and this was finally the moment when she might free herself of one of her most disastrous investments.

There remained one potentially large obstacle: her uncle Chris. He was the sole family trustee on the Article III trust of which she was a beneficiary. The trust owned 3.48 million super-voting shares in Dow Jones and therefore controlled 13 percent of the company's voting power. Chris Bancroft would grow weary of dealing with his cousins throughout the summer.

Two days after their meeting in Boston, the family reconvened on the phone to talk about their questions and have a "family-only" discussion away from the bankers and lawyers. On the call, Chris Bancroft, who had skipped the Boston meeting, said he was voting against the offer. He told his family he was against the deal with Murdoch, but Chris had previously sent messages through his Texas business partner to the Murdoch camp—Jimmy Lee, in particular—that gave the impression he might favor a sale. Murdoch didn't know about Chris's vote against the offer. He saw him as an important pawn in the negotiations; he thought he could sway him.

On the call, Buzzy Stevenson, married to Jean, one of the New England sisters, told his in-laws the offer was "not in the interest of the family." Leslie Hill held a different view. She said the offer needed to be explored, though she expressed her "regret, sadness, and disappointment" that it did. She was not saying she wanted to accept the offer, but she wanted to hear more about it.

Dow Jones's board wanted to know where the family stood. Throughout the discussion on the phone that day, it became clear that almost no one in the family was ready to vote yes to accept Murdoch's offer. Nor were they ready to reject it out of hand. If the Bancrofts weren't solidly against the bid for the company, the board wanted to start a dialogue; they had the "common" shareholders to think of. They couldn't be caught sitting on an offer this rich for shareholders unless they could put the blame for it squarely on the shoulders of their controlling family. For the Bancrofts, giving up a century of ownership would take a bit longer. In classic euphemistic style, Hemenway & Barnes came up with another way to gauge the family, one that would allow the Bancrofts to edge closer to Murdoch but maintain the appearance that they were still holding the line. Elefante asked them to say whether they were voting no or "not no."

The same day as the Bancroft family phone call, Thursday, April 26, Dow Jones chairman Peter McPherson received a fax from Murdoch, who was growing impatient with the lack of a response to his generous offer. McPherson had already responded noncommittally to his offer letter from the week before.

Since that response, Murdoch had received only radio silence from the family and the company. As the Bancrofts discussed their future on the phone, McPherson fielded another fax from Murdoch, asking the family for a meeting. He reminded McPherson that "we have a history of long stewardship of great newspapers (for instance, 'the Times,' 'The Sunday Times' and 'The Australian'). I always see my role as supporting the editors and publishers of these newspapers." He said News Corp. would be "the ideal partner to grow and expand your company, as well as protect such a vital public trust." Murdoch knew his reputation, and when he proposed a meeting with the Bancrofts, he reminded McPherson that he had family, too, as well as a group of top editors, whom it might be helpful for the Bancrofts to meet. "Such a meeting would at least give them better understanding and clear up many possible misconceptions."

The next day, Friday, April 27, Elefante knew the tally, at least so far, of those who had weighed in. Shockingly, it wasn't enough to rebuff Murdoch. Was it possible that this family, so long seen as an impenetrable fortress around the prized *Wall Street Journal,* was so easy to topple, so ready to sell out? Even Elefante, who knew all the fissures and weaknesses in his largest client, couldn't quite believe it was all moving so fast.

Elefante sent out a follow-up note to all family members informing them that given the votes counted so far, the family didn't have a majority to turn down Murdoch's proposal. That message rattled several Bancrofts, who had never seriously considered that their legacy might be taken away from them so quickly.

Two days later, on Sunday, April 29, at 10:00 a.m., Ann and Stephen Bartram, sister and brother-in-law to Billy Cox III, sent an e-mail to their relatives offering to buy out those family members who wanted to sell. They had talked to some of their cousins and aunts and uncles and signed their names to the proposal. Ann and Stephen Bartram didn't have the faintest notion of how to finance such a transaction, however, and many of the people whose names they signed on the letter were only theoretically interested in buying out their fellow family members. Still, Chris Bancroft sent an enthusiastic e-mail supporting the buyout proposal. But at 1:00 a.m., April 30, the family received another e-mail from the Bartrams, who, with the benefit of fifteen hours of reflection, retracted the offer. The Bancroft family was back to square one. Then, the morning of May 1, the Bancrofts ran out of time.

In journalism, the greatest crime is getting scooped.

David Faber, a reporter at General Electric's CNBC financial news channel, had been tipped off about Murdoch's offer. Faber e-mailed Gary Ginsberg at News Corp. the morning of May 1, 2007: "I know."

Ginsberg called Murdoch's office to tell him that they were about to be outed; things were about to change. The night before, Murdoch and his executives had met with their bankers. The stocks of both News Corporation and Dow Jones were acting up, and they had been bracing for the news to break. Murdoch, aware of McPherson's veiled threat in his last note to keep the news confidential, immediately sent him a fax:

Dear Mr. McPherson:

We have just been approached by email by a reporter from CNBC who claims to know something of our talks. We have not spoken to him. However, if you don't already know it I thought I should warn you.

In the event that something is broadcast, we should consider whether both of us say nothing or try to put together a bland joint statement. The danger is that so many bankers, lawyers and directors are now "in the know" something may be said which would not be in the interests of either side.

Sincerely,

Rupert Murdoch

But before he could hit the Send button, Faber's report was scrolling across the bottom of the screen (Murdoch had to turn from his Fox News channel to CNBC to get the story), so he quickly added a postscript:

As I sign this it is now on CNBC with the correct price!

When CNBC reported that News Corporation had made an unsolicited $60-a-share offer for Dow Jones & Company, the newsroom of the *Wall Street Journal* issued a collective shudder, not just because the unthinkable had happened—Rupert Murdoch had made a bid for the paper—but that the information was coming from a rival news outlet.

When CNBC broke the news shortly after 11:00 a.m., the *Journal*'s editors put media editor Martin Peers's story—in the works ever since *Journal* managing editor Paul Steiger received his e-mail from Murdoch nearly two weeks before—on Dow Jones Newswires.

As happened at many points during the summer, Mike Elefante was caught off guard by the breaking news. Although Elefante had spent the past two weeks polling the Bancroft family on how they felt about the offer, the family was so disorganized, and Elefante's communication with them was so strained, that even now, after the news that would change all their lives had broken, he was still uncertain about their stance as a group.

If the family turned down the offer immediately, the company's board would do the same, arguing that its hands were tied by its controlling shareholder. The family's super-voting stock, with ten times the voting power of a regular common share, had long gone out of fashion in corporate America. Such dual-class structures hung on in the newspaper industry as a vestige of a time when the press occupied a more respected rung on the societal ladder and family values trumped shareholder activism.

By 2007, that view was not only unpopular; it was mocked. Shareholders were demanding not great journalism but great financial returns. Newspaper company executives shared in the notion. Focusing on profits made the companies stronger, the argument went, and strong companies produced more and better journalism. The directors subscribed to a more extreme version of this idea: that Dow Jones existed to make money for its shareholders. They believed they were legally obligated to ensure that the company do so.

If the family was on the fence or in favor of the offer, then Dow Jones's board felt an obligation to carry out its "fiduciary duty" to the shareholders of the company who had entrusted them with their hard-earned dollars. Those shareholders weren't concerned about the Bancrofts' emotional attachment to the company, and they weren't about to subsidize it. As soon as the "common" shareholders found out that Murdoch had made such a dizzying offer for Dow Jones, the weight of all of Murdoch's $5 billion would fall on the Bancroft family.

Elefante couldn't corral the Bancrofts; he was still trying to tally the family's stance that morning when the news broke.

Zannino called him. "Mike, I need to know where the family stands," he said, desperate to know how he was going to handle this situation if they turned the offer down, incredulous that they might. "I'm going to need a bit more time," Elefante responded. "We're trying to get in touch with a few people and be as thorough as we can." The events were overtaking both men. After CNBC reported the news of Murdoch's offer, the New York Stock Exchange briefly halted trading in Dow Jones's stock, pending a press release from the company. The halt lasted less than ten minutes, and the release gave little information. "Dow Jones & Company today confirmed that its Board of Directors has received an unsolicited proposal from News Corporation to acquire all of the outstanding shares of Dow Jones common stock and Class B common stock for $60.00 per share in cash, or in a combination of cash and News Corporation securities," the release read. "The Board of Directors and members and trustees of the Bancroft family, who hold shares representing a majority of the Company's voting power, are evaluating the proposal. There can be no assurance that this evaluation will lead to any transaction."

After Zannino spent several hours sweating in his office while Elefante frantically called Bancrofts, Elefante was finally able to confirm that enough members of the family were against the offer that he could say no to Murdoch. "A substantial portion" of the family was against the deal, he told Zannino. But Elefante wasn't specific enough for Dow Jones's outside counsel, Fried, Frank's Art Fleischer. If the board was going to make all the rest of its shareholders forgo Murdoch's billions, the Bancrofts were going to have to be a bit more specific about how many of them were against the deal. The board was in, as one director inelegantly put it, "ass-covering mode."

Elefante spent several more hours tallying the total and came back with a stunning clarification: Bancroft family members representing "slightly more than 50 percent" of the company's overall voting power were against the deal. The slim margin showed that it would take only a nudge for the Bancrofts to sell the company.

By the end of the day, Dow Jones's shares had increased from $36, roughly where they had been trading for the past several years, to $56, a 55 percent increase. In that single day, more people traded the stock than in any day in the past thirty years, and more than two-thirds of the shares changed hands. The company, in effect, had been sold—not, for the moment, to Rupert Murdoch, but to a new breed of investors. These investors—hedge fund managers and arbitrageurs— were not Dow Jones's sleepy circle of shareholders. They were investors who looked for significant "events" to drive a stock price. Hanging on to shares for the long term wasn't part of their plan. They were betting Murdoch's offer would succeed, and they would do everything they could to make sure they were right. Zannino and every other member of the board felt that this shift would make Dow Jones "un-governable" if the sale fell through. Shareholder lawsuits would be plentiful. Directors would resign. The new shareholders would lobby to nominate their own directors, who would put the company up for sale. "It's going to be nigh impossible to put this genie back in the bottle," Zannino thought.

The *Journal*'s newsroom was hoping otherwise. The day after the offer became public, a reporter rallied his colleagues to communicate directly with the Bancrofts.

Investigative tax reporter Jesse Drucker urged his fellow report-ers and editors to appeal to the Bancroft directors—Lisa Steele, Les-lie Hill, and Christopher Bancroft—who would be the main people through whom the family needed to communicate. Noting that the family was under "enormous pressure," he wrote in an e-mail to his colleagues, "A short letter addressed to each of the three—make a separate copy for each—urging them to stand firm can only help our cause."

Chris Bancroft responded (in a letter he printed out on his letter-head: "Chris Bancroft Operations") by saying how much he appre-ciated the reporters' commitment to Dow Jones. But he was cryptic in his response. "I want to reassure you that my commitment to our common value has not changed and I will do all I can to preserve this special environment that encourages your work," he wrote. Such a statement left all his options open.

Shortly after the company confirmed the offer on Tuesday, the union representing the company's employees released its own state-ment against the bid. "The staff, from top to bottom, opposes a Rupert Murdoch takeover of Dow Jones & Co.," it said, expressing concern that Mr. Murdoch would destroy the company's editorial indepen-dence and would cut jobs as part of the deal.

The paper's reporters were desperate to preserve the unusual cul-ture of Dow Jones under Peter Kann and the Bancrofts. That sen-sibility, and of course Paul Steiger's, allowed the paper to ferret out stories that were off the beaten path and seemed arcane, until they became required reading. Ralph Nader, hardly a friend of the *Jour-nal*'s editorial page, once proclaimed that the *Journal* was "the most effective muckraking daily paper in the country . . . the main reporter in our country of corporate crime."

The *Journal* also pursued the unexpected feature and ignored the pressure of the pack, especially for sensational stories that were tabloid fodder. For example, in 1993, the *Journal* famously didn't report on Lorena Bobbitt for a month and a half, even as the news blanketed the pages of other papers. Then the paper broke its silence with a long profile of the urologist who reattached John Bobbitt's penis. That was the one and only mention of the Bobbitts in the *Journal* that year. Such aversion to the popular story would end under Murdoch, the newsroom knew.

Leslie Hill couldn't believe what she was hearing. Richard F. Zannino, the man she had advocated to become the CEO of Dow Jones just a year and a half earlier, was giving up. Leslie had helped push the early ouster of CEO Peter Kann and appointment of Zannino as his replacement. Yet here Zannino was, less than two years later, making the case for selling to Murdoch. Standing in front of his hastily assembled board on May 2, 2007, the day after the offer became public, Zannino looked out on the directors and knew he had to deliver a straightforward message that wouldn't be misunderstood. He wanted them to know the advantages of a tie-up with News Corp., and he also wanted them to realize what they were getting into if they turned it down. All Leslie heard was a man interested in selling out to avoid the hard work he had promised he would do to improve the company her family controlled.

The directors and advisers around the long wooden table represented an overlapping web of conflicting interests. Zannino had teed up this offer with his numerous meetings with Murdoch. The independent directors, though wildly different in their personal attachments to the company, felt they had little choice but to speak in favor of the deal; anything else might get them sued by the company's common shareholders. The family members on the board were their own mass of confusion and conflict. Not one of them was immune to the sentimental pull of their family's history with the company, but they took wildly different stances on what was best for the company.

Zannino's reaction to this assemblage of delicate alliances was to retreat to the familiar bland language of "shareholder value." Yes, there was "the potential risk of loss of journalistic independence," he told the group, but on the other hand, the benefits of the deal, the firepower News Corp. could offer the cash-strapped Dow Jones, would give the company the ability to go "to the next level" in a number of different businesses. Furthermore, the premium Murdoch was offering—the amount above the existing price—was beyond Zannino's wildest imaginings. He would be delivering shareholders a better deal than they ever could have imagined under Peter Kann. This last comparison wasn't explicit, but it didn't need to be. Zannino was the anti-Kann.

The meeting was disastrous. Zannino appeared, to almost all who attended, to have given up. A CEO was to protest a bit more when faced with his imminent irrelevance. Instead, Zannino seemed to embrace his defeat at the hands of Murdoch and profess immediately that he and his management could not offer what Murdoch could.

Hill listened to the man who she had hoped would deliver her company and her family a bright future. He was ready to give up and sell out. She looked at her cousin Lisa Steele, whose eyes were tearing up at the dismal prospects for Dow Jones. "Just when we were making progress," she thought, outraged.

From that moment forward, Zannino's board mistrusted him. Some, like Harvey Golub and some of the other senior directors, thought that Zannino was green, too inexperienced and uncreative to handle the myriad pressures facing him. Others believed, as did Leslie Hill, that he wanted to sell the company out from under the family and walk away with a big check. Leslie Hill and Harvey Golub both told Peter McPherson, the new chairman, that Zannino seemed out of line and in favor of a deal with Murdoch. McPherson told Zannino that some on the board were worried and urged him to write board members a letter to clarify his neutral position. Lewis Campbell, the CEO of Textron who was in favor of the deal from the get-go, told him, "You did it exactly right, but that crowd doesn't know that." Zannino began to worry. Five days after the meeting, he wrote a letter to the directors to assure them that "my sole intention in making these comments was to summarize the pros and cons of selling or not selling Dow Jones." He was furiously backpedaling in an attempt to maintain credibility with his directors. The letter continued:

As CEO I'm totally committed to doing everything in my power to help Dow Jones's continued success as we go forward. Please know that this is the way I felt last Wednesday when the family confirmed its decision not to sell. And it's the way I feel today.

More importantly, it's the way we are running the company, as my management team is likewise committed, engaged and focused. I also want to say I appreciate the confidence of the Bancroft family in this great company.

I look forward to seeing you all at next week's regularly-scheduled meeting. Until then, please feel free to contact me with any comments, suggestions or questions.

Sincerely,

Rich

The letter only served to highlight the awkwardness of what had happened a few days before in the boardroom. When portions of the letter appeared in the *Journal* a month later, it fueled Zannino's innate defensiveness and spread what would become the pervasive mistrust in the boardroom.

The finger-pointing inside Dow Jones began almost immediately after Murdoch sent his offer. But amid all the blame was an epic clash between the network of bankers and lawyers incentivized to make a deal and a group dedicated to the values of the old journalistic establishment. Mike Elefante, an unsuspecting lawyer with no experience standing up to the force of Wall Street's deal machine, was stuck between these two worlds. One of the most unapologetic members of the old establishment was Jim Ottaway, who had sold his father's community newspaper chain to Dow Jones thirty-seven years earlier and who had a year before retired from Dow Jones's board. Ottaway came to visit Elefante on Friday, May 11, to commiserate about the unfortunate situation in which the Bancrofts found themselves. Ottaway disapproved of Murdoch. Days before, he had penned an impassioned plea to the Bancroft family not to sell to Murdoch. His family was a sizable shareholder in Dow Jones. They owned 2 percent of the company's shares, some of which were super-voting B shares, which granted them control over 7 percent of the company's voting power. But Ottaway had been born with money and wasn't overly concerned with making too much more of it. A friend of the Sulzbergers, with whom he socialized in the raggedly upscale rural enclave of New Paltz, New York, Ottaway carried himself like a rumpled professor. He had owned an organic farm upstate, donated money to his alma mater, the Phillips Exeter Academy, and wore slippers when receiving visitors at his woods-surrounded home. "You can't make it up," marveled one of Dow Jones's advisers. That day in the Hemenway & Barnes offices, he voiced his strong aversion to Murdoch and his hope that the family would resist the temptation to sell.

Elefante showed up the next day, a Saturday, at his office to clear his head and work on potential structures to keep Dow Jones independent. He and Mike Puzo, another major Bancroft trustee at the firm, realized quickly that of the three branches of the family, two contained agitators who wanted to sell. Jessie Cox's grandchildren— among them the Hill brothers, Tom, Mike, and Crawford; and Billy Cox III, known in the family as Billy "three sticks"—were likely sellers. Then there was Elisabeth Goth Chelberg, who had long before given up her public agitating but still harbored concerns about Dow Jones. Elisabeth's uncle Hugh Bancroft III, the late Bettina Bancroft's half brother, seemed ready for a sale.

There were other factions steadfastly against selling to Murdoch. Chris Bancroft had told the family he was against Murdoch's offer. The three Jane Cook daughters would resist a sale, Elefante knew.

He started there and tried to figure out a way, as Ann and Stephen Bartram had fleetingly suggested, for some of the family members to buy out the others. Elisabeth was a beneficiary of one of the family's big trusts, Article III. Could she be bought out by other family members who were against the sale? Elefante wondered. How could trustees who didn't want to sell avoid getting sued by beneficiaries who wanted their money? Puzo and Elefante spent hours writing indemnity agreements to allow a trustee to hold on to shares and avoid getting sued. The Hemenway & Barnes partners had reservations about the Murdoch offer. As trustees on the vast majority of the Bancrofts' trusts, they enjoyed tremendous power over the Bancroft fortune and, in turn, Dow Jones. However, they had calculated that about a third of the family wanted out. Ignoring their point of view, Elefante reasoned, was perilous. "I'm not about to throw my net worth away to make a point," he thought. He didn't want to be sued, didn't want the firm to be sued, and didn't want to spend the next ten years of his life in court with the Bancroft family.

Murdoch was growing frustrated that he had heard nothing from the family since their initial refusal. He couldn't wait. Through their bumbling indecisiveness, the Bancrofts were turning out to be wily negotiators. Murdoch, impatient, began negotiating with himself. The same day Ottaway visited Elefante, Murdoch sent the family unsolicited additional sweeteners: a News Corp. board seat for one of them, and the promise of a protective structure for the *Journal* "exactly along the lines" of what was established at the *Times* of London. At that paper, Murdoch had agreed to a board of "directors" with the right to review the hiring and firing of senior editors.

Still, he received no answer from the Bancrofts.

Four days later, the business world added its own nudge toward accepting Murdoch's proposal: Thomson, a massive publisher of financial news and data, said it would buy international newswire Reuters PLC. Both firms were competitors to Dow Jones Newswires, one of the most profitable divisions of Dow Jones & Company. The tie-up was another reminder, at least to Elefante, that Dow Jones was outmanned. That impression was backed up by aggressive presentations in both Dow Jones's boardroom and family-wide conference calls with Merrill Lynch. Clare Hart, a Dow Jones executive who ran the company division that housed Dow Jones Newswires, presented the dire case for how newly combined Thomson and Reuters would cripple Newswires. Many in the boardroom thought she was exaggerating the damage and saw Zannino's hand in her frightening predictions. He had, by that time, lost the faith of many of his directors. But the presentation found fertile ground in the mind of Lisa Steele.

Initially, Steele had great hope for the search for a "white knight" for Dow Jones. But after Pearson PLC and General Electric Company briefly teamed up to contemplate an offer for Dow Jones, Steele realized that many of the potential white knights were in fact competitors to Dow Jones and would cut many more jobs than Murdoch if they merged with Dow Jones. To this Steele felt particularly sensitive. She felt she wanted to protect their jobs. She was slowly beginning to believe that Murdoch ownership might be the best way to do it. The merger between the Thomson Corporation and Reuters PLC would threaten to cannibalize the Dow Jones Newswires business. When Steele learned from CEO Rich Zannino and Clare Hart that as of July 1, 2008, Thomson would use Reuters's content exclusively instead of Dow Jones Newswires, she blanched. Sixty-five percent of Newswires revenue came from Thomson and Reuters, they told her, and that would dwindle to zero. What's more, Zannino reminded them, rival Bloomberg LLC was spending tens of millions of dollars hiring new reporters, and Yahoo! Finance was becoming an increasingly dangerous competitor.

Even the media were warming to the notion of a deal with Murdoch. Enthusiastic pieces about Murdoch's offer appeared in the days following the bid. Despite the aggrieved stance that Murdoch's team would take—claiming they had been vilified universally by the press—the howls of protest that greeted him this time around were far more muted than they had ever been. Murdoch was gaining respectability. Or at the very least, he seemed the best option amid the increasingly dismal future of newspaper journalism. Andrew Ross Sorkin, the head mergers-and-acquisitions reporter for the *New York Times,* wrote a lengthy piece on Murdoch's offer entitled "What to Do When Rupert Calls?" a short five days after its existence became public. Sorkin would have to answer this question himself months later, when Murdoch would woo him to come work for the *Journal,* but for the moment, Sorkin was focused on Dow Jones's predicament. The piece, with all the hesitation and hedges of an experienced reporter, made a proposal: "Mr. Murdoch may be the perfect publisher of *The Wall Street Journal.*"

11

Exploring Alternatives

LMOST A MONTH into the public's knowledge of Rupert Murdoch's bid for Dow Jones, Mike Elefante asked Peter McPherson if he could call a board meeting. "Any reason in particular?" McPherson queried, helpless before this diffuse family who controlled his fate. "I'd rather just cover it at the meeting," Elefante replied.

When the board convened via conference call at 5:00 p.m. on May 31, 2007, Elefante dutifully informed the directors why he had called them all to attention. The family had prepared a statement, he said. He read it to the assembled directors:

> As we have been since 1902, the Bancroft Family remains reso-
> lute in its commitment to preserve and protect the editorial inde-
> pendence and integrity of The Wall Street Journal, as well as the
> leadership, strength and vitality of The Journal and all of the other
> publications and services of Dow Jones.
>
> Since first receiving the News Corporation proposal, the Family
> has carefully considered and discussed among ourselves and with
> our advisors how best to achieve that overarching objective, while
> serving the best interests of the Company's various constituencies.
>
> After a detailed review of the business of Dow Jones and the
> evolving competitive environment in which it operates, the Family
> has reached consensus that the mission of Dow Jones may be bet-

ter accomplished in combination or collaboration with another organization, which may include News Corporation.

Accordingly, the Family has advised the Company's Board that it
intends to meet with News Corporation to determine whether, in
the context of the current or any modified News Corporation proposal, it will be possible to ensure the level of commitment to editorial independence, integrity and journalistic freedom that is the
hallmark of Dow Jones.

The Family also indicated its receptivity to other options that
might achieve the same overarching objective.

The board members and advisers on the call were stunned. The
wording of the release, pored over by Bancroft advisers and a lone
family member, Michael Hill, the youngest of the Hill brothers, may
have seemed benign, but to those who understood the language of
Wall Street, it hung a large For Sale sign on Dow Jones & Company.
After 105 years, the family was throwing in the towel.

Richard Beattie, the lawyer for Dow Jones's independent directors,
read one line of the family statement—"the Family has reached consensus that the mission of Dow Jones may be better accomplished in
combination or collaboration with another organization, which may
include News Corporation"—repeatedly out loud for the benefit of
the Bancrofts on the call. Didn't they see what they were doing? he
wondered.

The family was setting in motion something they didn't understand. They took the wording of their statement at face value, even
the throwaway lines at the end of the release that stated that a deal
might not happen. They thought they would see who was interested
in buying Dow Jones and then make a decision about whether or not
to sell the company.

That wasn't the way it worked. Beattie knew that the Bancrofts
had done something that required the board to make independent
decisions about the future of Dow Jones. No longer could the other
directors channel the needs of their majority shareholder. The board
was going to need to take action. It couldn't allow the family to float
this statement without starting a formal "process" of its own to sell
the company.

Mike Elefante did most of the talking for the family. Leslie, Lisa, and Chris said little. McPherson suggested that the four family directors hang up to allow the rest of the board to talk about the family's statement. Elefante quickly offered that the family would be happy to stay on and join the discussion if the rest of the directors agreed. McPherson conferred with Beattie, who said there was no way the board could reasonably discuss the family's position as the controlling shareholder in the company with the family directors participating. McPherson told Elefante that the family had to get off the call. The division between the Bancrofts and the board was deepening.

So, too, were the divisions between board members. Harvey Golub, the Campbell Soup chairman and Peter Kann loyalist who said privately that he hoped the sale wouldn't go through, suggested that the directors might not need to put out their own release saying they would "explore strategic alternatives," which was code on Wall Street for "For Sale." The family's statement could speak for itself and the board could remain silent, he told the group. Lewis Campbell, the chairman of the board's governance committee, wasn't going to take the risk. If the family was open to selling the company, he thought, the board's obligation was to sell it to the highest bidder. To stand in the way of doing so—and in the way of common shareholders getting their money—was inviting lawsuits. "We have a knife to our throats," he said, his southern twang hardening. "We have no choice." The other directors agreed with him, and they quickly crafted their own statement, which they planned to release at the close of the board meeting.

When the family directors rejoined the call, McPherson told them that given the family's stance, the board would release a statement saying that it had decided "to consider strategic alternatives available to the company, including the News Corporation proposal."

Chris Bancroft listened to McPherson, bewildered. "Wait a minute," he said. "My family didn't understand that this meant we were for sale." Beattie, now slightly amused and exasperated, repeated the section of the family's statement that seemed to indicate, unmistakably, that that was exactly what the family understood: "'The Family has reached consensus that the mission of Dow Jones may be better accomplished in combination or collaboration with another organization, which may include News Corporation,'" he read. "You're tell-ing the world the company's up for sale," Beattie said.

Chris was becoming increasingly agitated and turned to his cousins for support. "Lisa, did you understand that this is what this means?" he asked Lisa Steele. "Yes," she replied. "Leslie, did you?" he asked Leslie Hill. "Yes," she said. Harvey Golub directed a question to Ele-fante, eager for some clarity: "Does the family stand behind its state-ment?" he asked. Elefante replied with as much certainty as he could. "There is consensus in the family in support of this statement," he told the board.

By this time, Chris was desperate. "Is it too late for us to withdraw our statement?" he asked. Beattie had his laptop open on the confer-ence table in front of him and had been idly scrolling through the *Wall Street Journal* online. As he heard Chris asking his question, Beattie's eyes jumped to a breaking headline that appeared on the site: "Bancrofts' Statement on Dow Jones Bid." The *Journal*'s report-ers had obtained an early copy of the statement and put it out. "It's too late," Beattie said. "I'm looking at the statement on the *Journal*'s Web site."

Earlier that evening, before the statement had been released, Mar-cus Brauchli was sitting in the Osprey Room in the Four Seasons Re-sort Aviara in Carlsbad, California, on hold, surrounded by sea-green walls stamped with a paisley print, staring at a pitcher of water in the center of a white-tableclothed table, waiting for someone else to join him on the Polycom for a conference call.

He had been beckoned here by the CEO of Dow Jones, Rich Zan-nino, earlier that day. "Hi, it's Rich." The voice crackled on Brauchli's cell phone. "Oh, hi," Brauchli had replied. "Are you still in Califor-nia?" Zannino asked. "We just want to make sure you don't get on a plane. We need you on a conference call at 7:00 p.m. East Coast time." Brauchli was attending the "D: All Things Digital" conference, the Dow Jones–organized gathering of California media and tech-nology players. It was an unusually high-profile event for the usu-ally staid Dow Jones; *Journal* executives and top editors typically attended, but it was the rare Bancroft family member, with the ex-ception of Leslie Hill, who came every year. Brauchli took down the conference call number from Zannino and wondered what the call could be about.

Brauchli got his answer when Nik Deogun, ever helpful with intelligence, e-mailed him to tell him that the *Journal* had gotten a copy of a Bancroft family statement that would be released as soon as a Dow Jones board meeting was completed later that day. The statement said the family would meet with Murdoch. They would consider his and any other offers that would maintain the integrity of Dow Jones and the *Journal*. Brauchli knew that the upcoming conference call was obviously going to revolve around coming up with some kind of editorial "independence" from News Corporation.

Just then, Gordon Crovitz, the *Journal*'s publisher, called Brauchli on his cell. Brauchli told Crovitz of the family's statement, eliciting what appeared to be a surprised reaction. Again, Crovitz found himself on the outside of the information loop. That small irritation aside, the two understood they needed to prepare for a News Corporation takeover. They moved quickly to discuss how to create a structure to protect the *Journal*'s editorial independence as a unit of Murdoch's empire. Neither of them cared much, really, for the rest of the company. It was the *Journal* they needed to guard. If Murdoch was going to win the day, as looked likely, the precedents were disheartening.

His *Times* and *Sunday Times* of London each had an independent board watching over the publications to ensure the owner didn't interfere. Both, packed with Murdoch loyalists, were jokes. Crovitz quipped that the members all seemed to be related since they shared the name "Lord." The board had never blocked anything, the men agreed.

When Murdoch bought the *Times* of London in 1981, he promised new editor Harold Evans editorial independence. Evans memorialized Murdoch's behavior afterward in his book about his editorship, *Good Times, Bad Times*. When Evans confronted Murdoch about the guarantees in the editorial agreement, Murdoch shot back, "They're not worth the paper they're written on."

Crovitz and Brauchli batted around other possible structures such as the one at the *Economist,* which was controlled by an employee trust and Reuters's "golden share," which protected the company from a sale. That protection, too, was rendered meaningless by Thomson

Corp.'s just-announced agreement to purchase Reuters. The two men had their autonomy to defend, and they were united in purpose.

The conference call began a few moments later. Rich Zannino had gathered some of his executives. Leslie Hill joined Brauchli in the paisley-covered room at the Four Seasons, and her two cousins—Chris Bancroft and Lisa Steele—joined the discussion from Texas and Vermont, respectively. Paul Gigot, the editorial page editor of the *Journal,* called in from Istanbul, where it was two in the morning.

Chris Bancroft, still stung from what he saw as the betrayal and deception of the last call, led off the conversation, determined to take control. "We feel it is necessary we sit down and listen to Murdoch," he began. "The family needs to determine if there is any way to do business with this man." He articulated the question that was on everyone's mind: "How do you protect Dow Jones & Company if there is an owner other than the Bancroft family?"

Crovitz, ever mindful of the Bancrofts' power over his future, then thanked the family for their stewardship. "I don't know of any news organization with the independence we have here. We start from an unusual, maybe unique, position," he said. "And we all appreciate the independence we've had for a very long time." Crovitz was on a roll now, speaking in his hushed, professorial tone that made some on the call bend closer to their phones to hear him. He went through some of the structures he and Brauchli had just outlined. "What would it take to preserve the independence? That's where we should start," he said. The disembodied voices murmured their assent.

At a lull in the conversation, Brauchli broke in. He brought up his great fear that Murdoch's control of the *Journal,* simply by association, could tarnish its identity. If Murdoch started something called WSJ Television and had Roger Ailes, the former Nixon speechwriter and spiritual father of Fox News, run it, it could be more damaging to the *Journal*'s stature than any direct meddling in the paper's coverage, Brauchli thought. "The strongest protection I can imagine," he said, "is autonomy for the editors and some guarantee of job security. If we identify what it is that defines an editor's autonomy—from deciding how the brand should be used, to controlling content and story placement, to hiring—we can perhaps better protect the paper simply by ensuring editorial autonomy." Again, the assenting murmurs sounded, with Chris Bancroft agreeing emphatically. Lisa Steele, from her cozy Vermont quarters, chimed in: "It is critical that news and editorial be protected. We do not want to consider a deal with Rupert Murdoch if we can't construct something ironclad. We need to hear from you all who live and breathe it."

Zannino, who had been listening, then told Chris, Lisa, Leslie, and Elefante that the editors and executives would get back to them with suggestions for how to protect the *Journal*. The family, after their announcement, had quickly agreed to meet Murdoch that coming Monday. Chris Bancroft, anticipating the meeting, wondered if they could deliver those suggestions by Sunday, which was three days from the call. "Our objective is to find out if there's a reason to change our minds" about the meeting, he said.

Leslie, Lisa, and Chris hung up from the call. Leslie walked out of the room, leaving Brauchli alone. Zannino, ever focused on his role in this meandering discussion as well as his duty to his shareholders and his reputation as a CEO, took over. "Whether the family sells is really going to be a function of where they end up on the question of editorial integrity within News Corp.," he said. The difficulty now was that since the family had voiced a willingness to sell, the board was involved and obligated to sell to the highest bidder. It didn't matter to the shareholders if the highest bidder would ruin the company the day after the closing of the deal, just as long as they got their payout. It sounded cruel, but such was the code of Wall Street, and its adherents subscribed to it just as journalists prayed at the feet of objectivity.

Zannino was concerned that the family might reject the offer out of some unrealistic hope for independence for the *Journal* under News Corp. There could be a conflict, Zannino warned, if the highest bidder was somehow unpalatable to the family. "We have to look at it through a lens of the practical, not the perfect," he said. Brauchli flinched at this. While Zannino had maintained a public stance of neutrality on the deal, it was clear to Brauchli that he favored it. Zannino offered the listeners this final thought, cementing in Brauchli's mind Zannino's pro-deal stance: "There is something to be said for being part of a larger enterprise in terms of access to capital, access to platforms. This isn't the end of the world."

Just as the call was about to end, Brauchli asked Crovitz and Zannino to stay on. After the others had hung up, he told them that the recently retired Paul Steiger would oversee the coverage of the Dow Jones deal for the *Journal*. At last, he could delve into the story he had necessarily avoided for so long. Brauchli was recusing himself to focus on editorial protections for the paper. He wanted be involved in the question of editorial independence. The coming weeks would put him on conference calls with his CEO and publisher, shaping the future of his newsroom under a potential new owner. Brauchli gravitated to these power sources. But he was still ambivalent about his comrades in arms. "One other thing I want us to be very careful about," he said to them, "is the inherent conflict between the obvious interest of some people, and possibly the board, in getting a deal done at a high price, and the need to ensure absolutely that we are coming up with the best possible structure for preserving the *Journal*'s editorial integrity, even if it might lead the family to a conclusion the board might not agree with."

Crovitz concurred. Zannino appeared patient but was tiring of this chatter. What did these people understand, he wondered, about the pressure they were now under? The world had fundamentally changed. Fewer people were reading newspapers. Advertisers were buying fewer ads. Nobody had figured out the Internet. These could be Murdoch's problems in one fell swoop. Zannino told the two men that the best way to create the strongest possible structure was to act quickly to get some feedback to the family. He knew it would be corporate suicide if the Bancrofts turned the offer down, especially now that they had opened the door to a sale. Shareholders would sue the company in droves, and Zannino would be stuck at the helm of an embattled firm with no way out. "Life will be different and change will come" under Murdoch, he told Brauchli and Crovitz. But "it's a lot more fun to grow a business than to shrink it by a thousand cuts." With that, the men signed off, each to his particular set of strategies and objectives.

The following morning, Brauchli arrived back in the *Journal* newsroom and joined the news meeting in the small conference room next to his office to listen to the buzz of editors planning the day's big story: how the Bancroft family didn't know what it was unleashing with its announcement the previous day. Amid the chatter, an editor asked the group if there was a committee being formed to study how the editorial independence of the *Journal* might be protected. Brauchli was silent, realizing he had now entered a different sphere and wasn't really part of the newsroom anymore, at least not on this story. No one appeared to notice his silence and he quietly slipped out of the room. He didn't want to sit with his colleagues, withholding information they needed.

Over the course of the next several weeks, the number of people who became interested in the "editorial independence" of the *Journal* grew. Some were genuinely concerned with the independence of the *Journal,* but many others wanted a structure that would suit their own purpose. Zannino wanted the structure to work because he saw it as a means to getting a deal done; Brauchli wanted the structure to work because he wanted to protect his job and the paper he had inherited; Leslie Hill wanted the structure to work so she could stomach selling the company to Murdoch, even for a moment. Murdoch knew from experience that these structures were easy to establish and even easier to circumvent. As the inexorable progress of the deal machine moved forward, the editorial agreement became a useful distraction for the Bancrofts and the *Journal* newsroom. Crafting the agreement presented an illusion of control to those with little of it. They scarcely imagined how the *Journal* would evolve in the coming months, but for now, the Bancrofts appeared willing to believe anything Murdoch put on paper.

12

Family Meeting

THE RAINY MONDAY following the family's inadvertent statement, Murdoch got the meeting he requested. The gathering would bring him another step closer to his prize. Though Murdoch wasn't prone to much planning, he enjoyed musing about what he would do with various properties he didn't own. He had discussed the future of the *Journal* with his colleagues and fantasized about owning it for years. He had many changes he wanted to make in the paper, to make it more to his liking.

Those plans weren't what he would stress to the Bancrofts that rainy June 4 afternoon. He wanted to impress upon them that he, too, understood the importance of family. He asked James, the only one of his four grown children still employed at a News Corp. business, to join him. Murdoch's younger son quickly agreed. James was then the CEO of British Sky Broadcasting, a business that was 39 percent owned by News Corporation. He had gotten the job four years earlier when his father effectively appointed him to the post, a move that the British business establishment greeted unenthusiastically. The Brits, though ever loyal to the dictates of their classes, were not as friendly to the nepotism James's appointment represented.

Murdoch also asked two of his deputies, News Corp. general counsel Lon Jacobs and chief financial officer David DeVoe, to come with him to meet the Bancrofts. The two men were intimately involved in every step of Murdoch's negotiation of this deal. As much as Murdoch relied on Jimmy Lee to get the transaction done, his most trusted advisers were inside the News Corporation "family." Both men were part of the "Office of the Chairman" at News Corp., which meant they were in contact with Murdoch every day, many times a day. Particularly during a deal such as this one, where Murdoch's attention focused exclusively on his target, his underlings followed his gaze. On call at all hours, both DeVoe and Jacobs were fiercely loyal to Murdoch and were indispensable for meetings like this one. They were also there to make sure Murdoch didn't promise anything he would regret. While handlers were typically ineffective at reining in the "boss," as Murdoch was known inside the company, even Murdoch knew enough about himself to want these men to protect him from his own conversational meanderings.

On the Bancroft side was the legendary deal lawyer Martin Lipton. Three years earlier his firm had worked for News Corp.'s independent directors as part of a plan to move the media conglomerate's home base from Australia to the United States. He knew the players opposite him better than he knew the Bancrofts, who had hired him because they wanted "the best." He was hosting the proceedings that day. In his short professional biography posted on his firm's Web site, Lipton touted the fact that in 1982 he created the shareholder rights plan ("poison pill"), which was described by Professor Ronald Gilson of the Columbia and Stanford law schools as "the most important innovation in corporate law since Samuel Dodd invented the trust for John D. Rockefeller and Standard Oil in 1879." Lipton had done scores of deals and recognized a family in crisis. He foresaw that this particular deal was going to end with the family losing the company, and it was only a matter of how messy the process was going to be. He thought the sale to Murdoch could be an efficient exit for the Bancrofts, who were becoming unruly and too divided to be effective stewards of Dow Jones. But he was careful to keep his views from the family. Even though he was working for the Bancrofts, he had been talking to Murdoch, assuring him that the family would come around.

The meeting started haphazardly. Even though Dow Jones's chairman, Peter McPherson, had arranged to arrive early and meet for a few minutes with the Bancroft directors before going into the meeting with Murdoch, the driving rain disrupted the travel plans of most of the attendees. Because of the weather, people trickled in just a few minutes before the 1:00 p.m. start time. They filed upstairs to the main conference room Lipton had arranged for them and waited.

Leslie Hill arrived first. She had purposely come early to avoid any reporters who might be outside the building, taking a cab straight from Pennsylvania Station, where her Acela train from Washington, DC, had deposited her that morning. Her thoughts about the offer were complicated. While she wasn't particularly interested in selling, she initially thought the offer was exactly what the family needed. It might, she hoped, shake them out of practicing what she called "ancestor worship." She, like her brothers, had long been a critic of Dow Jones's management and Peter Kann. Murdoch knew this and initially believed she could be an important ally in convincing the family to sell.

Leslie had been interested in the meeting with Murdoch and felt the bid might wake up her cousins to realize they needed to focus on the company, demand more from management, and ask the kinds of questions Leslie liked to ask, the kind that were often followed with awkward silences and uncomfortable stares from family members and board members alike. She had grown so frustrated with Dow Jones's poor management under former CEO Peter Kann that she told people, "The only way to get rid of the guy is to sell the company!"

Lisa Steele, Leslie's cousin, and Michael Elefante arrived together at the Murdoch meeting from the airport. They had taken the shuttle from Boston. They sat down next to each other on the long side of a mammoth table in the main Wachtell, Lipton conference room. Steele had joined the Dow Jones board in 2001 and things had gone downhill ever since. The terrorist attacks of September 11 and the murder of Daniel Pearl were personal tragedies compounded by her growing sense of foreboding about the livelihood of many of Dow Jones's staff. The technology bubble that had buoyed the company's performance for so long had burst, and the firm suffered difficult layoffs and a dramatic curb in capital spending. Steele watched all the events with dismay and felt that while the company had been able to maintain high journalistic standards, it had less money to invest in important projects even as it increased its debt load. Steele saw the company shrink in what one of the Dow Jones executives told her was "a game of scale."

Steele had grown frustrated by the leaks within her family and on Dow Jones's board. What were meant to be private discussions turned up in the pages of the paper her family was supposed to protect. While she understood the reporters were doing their jobs, she grew angry at the breach of confidence, though she, seemingly unaware of the damage she could do to individual reporters' careers, told Rich Zannino about visits she received from *Journal* reporters lobbying her to oppose the deal.

She had been spending a lot of time with her sisters talking about the family business and was deeply affected by a day she had spent at the *Journal*'s headquarters in mid-May, when she spoke to the gamut of *Journal* managers, both inside the newsroom and out. She met with CEO Zannino and *Journal* publisher Gordon Crovitz, retired *Journal* managing editor Paul Steiger, Marcus Brauchli, and Clare Hart. At the end of that day, she couldn't find a single person who would tell her that the company would be better off not selling to Murdoch. "If these people are not against the sale, and in fact harbor great concerns about the future of Dow Jones as an independent company, then how can we turn this offer down?" she thought. She was also convinced by Mike Elefante's evolving view that Dow Jones needed to combine with another firm. Two weeks before in Boston, she had, again with tears in her eyes, told her cousins that her family didn't have the appetite for risk that an independent Dow Jones would require. It was a wrenching decision for her and her sisters, who descended from the mild-mannered Jane Cook and were, for years, blindly loyal to the *Journal*.

While they were still alone, Lipton passed out the family's draft of an editorial agreement they planned to present to Murdoch. This was the cage they planned to build around him if he took over the *Journal*. The agreement limited his ability to use the Dow Jones name. It protected the jobs of the existing publisher, managing editor, and editorial page editor at the *Journal*. It laid out how the family could sue News Corp. if Murdoch intervened in the operation of the paper. Each point reached far beyond what Murdoch had suggested in his initial letter to set up something "exactly along the lines" of what he offered the *Times* of London when he bought that paper twenty-five years previously.

Murdoch, Lon Jacobs, and David DeVoe walked into the meeting together and greeted the assembled crowd. The room dwarfed the attendees, and after exchanging pleasantries, Lipton invited them into an adjacent room to serve themselves lunch from the elaborate buffet the law firm had set.

As the group was filing into the other room, Christopher Bancroft arrived. The third member of the Bancroft family on the board, Chris was the most difficult to gauge—both for his relatives and for Murdoch. He had flown in from Denton, Texas, that morning. Leslie was furious with what she saw as his flakiness and inattention.

When the group sat down for lunch, the two sides faced each other. Murdoch opened the meeting with a welcome to the Bancrofts and praise for the *Wall Street Journal*. Because of the size of the room and the width of the table, at least ten feet across, his voice seemed faint to the Bancrofts on the other side. They leaned in closer to try to decipher what he was saying. He looked old, at least to Elefante, who was struck by how unassuming this giant of a businessman appeared in person.

Murdoch knew the reputation he had with the family: a meddler in news coverage; someone who used his papers to further his business interests; an apologist for China's repressive regime. He knew that to get to Dow Jones, he needed to woo the family. To woo them he needed to rehabilitate his image. He gave a meandering introduction, praising the Bancroft family and everything they had protected over the years. His advisers had coached him in the importance of flattery. In an uncharacteristic moment of self-analysis, he ventured an acknowledgment of his past. "I've made some mistakes," he said quickly. After a brief pause, he recovered: "But it's worked out pretty well in the end."

With a boyish face and closely shorn dark hair, James arrived almost two hours late. He had delivered a speech that morning in London at a breakfast to benefit the charity Jewish Care. It was a commitment he couldn't cancel, so even though the meeting with the

Bancrofts had come up at the last minute, he finished his speech in the morning in London and jumped on a private chartered plane right after breakfast to make his way to New York. A Harvard dropout, James had rebelled early (and smartly, his siblings thought) from the family business. He left Harvard, where he served on the editorial board of the satirical *Harvard Lampoon*, and then started up an independent hip-hop music label, Rawkus Records, with two high school friends. His father purchased the label in 1998, showing that for Murdochs, rebellions could end peacefully.

James was now firmly back in the fold. Prior to becoming CEO at BSkyB, James had been chairman and chief executive of News Corp.'s Asian satellite television business, Star TV. He had begun to think of how to make the family business last beyond his father, who had defined News Corp. through his opportunistic dealmaking and relentless personality. The senior Murdoch had lived through tougher days and reveled in provocation. James's business jargon made him seem un-Murdochian. "Pop," as he called his father, had never adopted such talk.

Once James arrived at the meeting, he walked the length of the mammoth conference room, past the Bancroft camp, to give his father a hug. To Leslie Hill, such overt expressions of affection, particularly in this kind of business meeting, smacked of showmanship. She knew the stories of the Murdoch family's rifts from years earlier when Murdoch's marriage to his much younger third wife, Wendi, divided his family. A skeptic by nature, she didn't quite believe the father and his son were as close as they were letting on.

The meeting continued, and halfway through what had been a polite gathering, Leslie began questioning Murdoch about China. Murdoch's reputation for sacrificing journalistic priorities to advance his business interests was exhibited nowhere better than in his dealings with China. Both the elder and younger Murdoch in the room that June afternoon had played a role in shaping that unfortunate reputation.

The elder Murdoch had spent considerable time in China since he visited Shanghai in 1997 and met his future wife, Wendi Deng, then a junior News Corporation employee based in Hong Kong. Wendi had served as his translator, and within two years, Murdoch had left his second wife, Anna Mann.

His initial business forays into China were less successful. Shortly after he bought a majority stake in the satellite broadcaster Star TV in Hong Kong for more than half a billion dollars in 1993, he made a speech in London that enraged the Chinese leadership. In it, he said Orwell was wrong. Mass communication would not subordinate the individual. On the contrary, he told his audience: "Advances in the technology of telecommunications have proved an unambiguous threat to totalitarian regimes everywhere." He was speaking, of course, of Star, which could beam programming to every corner of China. The remark (which Murdoch later said was written for him by Irwin Stelzer, the neoconservative U.S. economic and political columnist for Murdoch's *Sunday Times* of London) cost him dearly. Chinese premier Li Peng, enraged by Murdoch's comments, promptly outlawed private satellite dishes, which had once proliferated on China's rooftops. Murdoch rented a house in Hong Kong to get closer to his target and tried to make amends. His HarperCollins book publishing unit published a biography of Deng Xiaoping, the retired leader of China, written by his daughter, Deng Rong. To celebrate the book, which mainly recycled propaganda about Deng, Murdoch threw a lavish book party at Le Cirque. Star TV overhauled its programming to suit Chinese tastes. In 1994 it dropped BBC News, which had frequently angered Chinese officials with its reports on mainland affairs. (Murdoch insists that the decision was made for business, not political, reasons.) In a 1999 interview with *Vanity Fair,* Murdoch said of the Dalai Lama, whom the Chinese government considers a criminal, "I have heard cynics who say he is a very political old monk shuffling around in Gucci shoes."

James Murdoch, who ran Star TV from 2000 to 2003, joined in. He had a history of his own on these topics. In a speech in Los Angeles in 2001, James attacked the Falun Gong. That same year, the *Journal* won a Pulitzer Prize for its coverage of China's brutal suppression of the group.

Leslie knew about this history, and her mind focused on a letter written the previous month by the *Journal's* seven Pulitzer Prize-winning reporters in China that urged her family not to sell the paper to Murdoch. It read:

> We are correspondents who report from China for The Wall Street Journal, and we are writing to urge you to stand by the Bancroft family's courageous and principled decision to reject News Corp.'s offer to acquire Dow Jones & Co.
>
> There are only a handful of news organizations anywhere with the resources and the integrity to pursue the truth in matters of national and even global importance. Thanks to your family's committed stewardship, the Journal is at the head of this dwindling group.
>
> Our China team won the Pulitzer Prize for international reporting this year for a series of stories detailing the consequences of China's unbridled pursuit of capitalism—for China and for the rest of the world. Many of those stories shed an unflattering light on the government and business interests.
>
> The prize is a reflection of the Journal's substantial investment in covering what is perhaps the biggest economic, business and political story of our time: how China's embrace of markets and its growing global role are reshaping the world we live in. It is an important example of the coverage that we fear would suffer if News Corp. takes control.
>
> News Corp. Chairman Rupert Murdoch has a well-documented history of making editorial decisions in order to advance his business interests in China and, indeed, of sacrificing journalistic integrity to satisfy personal or political aims.
>
> Mr. Murdoch's approach is completely at odds with that taken by your own family, whose unwavering support of ethical journalism has made the Journal the trusted news source it is. It is fair to ask how News Corp. would change the Journal's coverage.
>
> In 2001, for example, our colleague Ian Johnson shared the Pulitzer for international reporting for his articles about the Chinese government's sometimes brutal suppression of the Falun Gong spiritual movement.
>
> Under Mr. Murdoch, these articles might never have seen the light of day. That year, Mr. Murdoch's son, James, the CEO of Brit-

ish Sky Broadcasting, delivered a speech in California echoing the line of the Chinese government in terming Falun Gong a "dangerous" and "apocalyptic cult," which "clearly does not have the success of China at heart."

Newspaper accounts of the speech say that James Murdoch criticized the Western media for negative coverage of human-rights issues in China, concluding that "these destabilizing forces today are very, very dangerous for the Chinese government."

We believe that it is important for all of us—from reporters and editors to you, the owners of the company—to keep constantly in mind the fact that the Journal is an institution that plays a critical role in civic life. We take pride in knowing that Journal readers trust us to uphold these principles, even in the face of risks.

Your family established and is now entrusted with a unique and important institution. Safeguarding it is a responsibility that you have fulfilled admirably for decades. Yours is the kind of stewardship journalists on the ground in China will require in the years to come if they are to accurately frame one of the world's most critical news stories. We have enormous respect for your continued willingness to defend the journalistic standards so important to all of us.

Leslie felt an obligation to grill the mogul and, typically, broached the topic directly. "How do you deal with coverage of China given your substantial business interests there?" she asked. She spoke glowingly of the *Journal*'s coverage of China. In praising *Journal* reporters' dedication to their craft, she invoked the death of Daniel Pearl.

Murdoch gave a rambling response and pointed out that the *Times* of London had done several stories critical of the Chinese government. James looked at his father and grew defensive of the old man. He was at a loss at what he was hearing. Here, the Bancrofts were acting like an august group on the other side of the table. "He has more work experience in his pinky finger," James thought of his father.

James quickly jumped in, speaking in his staccato tone. "Look, we were the only broadcaster in China to broadcast September 11 live," he said. "We were the only broadcaster to cover the Taiwanese election," he added. "We did it carefully, but we did it." News Corp. had journalists risking their lives all over the world, he thought to himself. He felt that American journalism smacked of self-importance. He remembered the *New York Times*'s Jayson Blair debacle in 2003, when the young reporter fabricated details and plagiarized others' work in his coverage of significant news events. When the *Times* assigned Blair to cover the story of the rescue of the prisoner of war Jessica Lynch, Blair co-wrote a story full of details from Lynch's home in Palestine, West Virginia. It turned out that Blair never went to Palestine, and his entire contribution to the story consisted of rearranged details from other wire services and papers. What James remembered from the incident was that nobody from the Lynch family did anything, even after they saw the story in the *Times* and knew neither of its authors had ever been to their home. To him that showed how far out of whack journalists' impressions of themselves were from those of the broader public. Leslie, he thought, was championing the same misguided self-importance. He didn't share the thought out loud. Instead, he went on to outline News Corp.'s business strategy and his personal view about opportunities. "If it doesn't make money, we don't do it," he said.

Then, perhaps to soothe fraying nerves across the table, the elder Murdoch reiterated his willingness to set up an editorial board as he had done with the *Times* of London twenty-five years earlier. He took a copy of the editorial agreement he had given the *Times* and pushed it across the table. In it, he proposed a board whose members were partly chosen by himself, a structure that had allowed him to force out the *Times*'s editor, Harold Evans, shortly after Murdoch took over the paper.

Elefante then handed over a copy of the family's proposal. Murdoch perused the document as Elefante ran through its main points. The Bancroft proposal suggested that the initial members of Dow Jones's editorial board be chosen by the Bancroft family, who would choose their own successors in perpetuity. It was their way of cementing control.

Murdoch furrowed his brow. Clearly, he didn't like the agreement in front of him. Under the current configuration of the *Times*'s board, he explained, he could appoint the paper's editor but the editor would need to be approved by the independent board. Similarly, he could not remove the editor without the concurrence of the board.

There was a wide distance between the two sides, but they continued to look for areas where they could compromise. Encouraged by the progress, Lipton said, "Maybe we should get back together tonight and see if we can't get this done."

The comment surprised Dow Jones chairman Peter McPherson, who thought the meeting was set up as a way for the Bancrofts to get more comfortable with Murdoch, not for them to sign any agreements or commit to any portion of a deal. He thought this meeting would be the first of many. So did the Bancrofts. Here, Lipton, supposedly the Bancrofts' adviser, was trying to hijack the process, McPherson thought, and get the deal done that day.

McPherson quickly suggested the two sides take a break and meet again in an hour and a half at about 5:00 p.m. The two sides agreed to do so, and Murdoch, with his son and his associates, left the room. "I don't think we want to sign anything today," McPherson told the family once they were alone. "I agree," said Elefante. "We have time to figure this out." Without saying where he was going, Chris left the building while his cousins, McPherson, and Elefante stayed in the lawyer's office to continue to look over the editorial agreements. His cousins, paranoid about press leaks, feared Chris had left to go talk to reporters. In fact, he left to get a break from his family and make some business calls. He had started to think about how he could come up with enough money to buy out his family members and preserve Dow Jones's independence. The meeting reconvened, but only briefly, and the two sides left Lipton's office without committing to anything. The Bancrofts would take a look at the *Times* of London proposal and then spend some time coming up with a revised proposal of their own for News Corporation. When Murdoch left the building that day, photographers and television cameras greeted him. He told them blandly that after more than four hours in the conference room together, "we had a very long, constructive meeting, and we've both gone away to consider both sides." He and his cohorts went to a cigar bar around the corner afterward to celebrate.

The meeting would turn Leslie Hill completely against Murdoch. She felt he had dodged her questions about China. She didn't trust him. She would spend the rest of the summer scouring the East Coast trying to find alternatives to Murdoch.

13

Editorial Independence

I N THE ABSENCE OF any real power over the deal proceedings, people started grasping at Murdoch's promise of editorial protections for the *Journal*. The morning after Murdoch's meeting with the Bancrofts, Marcus Brauchli picked up the *Journal* at 5:30 a.m. on his way to the gym, gazing with satisfaction at the four-thousand-word story stripped across the paper's front page, outlining the many ways in which Rupert Murdoch had interfered with his newspapers and editors throughout his career. This kind of story was, he thought, what it meant to work at an independent paper. He then read the *New York Times*'s account and his own paper's account of the previous day's meeting, frustrated that the *Times*'s was more complete. Especially with this story, he wanted his paper to beat the competition every day.

His frustration grew as he realized the Bancrofts had walked into the meeting with Murdoch without any representative from the newsroom, or even an executive who might have understood how the *Journal* operated. "There's such hypocrisy in talking about editorial independence and making it an issue," he thought, and then not worrying about how it is actually implemented. Eager to mine his own sources of information and exert some influence on the proceedings, he texted Robert Thomson. The two had a competitive but friendly rapport, each respectful of the other's intellect and talent. Brauchli wanted to tell Murdoch that whatever the Bancrofts had said in the meeting, they had done it without the support of the newsroom. In his text, Brauchli was almost painfully obscure: "What if Lord Macartney had visited the Qianlong Emperor without having the Parliament who make the laws and organize society behind him?" It was the typical kind of intellectual jousting Brauchli liked to engage in. He was referring to Britain's first envoy to China, who tried, and failed, to establish trade relations with the Chinese. His message: What if the representatives in the meeting yesterday didn't represent the *Wall Street Journal* journalists responsible for putting out the paper? Thomson, married to the daughter of a general in the Chinese army, kept up effortlessly: "The Emperor would assume that the King's emissary represents the King, and the parliament is His Majesty's." Thomson's response was clear: Murdoch would not see it as his problem if the Bancrofts agreed to a deal that the journalists didn't like. Brauchli attempted to extend the now tortured analogy by saying, "Of course the rifts of the Macartney mission doomed it and later produced the Opium Wars that weakened the Qing." Even as he typed it, he knew his attempt was too obscure. Brauchli knew, too, that Thomson had little sympathy for the *Journal* newsroom.

Leslie Hill wasn't going to let this slide. Fresh from the meeting with Murdoch, she felt disgusted by the man whose company she had just left and increasingly annoyed by her cousins. Lisa followed Mike Elefante blindly, she thought. Chris was impossible to read and seemed not to know his own mind. She didn't like Murdoch's response to her questions in the meeting, nor did she trust that he was even telling the truth when he spoke. She had asked him three different ways to explain how he would treat China once he owned the *Journal*, and he kept dodging the question, she thought. She didn't trust Marty Lipton, who seemed ready to sign a deal before they had even begun negotiating. Elefante was doing his best, but he himself admitted that doing deals wasn't his specialty; he was, in the Bancrofts' long tradition, leaving it to the "professionals." Meanwhile, her brothers were agitating to explore a sale. Her brother Tom said it most succinctly: the family had stopped benefiting from the company and the company had stopped benefiting from the family. It was time to part ways.

Leslie wasn't entirely convinced of that point, especially now that she had met Murdoch. Her first step was going to be to talk to Marcus Brauchli. She wanted to know more about the editorial agreement he had mentioned. An editorial agreement offered a tantalizing possibility for her family. It could allow them to extract themselves from the disastrous business of Dow Jones and newspaper publishing and still feel they had played a role in preserving the integrity of one of the nation's great papers. At best it would really protect the *Journal;* at worst it was a salve on a guilty conscience.

The family had little reason to believe any of Murdoch's promises to abide by the editorial agreement. Leslie knew what had happened to Harold Evans. Still, the Bancrofts wanted to believe. Leslie, tired of feeling as if she had been led around by the lawyers and executives surrounding her, was determined to take a leading role. "If we're going to protect these people, shouldn't we ask them how they want to be protected?" she asked herself. On June 7, the Thursday after she and her cousins had sat down with Murdoch, she spoke to Brauchli on the phone. Leslie had gotten a copy of the editorial agreement the Bancrofts were considering from Elefante and ran Brauchli through it. It didn't bear any resemblance to the agreement Elefante had given Rich Zannino, Brauchli told her. At that time, the flurry of potential agreements traveling among Elefante, Zannino, and others was almost comical. All of them felt they could come up with a structure that would keep Murdoch at bay. Leslie wanted to know if it was possible to give the editor of the *Journal* veto power over how the *Journal* brand would be used. She didn't trust Murdoch, she told Brauchli. He hadn't done much to win her over, and what charm he attempted, she found false. Brauchli told her Murdoch was like an escape artist. "We're all trying to put Murdoch in a straitjacket, wrap him in chains, put him inside a lead box, padlock it shut, and drop it into the East River," Brauchli said. "And five minutes later he will be standing on the bank, smiling."

While the Bancrofts worked and reworked the editorial agreement during the month of June, Murdoch waited. He became frustrated with the prolonged time frame. "The final approval is in the next two, three weeks' time or not at all," he told Reuters in late June during a trip to Warsaw. "Everything is done. We are just waiting for a final approval of the Bancroft family." He made the pronouncement just as due diligence was beginning on the deal, a sign of how little the business results of Dow Jones—good or bad—were likely to sway his resolve to own the company.

Almost daily, advisers for the Bancrofts and Dow Jones sent (hopeful) signals that the family was about to send their revised version of the editorial agreement to News Corporation. And every day, the agreement stayed mired in the back-and-forth among Leslie Hill, Elefante, Brauchli, Crovitz, Stuart Karle, the *Journal's* general counsel, and any number of consulting players who were brought in to weigh in. Dow Jones's chairman, Peter McPherson, had started looking for individuals who might people the editorial board. He was consulting Peter Kann. Elefante was busy acting as the intermediary between Zannino and the family board members. He was talking to Jimmy Lee, News Corporation's banker, who would call him daily to check on the family's progress.

Three weeks after they met with Murdoch that rainy June afternoon, the family just gave up. Exhausted from the to-ing and fro-ing over the structure of the editorial independence agreement, the Bancroft directors handed their negotiating power over to Dow Jones's board. While they had once been set on maintaining control over the discussions with Murdoch, their own internal weaknesses had only grown since they sat down with the aging mogul. After 105 years of ownership, the Bancroft stewardship of Dow Jones was over. All that remained was the signing of the papers.

It took just three days for the Dow Jones board, eager to see these proceedings come to a close, to send the agreement to News Corporation.

Marty Lipton, the Bancroft family's lawyer, had been telling the Murdoch camp for weeks that the proposal was forthcoming. Finally, at 3:00 p.m. on Friday, June 29, Rupert Murdoch received the call from Rich Zannino. "We're sending over the editorial independence proposal," he said, his voice relaxed and easy. "I think you're going to be happy with it." Murdoch alerted his entourage, who gathered for the momentous event. The day's proceedings were lent an air of siege, thanks to a burst pipe on the tenth floor that had flooded the three floors below. On Murdoch's eighth floor, dehumidifiers had been humming and roaring for three weeks, and executives decamped to drier offices to escape the growing scent of damp and mold. The executives gathered around Murdoch—general counsel Lon Jacobs, corporate communications executive vice president Gary Ginsberg, and deputy CFO John Nallen—were drawn into the drama of the moment.

The fax, sent from Goldman Sachs, arrived in Lon Jacobs's office; it boded ill from the beginning. That it was marked for the attention of "Rupert Murdock" was the start of a series of absurdities Murdoch perceived in the document. He had offered the protections as a sop to the Bancroft family but never expected them to be so earnestly attached to the details. Such niggling was absurd, especially for a piece of paper he had little intention of taking very seriously. He knew the agreement could offer some protection for the *Journal*'s reputation among the self-appointed media police, but he intended to change the paper and had said as much in an interview with the *New York Times* just two days after his offer became public. Unlike in an interview with the *Journal* a month later, he had been unscripted: "I'm sometimes frustrated by the long stories," he told the *Times,* adding that he rarely managed to finish some of the paper's longer stories. "I might put more emphasis on Washington," he said, and later confided that he was not a fan of the Saturday edition of the paper, which had been launched in 2005. Murdoch said that if it was legally possible, he would rechristen his planned Fox Business channel with the *Journal* name in it. His intentions were clear from the beginning, and what the Bancrofts were asking went far beyond what he was willing to offer.

As written, the proposal suggested that the Bancrofts would maintain a connection with the company through two board seats that would stay under Bancroft family control forever. Murdoch thought he had signaled his displeasure with that attempted power grab when they met weeks before. Furthermore, News Corp. would have to clear its nominations to the editorial independence board through the Bancrofts. News Corp. executives would have to check in with the managing editor of the paper and the publisher if News Corp. affiliates wanted to use the *Journal* name. The document suggested that the *Journal*'s publisher retain authority—including budgets—over the news and editorial pages and be responsible for ensuring "that business operations do not interfere with journalistic and editorial integrity and independence."

Rarely did Murdoch allow himself to feel truly slighted. But this, if nothing else, tried his patience. He had been waiting for weeks and had begun to think that the deal, which seemed so certain at the outset, might not happen. He had taken hits in the U.S. media over the past two months at a level he hadn't seen since his take-over of *New York* magazine thirty years before. That Friday afternoon his underlings, the vaunted members of the "Office of the Chairman," which operated inside News Corp. like a cool-kids clique, gathered around to craft a response. Gary Ginsberg called *Time* magazine's Eric Pooley, who had been working on a story about the takeover effort. "You might want to come over here. This is going to be the moment of reckoning," Ginsberg said. As with all things Murdoch, there was an appreciation for the media's take.

Then Murdoch got on the phone and called Zannino back. He called Marty Lipton, the family's lawyer at Wachtell, Lipton, and Greg Lee, the banker handling Dow Jones at Goldman Sachs. He called his son James on a yacht in Valencia. He called Dave DeVoe, his chief operating officer, on his way to Albany. "Dave, you can put the $5 billion away."

Jacobs and Ginsberg hovered around Murdoch as he worked the phones, and Pooley sat by, noting the events. James, on an eighty-foot yacht waiting to watch the America's Cup, had to walk to the opposite end of the boat to field his father's calls and avoid being heard by his fellow revelers. He had been growing weary of what he saw as the constant barrage of negative press for his father and the company. A child of his generation, James was perhaps more sensitive to the barbs of the media than his father. In that moment, hearing the rundown of the Bancrofts' requests, he wanted his father to publicly take his toys and go home, leaving the Bancrofts to wallow in regret after the bid was withdrawn and Dow Jones's stock price plummeted.

His father almost listened. "If we clean this up to our satisfaction, the family will reject it," Murdoch mused aloud to his cohorts. "So why don't we just reject them?" His phone buzzed. It was Zannino. "Hello, Rich. I've read it," Murdoch said. "I don't know what you were thinking. Why would we be happy with this?" He told Zannino that the proposal was outrageous because it attempted to keep the Bancrofts in control of key aspects of the business and allow not only the managing editor, but the existing publisher, too, to call the shots on editorial independence under News Corp. The proposal was reasonable to anyone but someone who had an idea of the changes he wanted to make. "Oh, yes, we reject this," he said to Zannino.

Almost immediately, Ginsberg sat down to work on a withdrawal letter, previous versions of which had been drafted by Jacobs and James Murdoch. It was something he doubted Murdoch would use, but something that might serve to vent some of the frustration in the musty room. Ginsberg mustered his best posture of the aggrieved, one he had perfected during years in politics and a position he found quite effective. Though able to twist the truth when necessary, Ginsberg had managed over the years to perfect high-minded indignation if someone questioned his or his boss's honor. It could only have been mock fury, then, that fueled his creative energy.

"68 days ago News Corporation submitted an unsolicited but friendly offer to the Board of the Dow Jones Company," Ginsberg typed, using the most generous definition of *friendly* to suit the purpose of the moment. Murdoch and the three other executives still in the office that Friday night gathered around, playing with how much vitriol they could add to the withdrawal. They came to call the document the "Fuck You Letter." Part of the fun of composing it was that they were all on the same team and defending Murdoch's honor to boot.

With a few exceptions, Ginsberg never felt the press coverage of Murdoch's offer had been so terrible. He had welcomed the positive coverage from high-profile reporters at the *Times* such as media writer Richard Siklos and mergers-and-acquisitions editor Andrew Ross Sorkin. He felt Martin Peers at the *Journal* had given Murdoch a fair shake. He had great hopes for the Dow Jones deal and what it could do to Murdoch's reputation. It might, Ginsberg thought, solidify Murdoch as the only real visionary in the media space today. Crying foul, acting hurt, and walking away would have set back the significant gains Ginsberg felt the company, and Murdoch, had made in the public's eye over the past two months. But he sublimated those feelings to please his boss and play along. Sitting next to John Nallen amid the noisy fans running to dry out the flood on the executive floor, he continued:

> Our expectation, born of 50 years of building a great media company, was that the process for weighing our offer would be rational, orderly and, most of all, fair. I was not so naïve to think emotions wouldn't play a role; when a newspaper is in play, especially one such as The Wall Street Journal, emotions almost always are a factor. What I did expect, however, was that at the end of the day, our offer would be accepted or rejected based on facts, rather than innuendo, false accusations, and fear.
>
> How wrong I was.
>
> For the past seven weeks, my company and my 57,000 professional colleagues have been subjected to a drumbeat of stories that cast us more as villains than as creators of one of the world's most innovative media companies. We've been caricatured as meddlers, misanthropes and sops. If believed, at various times we've tried either to topple benevolent governments or prop up despotic tyrants; no editor was free from my intervention, no newsroom impervious to my politics. Without stringent controls put on my ability to interact with an asset I am generously offering to acquire, the credibility and integrity of those assets—their most valuable currency I should add—would be lost forever.
>
> We patiently accepted this vitriolic abuse as part of the price of being an agent of change.
>
> And it might even have been amusing were it not so insulting and wrong.
>
> What's been lost in this noise is any sense that over the past fifty years, no other media company has done more to give newspaper readers, television viewers, moviegoers, book readers and internet users greater diversity of information than News Corp. No media company has salvaged more failing newspapers, and nurtured them to health, than News Corp. No company has provided for more jobs for journalists, or fresh voices to stale markets, all accomplishments for which we are proud.
>
> If in providing all this choice we've proved too popular, I make no apologies. If we've at times upset the Establishment to give consumers what they want, then I've done my job.

Armed with a steadfast confidence that we are not only a proper —but uniquely suited—suitor of Dow Jones, we proposed as a condition of our ownership the establishment of an editorial committee of the board to ensure that the business would continue to represent the highest standards of integrity and trust. We have some history in this regard. As a condition of our acquisition of The Times of London and The Sunday Times, we established a five member editorial board to ensure their editorial independence and integrity. That board has safeguarded these world-renowned brands throughout our 27 years of ownership. It was this structure that we offered to establish in our sole face-to-face meeting with some senior members of the Bancroft family nearly a month ago.

Despite our proven track record, the Bancroft family chose to put their own interests—and their own misguided conceptions of who we are and who they are—ahead of sanity and reality. In conveying their proposal, made after nearly a month of intense deliberations and consultation, they have communicated unworkable conditions on our future ownership that effectively enable them to retain control of an asset for which I and my shareholders had been willing to pay dearly.

In spite of our encouragingly friendly meeting, which was promised to be quickly resumed, we have now received, after weeks of waiting, a four page list of demands in which the family has insisted that they have the effective power to appoint five of the seven members of a proposed editorial board, a board that would control—in perpetuity—the key editorial positions and operations of the Wall Street Journal and Dow Jones Newswires. Equally astounding, that board would have the power to determine who will serve as Managing Editor, Publisher, Editorial Page Editor, and Dow Jones Newswires Editor. These key figures would then have the authority to run the paper, including how the brand is deployed and resources are allocated. As a final insult, they are demanding the power to appoint two Bancroft family members to the Board of News Corp., where we had invited as a courtesy one Bancroft to join us.

In essence, the Bancrofts are seeking to reserve for themselves a new role as the sole controller of the content of the newspaper, as they take our $5 billion.

We believe our offer made sense for both Dow Jones shareholders and News Corp. shareholders. Dow Jones has been starved of investment in a marketplace that demands constant investment and creativity. Without an owner willing to commit to the necessary investments, Dow Jones, a steward of some of the world's greatest brands, risks irrelevance and ultimately, extinction.

This is a time of special difficulty for the printed word, faced as it is by the most disruptive technology since Caxton. More than any other company, we know how fragile a great creative institution is. This drawn-out process, with no obvious path to resolution, risks damaging Dow Jones' business, and more importantly, the morale of its employees. We would never want to be a part of that. Nor for that matter do I want to continue to subject my colleagues to unwarranted attacks and false hopes.

On April 17th, I submitted my letter to Dow Jones' board outlining my offer to acquire the company. Today, I withdraw that offer.

It was the night of the premiere of News Corp.'s 20th Century Fox division's latest addition to the *Die Hard* franchise, *Live Free or Die Hard*, at Radio City Music Hall, so as soon as he had finished the letter, Ginsberg rushed to meet his wife and two sons, arriving just as the lights went down. He felt a sense of accomplishment, having batted out the letter and managed to meet his family. But back at home after the premiere, Ginsberg couldn't sleep. It seemed foolish to let the deal—and the big reputational boost it might bring—fall apart. Besides, Ginsberg was harboring fantasies of becoming directly involved in the *Journal*. He had come to News Corp. from the respectable world of Democratic politics. Ever since *George* magazine, he had toyed with returning to journalism circles, this time to a more prestigious perch. He had to be able to bridge this absurd misunderstanding about the editorial agreement. At 2:00 a.m., it hit him: "I can deal with Dick," he thought. If he could have a conversation with his old boss Dick Beattie, Ginsberg felt reasonable heads would prevail. There were three things Murdoch found particularly bothersome in the Bancroft proposal: the means of selecting editorial committee members, the number of board members, and the broad powers over budgets granted to the publisher of the *Journal*. In all the back-and-forth between James and Gary and Lon and DeVoe and Murdoch, "it was all fuck 'em, fuck 'em, fuck 'em," Ginsberg thought. "If I can talk to Dick we can make this right," he resolved.

In the early hours of Saturday morning, Ginsberg e-mailed Murdoch's wife, Wendi, whose BlackBerry Murdoch relied upon for e-mails on weekends and after hours. Once he got in touch with Murdoch, Ginsberg told him he wanted to call Beattie, to see if Beattie couldn't get the Bancrofts to back off on some of their demands. "Fine, get him," Murdoch said. Still, Murdoch asked Robert Thomson to edit Ginsberg's letter, so it would be ready to go.

Ginsberg knew that the threat of pulling the bid would mean something to Beattie, who was the lawyer for Dow Jones's independent directors. He knew that having the letter written gave him some leverage. He immediately phoned his old boss. But Beattie didn't pick up, and Ginsberg left a message for him. "It's urgent you call me. Everyone wants to withdraw, but I think we can put this right." Meanwhile, another banker on Murdoch's team, Blair Effron of the boutique investment bank Centerview Partners, called Rob Spatt, Beattie's partner at Simpson Thacher, to try to get in touch.

Once Ginsberg told Murdoch about his plan to call Beattie, Murdoch latched onto the idea and called in regularly, almost hourly, to see if Ginsberg had reached him. In the absence of any meaningful dialogue, Murdoch could be almost autistic in his repetitive and unrelenting focus. "Here I am talking about how close I am with Dick," Ginsberg thought, "and I can't even get him on the phone." Saturday evening, while out to dinner with his kids, Ginsberg received a call from Murdoch. "Did you talk to Beattie?" he asked. "No, I haven't," Ginsberg said apologetically. "I'm still waiting to hear back from him." Murdoch called Thomson in London to check on his edit of Ginsberg's letter. They would move ahead with the plan to send it at 3:00 p.m. on Sunday. During the dinner, Ginsberg's phone rang again. It was Beattie.

"Where the fuck have you been?" Ginsberg cried.

"I'm in Montana, fishing with my grandkids," Beattie replied, slightly amused at the unlikely circumstance.

"We have twenty-one hours," Ginsberg said. "We have a letter to withdraw the offer." He explained his objections to the editorial agreement from the Bancrofts.

"I haven't even seen the proposal. McPherson never sent it to us," Beattie replied. "I just got a copy faxed to me so let me look at it." On the phone, the two went over the three issues Ginsberg raised. Beattie thought they seemed minor and could be resolved. The two got off the phone and Ginsberg immediately called Murdoch, who had by then flown to the Mediterranean to his *Rosehearty* yacht, to give him the update.

At 5:00 a.m. Sunday, Ginsberg woke with a start to the ringing of his cell phone. It was Murdoch. "The deal's done," he said. "Lon is going to talk to Joe Stern." Like Ginsberg and Beattie, News Corp. general counsel Lon Jacobs and Dow Jones general counsel Joe Stern had known each other for years. They had worked together on numerous deals when Jacobs was on the board of Sky Mexico, and Stern represented one of the country's wealthiest businessmen. After a series of meetings with a small core group of Dow Jones directors, Stern trudged over to News Corp.'s headquarters Monday afternoon to meet Jacobs. The two men reached a compromise on the editorial independence agreement. News Corporation won most of the concessions, and Murdoch would later remember the compromise as one in which he gave up very little: "They caved on everything," he said. "They gave us everything."

The Bancrofts felt they had gotten Murdoch to agree to more than he ever had before. They thought they had the best editorial independence agreement that one could craft. Leslie had spoken frequently with Brauchli about the content of the agreement and hoped that he would stand up for the newsroom. Brauchli, who had tackled the creation of the agreement like a research project, doggedly looking at a wide range of independence agreements at publications across the globe, felt satisfied by how much better the agreement was than the others.

14

Decisions

THE LOBBY OF THE Hilton hotel in Boston's Financial District, flanked on both ends by revolving glass doors, made it difficult for the Bancroft family members meeting inside to hide from the reporters gathered around both exits. To reach the restrooms from the windowless conference room on the ground floor in which they sequestered themselves, family members had to cross both the length and the width of the lobby, leaving ample time for ambush. The more press-averse members of the family asked hotel security for accompaniment from the conference rooms to the restrooms and back. They didn't want to be questioned. Not today.

It was a Bancroft family reunion, but one far different from that at which many of these same adults had gathered twenty-five years before around Jessie Cox's magnetic presence in the '21' Club in New York. This time, the family, already naturally divided by its three branches, had nearly splintered under the strain of the offer thrust upon it by Rupert Murdoch and his News Corporation. It was the family's last reunion. With virtually nothing else in common except their ownership of Dow Jones & Company, the entirety of the Bancroft clan would have little reason to gather once Dow Jones was gone. Even now, as the decision loomed whether to sell the company their founder Clarence Barron had willed to them, several of them didn't deem the discussion important enough to attend in person. Vacations had been scheduled, and not even the fate of one of America's most vital newspapers would keep some in the family from their Spanish cottages, Sardinian cruises, or other relaxing summer pursuits.

The summer had begun to drag on with the efforts to find alternatives to Murdoch. In all, Dow Jones's advisers had been in touch with twenty-one potential suitors for the company but had received only one bid, from News Corp. General Electric Company and Pearson PLC had fleetingly joined together to make a bid for Dow Jones, but never followed through. Brad Greenspan, the former CEO of Intermix Media, Inc., the parent company of MySpace, and supermarket magnate Ron Burkle had teamed up to bid for a portion of Dow Jones, but nothing concrete ever materialized. Even the state-controlled Russian oil and gas giant Gazprom briefly considered an offer.

Finally, in mid-July, in what appeared to be an exhortation to the Bancrofts to wind it up, Peter Kann told the *Journal* that, while he still hoped the family would keep Dow Jones independent, "if the family is going to sell I see no point in pursuing industrial conglomerates, Internet entrepreneurs, supermarket magnates and real-estate developers. None know anything at all about journalism. As to Mr. Murdoch, at least he loves newspapers, presumably would invest in the WSJ and Dow Jones, and would seem to have little incentive to tarnish a trophy he has coveted for so long." Even Kann was pushing them into Murdoch's arms.

The week prior to the meeting in Boston, Dow Jones's board of directors had voted to accept the $5.6 billion offer from Rupert Murdoch's News Corporation. (Murdoch had agreed to assume $600 million in Dow Jones's debt, which boosted the value of the offer.) Dow Jones director Dieter von Holtzbrinck abstained from the vote and relinquished his board seat in protest. "Although I'm convinced that News Corp. offer is very generous in financial terms," he wrote in his resignation letter to directors, "I'm very worried that Dow Jones unique journalistic values will long-term strongly suffer after the proposed sale." He continued, "I do not believe that the 'Special Committee' can finally prevent Mr. Murdoch from doing what he wants to do, from acting his way." His resignation, though symbolic, was quietly celebrated by the deal's opponents, and all eyes trained on the Bancrofts.

Now, the only step left to make Murdoch the owner of Clarence Barron's old paper was the approval of Barron's descendants. The reality of the Bancroft family that damp Monday in July 2007 hardly lived up to their mythic possibilities as one of America's great newspaper families. They faced an important decision—whether to end 105 years of independence for the *Wall Street Journal* and add it to the media conglomeration of the Fox News television channel, the *New York Post* newspaper, and the MySpace social networking site.

The afternoon meeting had kicked off with a welcome from Mike Elefante, whose friendly eyes were sagging with weariness, punished as they were by the summer's proceedings. Not only did he have to act as the intermediary among Zannino, the Dow Jones board, and the rest of the Bancroft family, all of whom seemed to have different agendas, but he was juggling the Hill clan, who were in the midst of pulling their money out of his law firm, Hemenway & Barnes. He found his best strategy was to appear as opaque as possible and say very little to anyone questioning his motives or position. He dealt with Murdoch's banker Jimmy Lee—who still called him almost every day in hopes of gleaning some information—in much the same way he dealt with his own clients: be friendly and accommodating, but never say what you're really thinking. The strategy had served him well enough so far, and he hoped he was nearing the end of this hellish ordeal. He had barely had a summer at all. Instead of heading to his country house just outside the city on weekends, he spent Saturday and Sunday on endless calls with his fellow trustees at the firm and coaching Bancrofts through their decision. He had also been dealing with one of the peskiest of the Hills, Michael, who was the youngest of the three Hill brothers. Mike Hill appeared to have determined that Hemenway & Barnes was the root of all the Bancroft family's ills. Early Bancrofts designed the trusts that held their money so trustees could be removed only through a court order. The Hills had been battling to kick Hemenway & Barnes lawyers off their trusts and pull their money out of the firm since before the Murdoch offer surfaced. Hemenway & Barnes refused, not wanting to lose one of its biggest clients and suffer the negative publicity that was certain to come from such a move. But slowly the two sides had come to an agreement: to get their money out, the Hills would agree never to speak of their dissatisfaction with Hemenway & Barnes. The relationship would remain, as Hemenway & Barnes needed it to be, pristine in the eyes of the rest of Boston's wealthy families.

At the meeting, Elefante's bland introduction was fitting for a man whose primary goal was to ignite no great passions in his audience. Emotion, he knew, was his enemy at this stage of the game. Standing at a scuffed podium at the front of the cramped and windowless twenty-five-by-forty-foot conference room, he stared out on the rows of stained, gold-patterned chairs filled with the family he had come to resent. He introduced his fellow directors—chairman M. Peter McPherson and Lewis Campbell—to this motley bunch. Campbell, the CEO of Textron Inc., had fashioned himself as something of a consigliere to Leslie Hill. He appeared the homespun family man who understood the value of blood ties and legacy. And yet as the CEO of a successful aeronautics firm he could talk to the bankers on Wall Street as one of their own. He had, in fact, played both sides of this crowd successfully, chatting with Murdoch one afternoon and taking Leslie Hill to lunch the next. He knew that if this deal fell through, he would have to resign from the board. His mantra as CEO of Textron was "shareholder value," and he used the term constantly for his shareholders and fellow CEOs. If he let a deal like Murdoch's slip through his grasp, he would be ashamed to face any of his cohorts again. Leslie's opposition to the deal was a problem, he knew. But he determined early that it would be easier to jump through Leslie's hoops than to attempt to persuade her stubborn mind, so he had urged Zannino and the rest of the board to entertain—throughout the drawn-out summer negotiations—the cockeyed offers from the likes of kid-CEO Greenspan and Ron Burkle. Today, he knew, would involve a bit of pandering to the crowd, but he was determined to close the deal.

The conference rooms in the interior of the hotel's ground floor didn't provide the kind of accommodations Elisabeth Goth Chelberg was used to. Accustomed to more civilized shelters such as Claridge's in London and the Carlyle in New York, Elisabeth had borrowed a friend's plane for a few hours to make this family meeting and was staying in Boston only for the day. Draped in a buttery yellow cashmere wrap, she looked out of place among her relatives, who wore nubby fleece zip-up jackets and slip-on rubber-soled shoes. More than a decade after her mother died, this meeting seemed the culmination of what Elisabeth had started so many years before with Ira Millstein, Warren Buffett, and her cousin Billy. The family, though still divided, was coming to terms with its inadequacy as a steward of Dow Jones, she thought.

After Mike Elefante defended the deal he had initially opposed to the assembled Bancrofts, Lisa Steele followed him at the podium. With graying curly hair and attire that announced its Burlington, Vermont, origins, Steele looked warily around a room full of the relatives she had grown tired of dealing with over the past two months. When the offer from Murdoch first surfaced, she was deeply against it. She had inherited an independent *Wall Street Journal* and along with it, the notion that its independence should be defended at all costs. The summer had been long and painful for her, and she rarely imagined her family would have to face this kind of hopeless scenario in her lifetime. She felt she had worked hard—unlike many of her cousins—to get the facts right on this deal, mainly through talking to Elefante, who was, by that day at the end of July, the only person she felt she could totally trust. She had made a list of the pros and cons of retaining Dow Jones's independence versus selling the company to Rupert Murdoch. When she looked at the lopsided lists, she felt the deal was a no-brainer.

The decision, desperate and discouraging as it seemed to her earlier in the summer, had long settled into inevitability, and by that late-July afternoon, she arrived ready to defend her view. Despite warnings from some of the *Journal*'s reporters, Steele felt that the future without Murdoch would be much bleaker than one with him. She saw her family, through leaks to the press and indecisiveness and internal infighting, as unable to stand together.

Steele didn't realize, as she took the floor after Mike Elefante, that one of her relatives was reporting the meeting in real time to Murdoch's unofficial lieutenant Andy Steginsky. Steele told her family that she had done "her own due diligence" on the deal and had come to the painful conclusion that it was time to sell the company. Her words—"It will be irresponsible to walk away from this deal"—were welcomed warmly in the News Corp. camp.

Leslie Hill's opposition to the offer had blossomed over the past two months since her last meeting with Murdoch. She had been deeply affected by letters sent earlier in the summer from *Wall Street Journal* reporters urging her and her family members to reject Murdoch's offer. She had, by the time her family gathered for this meeting, grown entirely mistrustful of Dow Jones's advisers and many on the company's board.

When Leslie stood up after her cousin's comments, she walked to the front of the room and then stopped. "I have two speeches I could give," she said, "but I can't give either one of them." She then held up a manila envelope, a half-inch thick, stuffed with letters from *Journal* reporters who protested the deal and wrote to her and her cousins to urge them to reject it. "These are letters from *Wall Street Journal* reporters," she said, her deep voice quavering. "They wrote to urge us not to accept this offer. I could say a lot of things about this deal," she continued, "but it is their voices that matter." She was waving the manila envelope, clearly choked up. "We owe it to them not to sell."

Following Leslie was Chris Bancroft, who wore a blue baseball cap embroidered with a fishing lure and a not-so-subtle message to his relatives: *Bite Me.* He had hired his own lawyer and banker and was becoming annoyed at the money he was spending to explore the options he felt the company's advisers were allowing to pass by unexamined. He knew time was running short and Zannino was moving ahead with due diligence with Murdoch. If he could find a way to take a principled stand and still have the deal go through, that might solve his dilemma. He stood up and walked to the front of the room and didn't stop pacing until he finished his short talk. "We're not broken," he told his family. "Dow Jones is doing just fine, and if Rupert is offering sixty [dollars a share] then it must be worth a lot more," he said. "Selling now is like selling the milk cow for beef," he said, his voice rising.

Chris made it clear in his speech that he wasn't in favor of the offer, but he also delivered a message that showed he was as much a pragmatist as the advisers he so mistrusted. "I am going to vote no for the family shares I control, and I'm going to take the advice of my legal counsel for my votes as a trustee." The legal counsel for such a lucrative deal would almost certainly be to vote yes for the deal, Chris knew. If he voted yes for those shares, he would deliver the company to News Corp., since the vast majority of the shares he controlled were in Article III, which he oversaw as a trustee. But he couldn't bring himself to vote for this deal on his personal shares. His older brother, Hugh, was in favor of the deal, as was his niece Elisabeth Goth Chelberg, making his stance all the more controversial within his own family.

After Chris, the elders had their say. Jane MacElree, the Hill family's matriarch whose seven children were split over what to do with Dow Jones, approached the front of the room, her soft, round cheeks framed by a simple gray bob. Dressed in a soft purple sweater, she looked the part of the kind grandmother. Her mother, the boisterous and foul-mouthed Jessie Cox, would have had harsher words for a day like this, but MacElree was subdued. "We are lucky that we inherited the stock we have," she told the group. "We are blessed because of it." The journalists at the *Journal* "risk their lives every day," she continued. She couldn't help but mention Daniel Pearl. "He put his life on the line for the paper," she said, pausing to hold back tears. She spoke as if she were giving the eulogy for the *Journal*. She told the group a story of a man she had met several years ago when she and her daughter Leslie took a course at Harvard Business School for family-run companies. The man, she said, felt the weight of his grandfather on one shoulder and the weight of his great-grandfather on the other. "I feel the same weight of the past on me now."

But MacElree, too, had pragmatic considerations. Her considerable voting power over Dow Jones came from her role as a trustee over trusts controlling nearly 15 percent of the company's shares. In keeping with the Byzantine trust structure controlling Dow Jones, some of the beneficiaries of MacElree's trusts were the women of another branch of the family: Martha Robes, Jean Stevenson, and Lisa Steele, who, guided by Steele's painstaking deliberations, had come to favor the sale. MacElree's brother, William Cox Jr., whose frequent exhortations that the *Journal* was "the best damn paper in the country," spoke briefly. He remained, he told the crowd, against the deal.

Everyone in the family realized, to varying degrees, that the power over Dow Jones and the Bancroft family's fortune lay not with the people with Bancroft blood running through their veins, but with the law firm that had advised them for so many years, Hemenway & Barnes. The earliest Bancroft trusts dated back to the mid-1930s and were established for the three grandchildren of Clarence Barron: Jessie, Jane, and Hugh. The Bancrofts hired Hemenway & Barnes in the 1940s and had relied on them for counsel ever since. Mike Elefante informed the thirty-three Bancrofts in attendance that they had a deadline of about a week from that meeting to vote on the deal.

That week was a frenzy of activity and great stress. In the days leading up to the deadline for votes, William Cox Jr. went into diabetic shock. Leslie Hill, principled to the end, resigned her Dow Jones board seat in protest of the now inevitable decision.

Chris Bancroft took a different path from his cousin. Having made it known that he was going to straddle the offer, he realized that through their endless wavering the Bancroft family had forgotten the first rule of bargaining: if you are selling, ask for more. He and others made a last stab to get Murdoch to raise his offer. By then it was too late. The News Corp. camp knew they had the company at $60 a share, not a penny more. In an embarrassing denouement, Chris tried to chisel out of News Corp. a pledge to pay his legal fees.

Over the next several weeks, the Bancrofts suffered a final ignominy. After the deal was signed, they attempted to choose their representative to the News Corp. board, the family member who was to preserve Barron's legacy. Fractious as always, the Bancrofts missed their deadline. Murdoch made the choice for them, vetoing the family's first selection and instead picking a twenty-seven-year-old opera singer, Natalie Bancroft, whose greatest qualification for Murdoch was that unlike some of her Hill and Goth cousins, she held the right surname and wouldn't raise a fuss in the boardroom.

15

First Day

ON AUGUST 1, 2007, the morning of Barry Diller's party, Steiger was not the man in the newsroom's big office. Three months before, Steiger had retired from his role and handed the reins to his successor, Marcus Brauchli. Now, the morning meetings were more businesslike and less political. But another presence, though not in the room, loomed over the proceedings. That particular morning, after 105 years, Dow Jones was promised to a new owner, Rupert Murdoch. The news of the offer dominated the *Journal*'s own front page, a sign that even this paper could make accommodations to the day's news. Murdoch was a man widely mistrusted and quietly despised in the newsroom. The editors in the meeting, few of whom had made any feeling toward Murdoch known throughout the long battle for ownership of the paper, were skittish. They worried about the future of the newspaper business and they feared for their own employment. The new regime would come to see their morning gathering as a sleepy vestige of the *Journal*'s stultified past. Under Murdoch, the meeting would shift to mimic those in countless newsrooms across the country. They would talk about the biggest news of the day and those stories—scoops or not, fresh or not—would go on the front page.

Brauchli had yet to develop into his new role, though he had been training for it for years. He still seemed uncomfortable standing in the spotlight rather than sitting in the peanut gallery with everybody else. Every new editor is deemed unworthy at the start, and Brauchli was no exception. He was much younger than some of his erstwhile rivals, and his methods sometimes left the vanquished feeling stung. "You have to remember how Marcus rose to power," they would say. "It wasn't through building alliances; it was through proving that he was smarter than the rest of us." Brauchli seemed younger than he was and did little to change others' impressions of him. He tried to remain chummy in the newsroom. While Steiger took a car service to work, Brauchli still hopped on the subway every morning, and if he ran into a colleague, he would regale the listener with his latest take on the economy or finance or the odd dinner he had had the night before.

His most important quality, however, at that moment, the morning when the *Wall Street Journal* became a Murdoch paper, with its attendant stigma, was that Brauchli was one of those in the newsroom who knew and loved the old *Journal* and appreciated the old way of doing things. Though Brauchli had campaigned hard for his job and made some sacrifices to get there (spearheading an effort to shrink the width of the *Journal* in an effort to save money and win favor with his bosses), he was a more trusted source than the mogul waiting uptown.

Earlier that morning, Brauchli had sat at his desk in his corner office on the ninth-floor newsroom staring at an e-mail he had written the previous weekend. Just three months earlier he had moved in, and the office was barely unpacked. Boxes and papers sat on the floor, and the shelves held a few stacks of files and a handful of books, but there were no family photos, no happy souvenirs to mark his short tenure in this prestigious post. The entire summer had been an exercise in political survival. He had advised the Bancroft family on an editorial independence agreement they wanted in order to protect the *Journal* from Rupert Murdoch, while at the same time he had back-channeled with his friend and Murdoch intimate Robert Thomson to protect himself. If you were lucky enough to find him in his office at all that summer, he would often be rubbing his hands to stay warm in the air conditioning, looking more tired than was humanly possible for a man of forty-six and, in private moments, a bit stunned by the turn of events.

As people filed into the 10:30 meeting, Brauchli thought back to the very early morning. He had sent his e-mail to the staff at 6:45 a.m., having reread it and rephrased it before finally hitting Send. An exercise in management-speak crossed incongruously with precise journalistic prose, the note urged his staff to stay focused on their jobs and not be distracted. With a simple subject line—ON THE NEWS—the e-mail began:

Today's news that a decisive proportion of Bancroft family trusts will vote in favor of News Corp.'s proposed acquisition of Dow Jones begins a process that will affect us all, but won't change what we do in the newsroom.

As journalists at Dow Jones and The Wall Street Journal, we have always focused on maintaining the high quality and integrity of our work, without regard to our ownership. We will continue to do so.

Our journalism defines the Journal. A change in ownership won't change our understanding of what's important; our ability to compellingly explain the world, politics and business; or our commitment to reporting that is accurate, honest and free of slant.

We know that a successful news organization's first obligation is to its readers. We must serve them, recognizing that their interests and needs change constantly, and that we will have to change with them.

It is too early to know how or even whether News Corp. ownership might alter priorities or structures at Dow Jones. Our current and likely future owners have given formal assurances, however, that the newsroom will retain its independence.

An owner who values editorial independence is essential to the Journal's success. Yet it is we who ultimately will ensure it, through the continued quality and integrity of our work.

Clarence Barron's heirs in the Bancroft family have been loyal and proud stewards of The Wall Street Journal for nearly 80 years. The Journal today, in print, online and in new media, in the U.S. and internationally, sets the highest journalistic standard thanks to their long support. I hope you share in my deep gratitude to them.

Regards,

Brauchli, New York

The language was characteristically understated for a twenty-year veteran of the *Journal,* where euphemism approached an art form.

It fell to Brauchli to hold things together in the newsroom. He was barely perceptible to Murdoch, who in his career had encountered and dispensed with many more established editors. But Brauchli hoped and believed that he could outwit the cadre of News Corp. higher-ups who governed his future. He shifted immediately into a protectionist mode. The incredible thing about Brauchli's note to his staff that morning was not its astonishing banality and familiar corporate-speak of the conquered, but that in a newsroom full of gimlet-eyed cynics, so many people believed it.

As he began the morning meeting, Brauchli kicked things off with a joke about the wide range of the *Journal*'s coverage in the current edition. That day, the paper was filled with stories about Dow Jones as if little else in the world mattered. He urged the editors to continue, despite uncertainty around the future of the paper, to focus on doing what they did best: produce stories the paper could be proud of. Just then, Brauchli's assistant appeared at the door.

"Rupert Murdoch is calling."

And there it was, the new order. Her words interrupted the usual banter. Brauchli jumped to take the call. The first news meeting of the Murdoch era, and already the old man had interfered with the process. This would become a familiar ritual in the coming months. The remaining editors couldn't help but note the irony in the moment. Then they continued on, amid nervous laughter, to discuss the contents of the next day's paper.

When he walked back to his office to pick up the phone, it turned out his haste was unwarranted. Murdoch left him on hold for a few minutes before picking up. The mogul gave a terse apology, quickly moving to the business of the call.

"I hear you are worried about people leaving the paper," he said. He knew his reputation and had been reminded of it in the past three months as every major media outlet in the country scrutinized his record. He and those around him saw the coverage as an attack from a biased media. Murdoch would later say he withstood the barbs due "a genocidal tyrant." Media critic Jack Shafer of Slate.com would adopt the phrase as his pet name for Murdoch, who nursed a sense of aggrievement. This attitude helped fuel his perennial exhortations to staff to challenge the establishment and helped him galvanize his almost sixty thousand employees. It gave the company, an otherwise inexplicable jumble of media and entertainment properties, its identity. News Corp. grew thanks to Murdoch's opportunistic and haphazard acquisitions, but it never had a coherent reason for being as a business. The company did what Murdoch wanted. Despite some very high-profile mistakes (near bankruptcy in the early 1990s and disastrous acquisitions such as Gemstar and *TV Guide*), everyone had benefited. Now he was nearing eighty years of age. Newspapers were dying. News Corp.'s stock price had plummeted. The old titan still dodged questions about his succession. But some in his circle had started to think, gingerly, about how to define the company beyond the man.

Anyone assessing Murdoch's bid for the *Journal* that summer felt obliged to mention, ominously, that "the alternatives" to Murdoch were grim. The Bancrofts had grown up with the implicit assumption that the moment they decided to sell the paper they would face an eager line of buyers. However, when they finally realized they were ready to sell, they saw it was too late for all that. Their erstwhile suitors had problems of their own, and if they didn't, the *Journal* was no longer as attractive a partner. They judged Murdoch not solely on his merits but against the dearth of other options.

The *Journal*'s newsroom hadn't launched a serious revolt against Murdoch's bid, a signal of the staff's weak position in a shrinking industry. Murdoch's reputation in the United States had benefited from his longevity. As Noah Cross said in *Chinatown:* "Politicians, ugly buildings, and whores all get respectable if they last long enough." He could have added newspaper barons. At other outlets, such as *New York* magazine, the staff had staged a deadline walkout to protest Murdoch's imminent takeover of their publication. At the *Journal,* a lonely group of reporters tried to drum up a protest to the offer and were admired but largely ignored by the nervous staff. Most were too busy watching counterparts at other struggling papers lose their jobs as newspaper executives more fearful than Murdoch retreated from the industry even as he dove in. Still, the group had coaxed a good many of the *Journal*'s staffers to write letters to Bancroft family board members urging them not to sell. And those letters were the weapon Leslie Hill chose to brandish when she stood in front of her family and urged them, fruitlessly, not to sell the company her great-grandfather had bought and her family had controlled for 105 years. Brauchli was worried that each person who had penned an impassioned plea against Murdoch might walk out now that the deal was signed. "I'm more concerned about people feeling morally obliged to resign because they campaigned against you," Brauchli replied.

But Murdoch, whose relationship to most reporters who worked for his papers was that of a man to his desk chair—"Murdoch looks upon you as furniture," the mogul's lawyer told Ken Auletta during the *New York* magazine takeover—urged Brauchli not to worry. "You shouldn't hold on to people to just hold on to them," he said.

Wanting to quickly acquaint himself with this editor at the top of the crown jewel of his $5-billion-plus purchase, Murdoch invited Brauchli, whom he had never met, to breakfast or lunch that coming Friday. Perhaps in retaliation for waiting on hold for a few minutes and perhaps because he needed some time to think about the shark before he climbed into his tank, Brauchli told Murdoch he would have to check his calendar and give him a call back.

That afternoon, Dow Jones CEO Rich Zannino came down from the executive eleventh floor to the newsroom to address the staff about the morning's announcement. In a French blue shirt with linen trousers and brown loafers, he was improbably tan and healthy given how much time he had spent these past three months in conference rooms negotiating to sell the company. Next to him, Brauchli looked pale and thin, a mien that would only amplify in the coming months. Zannino's message about the deal was simple: "A lot's been written, a lot's been said about it, and as I think about it and as I cut through it all, my summary of it would be: this deal makes a tremendous amount of sense for Dow Jones. It's a terrific opportunity for the company; it's a terrific opportunity for our shareholders; it's a terrific opportunity for all of us as employees of Dow Jones." He didn't mention his $16 million severance payment, which made it a terrific deal for him, but the crowd before him didn't need to be reminded. He went on for just a few minutes and then asked for questions. As Zannino fielded them, and passed many of them on to the new managing editor, Brauchli felt all the responsibility for the *Journal* accumulate at his feet. It was his paper to protect, not Zannino's, he realized.

On August 3, Brauchli arrived in one of the small executive dining rooms on News Corp.'s third floor for his appointed breakfast with Murdoch. He saw the scalps of former conquests hanging on the walls around him: dust jackets of HarperCollins books and corporate paraphernalia were the décor. The two chatted about the economy, and Murdoch grilled Brauchli on his opinions. It was clear to Brauchli that Murdoch was testing him, seeing how much or how little he enjoyed his new editor's company.

Then he laid out for Brauchli his vision for the paper, one he had shared broadly during the deal negotiations: "The *New York Times* sets the national agenda, and we should," Murdoch said, already slipping easily into the role of owner. Brauchli smiled imperceptibly at Murdoch's mention of "we." He wasn't used to the concept of him and Murdoch being on the same side. Brauchli wasn't surprised that Murdoch wanted to attack the *New York Times;* he had received ample warning of that desire. But the *Journal's* sensibility was more subdued, and strategic. *Journal* editors picked their shots; Murdoch wanted all-out war. Traditionally, the paper had been a newsroom of midwesterners in the center of New York, a group happy to exist outside the glamour of the city. The *Journal* was well read in flyover country and in the investment banking corridors of Wall Street, but among the literati and the culture set of Manhattan, it was viewed with a certain disdain, almost as if it were a trade paper. The reporters and editors often thought that was part of the beauty of the place. The *Journal* told its readers stories they never knew they wanted to hear. The paper revered surprise, running a quirky, often hilarious story every day down the middle of the front page, internally called the "A-Hed." The *Journal's* investigative reporters often remarked how welcomed they were by corporate executives, who thought that the paper was a friendly outlet. One of the paper's great special-ties was the "tick-tock," often riveting reconstructions of significant events that had occurred months earlier. Almost to a fault, the *Journal* avoided using the influence of its news pages to full effect.

Murdoch wanted to wipe all that away. He wanted the *Journal* to lead the media pack. It was antithetical to the *Journal* ethos. "Even if you're leading the pack, you're still part of the pack," Peter Kann, the *Journal*'s former CEO, liked to say. "If there's something everyone is talking about, that should be on the front page of the *Wall Street Journal*," Murdoch told his aides.

He continued his list of priorities for Brauchli. "We should break more news," he said. Already Murdoch had planned to add four pages to the paper to accommodate the expanded political and general news he wanted to see in it. While Murdoch had been sipping cock-tails on Diller's yacht, a bridge had collapsed in Minneapolis, kill-ing 13 rush-hour commuters and injuring 145. The *New York Times* and the *Washington Post* had splashed the story on their front pages. At the *Journal*, however, it had appeared in a 117-word brief item in the "World-Wide" column, a list on the paper's front page where the *Journal* relegated non-business news. "We should cover the bridge collapse in Minneapolis," he continued. "It's a big infrastructure story. I could see that on the cover of 'Marketplace' [the paper's second sec-tion]." Brauchli wanted to point out that the very morning of their breakfast, the paper carried a lengthy story on the front of the "Mar-ketplace" section discussing how the collapse had revived the infra-structure debate in the country. Murdoch either missed that story, or it had come too late. When the *Times* had a color photo of the bridge collapse the day after the event, the *Journal*'s brief mention was in-sufficient, Murdoch felt.

Talking about the paper's international coverage, Murdoch was less precise. He wanted to beef up the European and Asian editions of the *Journal* but didn't have specific prescriptions for how to do so, and he wondered aloud if the paper should combine its foreign bureaus with those of the *Times* of London, another of Murdoch's "quality" papers. Brauchli knew that even a cowed *Journal* newsroom would be appalled by the suggestion. He pushed back, suggesting that the two papers could have access to one another's content and share certain stories but only if they were properly labeled to identify the difference between *Journal* content and articles from the *Times* of London. He wouldn't become "we" so quickly.

Murdoch spent much of the meeting recounting News Corp.'s strategy. Brauchli asked Murdoch if he had decided on a CEO structure for Dow Jones, and Murdoch said he hadn't thought about it yet. He delivered a damning pronouncement about Zannino: "He's not a media man. He doesn't know media." Like everyone granted a moment with a powerful ruler, Brauchli attempted to save his friends. He encouraged Murdoch to get to know *Journal* publisher Gordon Crovitz and Todd Larsen, chief operating officer for half of Dow Jones—two executives Brauchli liked and hoped wouldn't be fired. Murdoch said he would, just as soon as he got back from spending the month of August on his boat in the Mediterranean.

As he stepped out of the nondescript News Corp. tower onto Sixth Avenue and into the August morning sun, Brauchli felt encouraged. He thought that there was plenty of overlap between his vision and the baron's.

16

Meet Mr. Murdoch

RUPERT MURDOCH visited the *Wall Street Journal*'s newsroom for the first time as its future owner on September 12, after a relaxing month aboard his *Rosehearty* yacht. To prepare for his arrival, reporters festooned the newsroom with enlarged "hedcuts" of Murdoch—ink portraits the paper used to illustrate its stories instead of photos—accompanied by the caption "Show Us the Money." Negotiations between Dow Jones's management and its small, ineffectual union were ongoing, and the reporters wanted to pressure Murdoch into treating them fairly. They knew of his reputation. A union buster, he had singlehandedly broken the British print unions back in 1986 by dismantling the legendary presses on London's Fleet Street with his Wapping complex in East London. But they hoped—against hope—he would put on a friendlier face for his takeover of Dow Jones and the *Wall Street Journal*.

Once inside the door of the paper he had sought to own for as long as any of his associates could remember, Murdoch was not the evil genius many expected him to be. While he was no friendlier to unions or patient with the "respectable" American newsroom he saw rife with self-importance, he cut an almost grandfatherly figure. His hands, worn down by years of pampering, had grown papery and soft, and the deep crevasses in his face made him seem frequently tired, even when he was full of energy, as he was the day he stepped into One World Financial Center to visit his prize.

He had come the week before to see Dow Jones's executives. CEO Rich Zannino made sure he would feel welcome in part by turning the televisions from CNBC to Fox News. Zannino had also set up an office for Murdoch just two doors down from his own. The maintenance staff in the building initially marked the office with a nameplate for "Rupert Murdoch," but Zannino scolded them—such a welcome was too obvious and crass and, frankly, modest—and they took it down.

Brauchli was jittery on this first day with his new boss. He pulled Murdoch from meeting to meeting, introducing the editors and showing off the newsroom. Brauchli believed in the *Journal* and wanted Murdoch to be impressed. Brauchli especially wanted to display the planned launch of a glossy magazine called *Pursuits*, unabashed advertiser bait that would mimic the profitable ventures at the *New York Times* such as the fashion-focused *T* magazine. Dow Jones executives and *Journal* editors would unveil a prototype of the magazine to Murdoch. Even though he wasn't yet officially the owner, they wanted his approval for the project. Since it would be his decision ultimately whether the magazine would launch, and in what form, it only made sense to include him, Zannino reasoned.

In the meeting, Murdoch's mind was elsewhere. "We've got to have a much smaller meeting and figure out how to cripple, really cripple the *New York Times*," he said quietly as the group sat down to begin. The editors showed him the prototype, and Murdoch nodded occasionally, providing his own commentary. "We've got to lower the advertising rates to make them comparable to the *Times*'s weekly magazine," he said. He leafed through the prototype, and the attendees from Dow Jones craned their necks closer to better understand his rumbling speech. He told them that there should be more beautiful women in the advertisements in the magazine. "My wife brings home these magazines and just pages and pages through them, looking at the ads," he said, with contented befuddlement. "She loves it." When he spotted a photo of an older CEO in the prototype, Murdoch exclaimed, "He's really shrunk." The others laughed, a bit nervously. "I've shrunk. I mean, you'll shrink," he continued, pointing to one of the younger editors in the room. "But why is it that some people shrink?" The attendees, including Zannino, Brauchli, Gordon Crovitz, and the

Journal reporter who had done the lion's share of the work on the prototype, Robert Frank, said little, offering an occasional comment, though never a contradictory one. This was not the razor-sharp titan of legend. Murdoch said he wanted Leonard Lauder, the chairman of Estée Lauder Companies, to advertise in the magazine. "But Len always asks for coverage in exchange for ads," Murdoch mused, "and I'm going to be the one who tells him no. That'll be fun."

Murdoch and Robert Thomson would appoint their own editor of the magazine, Tina Gaudoin, who had worked for Thomson at the *Times* of London as editor of that paper's upscale *Luxx* magazine. Slim and fashionable, Gaudoin came from a world where magazine editors accepted gifts from fashion designers. The *Journal*'s "Code of Conduct," which applied to every employee from the chief executive down to the news assistants, prevented such fringe benefits. Gaudoin appeared loath to give up the perks.

She had told colleagues that the strictures at the *Journal* against accepting gifts made life impossible for an editor like her. On an editor's salary, one couldn't traffic in the appropriate circles without taking advantage of the generosity of the magazines' advertisers and article subjects. Deep discounts on fashion were common for editors at many women's magazines, in both the United Kingdom and the United States.

Gaudoin appealed to the *Journal*'s ethics czar, Alix Freedman, who had won a Pulitzer Prize for the paper years before for a series in which she investigated the efforts of tobacco companies to increase smokers' intake of nicotine. In a contentious meeting in Freedman's office, Gaudoin made her case, gesturing to her handbag and other articles she was wearing. She had done things quite differently in London.

Freedman said there would be no exceptions. The story quickly circulated in the *Journal* newsroom as evidence of the culture clash between an institution with ethical standards and ones without them. In any event, Gaudoin signed the Dow Jones Code of Conduct (which she later said she was happy to do). She gave up the perks of her old life.

17

Interregnum

FOR THOSE FIRST MONTHS before he had officially taken over, Murdoch reveled in his position. Everyone inside Dow Jones, from Rich Zannino on down, acted as if Murdoch were already in charge. Marcus Brauchli had started back in June assembling his new team of editors to lead the paper, and his activity since the announcement of the deal had only accelerated, now that the Bancrofts were no longer a concern and he had more time to devote to the internal workings of the newsroom. He didn't make a move without considering Murdoch, of course, though he still hoped he could impress the mogul with the *Journal's* homegrown talent and way of doing things. He urged his editors to think of every possible suggestion News Corp. might have for the *Journal* in order to come up with a response that would allow the *Journal* to fashion its own destiny under the conglomerate. Even though he thought of them often, and how to protect them, he grew more distant from his editors during this period; he was so busy strategizing how to save the paper that he spent little time with the people who were putting it out. He was practicing the age-old strategy of "managing up" and spent hours with Murdoch, attempting to charm him.

No matter what Murdoch would tell his board or his investors about the rich array of businesses at Dow Jones, it was the *Journal* that he wanted and the *Journal* he watched. So Murdoch was willing to allow Brauchli to stay in his position as long as Thomson was the one with real control. Over time, however, it became clear to him that Thomson wasn't running the paper with a free hand, and Murdoch wasn't allowed the fun he thought he would have—daily chats with his editor and a ringside seat at the inner workings of the daily diary of the American dream—while Brauchli was in charge.

Brauchli continued to work feverishly on a plan to redesign the *Journal,* in hopes his stamp on the paper would be to Murdoch's liking. Brauchli was a fan of wonky political and financial reporting. His taste for corporate dramas paled in comparison to his liking for analyses of the global financial system or a quirky tale about a corrupt foreign dictator. He wanted to bring more political reporting into the paper, a goal that jibed with Murdoch's vision. The internal name for the planned redesign, which was in the works before Murdoch's bid even surfaced the previous April, was "Project Kilgore," a reference to the famed Barney Kilgore, who transformed the *Journal* from its narrow stock-tip roots to a national daily that covered a wide range of business and society. Project Kilgore would bring more politics to the front page of the paper; refocus the entire front section of the *Journal* more toward politics, culture, art, and science; and move corporate coverage to the second section of the paper. That second section, "Marketplace," had been a home for media, health, and technology feature stories, but in the redesigned *Journal* the biggest corporate news stories of the day would reside there.

Brauchli insisted to anyone who would listen that the changes he planned to make were his and his alone; he had talked about what he wanted to do with the paper for years, he said. Some of his friends backed him up. But even he admitted that Murdoch was coloring his every move, and Brauchli began to suffer from the disease that plagues every Murdoch editor: whether he made his own decisions or not, nobody believed he had a thought or utterance that didn't originate from Murdoch.

The newsroom of the *Journal* had never been full of firebrands, and the interregnum—when Dow Jones was promised yet not delivered to Murdoch—was no different. Paranoia suffused the newsrooms and the corporate offices. Though Murdoch thought little about the individuals in One World Financial Center—he had, after all, taken over newspapers many times before and heard howls of protest, only to overcome them—their minds were preoccupied by his every utterance and perceived preference.

He was particularly outspoken about his desire to change the one successful business strategy for which former CEO Peter Kann could claim credit: a paid subscription model for WSJ.com. Murdoch didn't like how it limited the audience for the *Journal*'s Web site. He viewed the success of his media properties largely through one lens: the size of their audience. On Fox's hit show *American Idol,* the audience, not the judges, voted for the winner. That was the real measure of success. Both properties needed to win large audiences to be successful. He wanted to harness the power of the *Journal*'s brand and use it online. Unlike other CEOs who would evaluate the financial implications of such a move before talking about their plans, Murdoch, with his characteristic disdain for such dithering, talked openly about making WSJ.com free before consulting anyone at Dow Jones about the move, or finding out how much it might cost the company. In mid-September, he told investors that a free WSJ.com "looks like the way we are going." The comments made Dow Jones executives, who prided themselves on their carefully constructed online strategy, apoplectic. They hadn't had a chance to present Murdoch with their evaluation of what such a move would mean financially. That didn't stop Murdoch from speculating aloud to an investor conference: "Would you lose fifty million in revenue? I don't think so . . . But you'd lose some tens of millions to start with. Then, if the site is good, I think you'd get much more than that back just in textual search. And I think you'd get not one million paying customers, but, around the world, you'd get ten to fifteen million regular daily hits on it, and that would be the most affluent, the most influential people in the world . . . And I think that could grow," he said. His numbers were all off, but no one with the real numbers had a chance yet to tell him, nor did they want to. After all, it was Rupert Murdoch, who had built a then $9 billion fortune from a single newspaper in Australia, they thought. Who were they to contradict him?

That fall, Murdoch continued on his tour of the *Journal,* meeting with everyone Brauchli would provide to him. He paired up News Corp. executives with their counterparts at Dow Jones and urged them to swap information. Though there was an army of executives coming from News Corp. to scout out Dow Jones, there was only one person whose opinion mattered, and that was Murdoch's. The executives at Dow Jones weren't certain about how to deal with the new focus. They were used to lengthy meetings, complete with ordered presentations and formal strategy sessions. Murdoch detested such formality. He ran News Corp. like a small club.

In early October, Brauchli arranged for Murdoch to meet with top editors from Dow Jones Newswires, MarketWatch.com, WSJ.com, and the *Journal.* They gathered in Harborside, New Jersey, in the Newswires headquarters. The discussion ranged widely, and as he often did, whether alone or surrounded by *Journal* editors or News Corp. executives, Murdoch went page by page through the *Journal,* critiquing the stories, their placement, and their length. At one point in the gathering, discussion turned to MarketWatch.com, a site Dow Jones had purchased in 2005. MarketWatch published short pieces of financial news and opinion but didn't charge for access the way the *Journal* did. Buying MarketWatch was supposed to give the *Journal* exposure to the growing online advertising market, which the *Journal* couldn't really access because of its paid subscription model online. David Callaway, editor in chief of MarketWatch, was telling Murdoch about Dow Jones's takeover of MarketWatch and the fevered interest in the site in 2005.

"You had a lot of people after you," Murdoch remarked, responding to Callaway's enthusiastic discussion of the pursuit. Both Dow Jones and the New York Times Company were circling the site back then, Callaway told Murdoch.

"How much did you make in profit last year?" Murdoch asked him flatly.

"Four million," Callaway replied.

"And how much did Dow Jones pay for you?" Murdoch asked.

"Five hundred and twenty million," Callaway said.

Murdoch paused, his mouth dropping into a reflective frown. "That's almost as bad as me paying five billion for Dow Jones," he said. An almost imperceptible smile from Murdoch gave the editors permission to laugh, and the group erupted.

● ● ●

In November, Paul Steiger got his official Dow Jones retirement party. Treasury secretary Hank Paulson, New York mayor Michael Bloomberg, New York Times Company chairman Arthur Sulzberger Jr., and other luminaries showed up to toast and roast Steiger. Murdoch had said he might come but wasn't able to because of another engagement. Steiger closed the evening with comforting words for the staffers assembled. He knew some of them were nervous about what the future under Murdoch would bring, but he urged them to maintain the same standards that had defined the *Journal* for decades: "In the coming months and years, I am sure you will uphold the long-standing traditions of the *Journal*," he told the assembled reporters and editors. "Some of it's going to be scary. Some of it's going to be wonderful," he said. He spoke in his same halting tone, the one they had grown to trust during his sixteen years at the top of the paper. Following him, the comedian Andy Borowitz took a less sanguine view with his short close to the evening: "Some of it's going to be scary. Some of it's going to be wonderful. But mainly it's going to be really fucking scary."

In early December, as the deal was about to officially close, Murdoch made his executive appointments. The most significant announcement for the company's future was that James Murdoch was taking over as CEO of News Corp. for Europe and Asia (he got everything except the United States and Australia, where Murdoch's son-in-law, Alasdair MacLeod, and his elder son, Lachlan, resided). The moment marked James's true ascension to heir apparent of News Corp., though as anyone who knew James's father understood, such things were never set in stone.

Simultaneously, Murdoch named Robert Thomson publisher of Dow Jones. Thomson, fresh off six years of running the *Times* of London newspaper, was Murdoch's man for the *Journal*. Thomson's job as publisher, designed specifically to subvert the carefully constructed editorial independence agreement, gave him authority over a wide array of Dow Jones's businesses, including the digital properties and Dow Jones Newswires. Murdoch was focused on the *Journal*, and he held Thomson responsible for it. Leaving Brauchli in place, he reasoned, might create less upheaval, but in Murdoch's mind, Thomson was in charge.

A week after Murdoch's executive appointments, at ten o'clock in the morning on a cold, blustery December day, Dow Jones convened its last shareholder meeting. It was here that Murdoch's deal for the *Journal* officially closed. In the "grand ballroom"—actually a windowless conference room with a small stage of the Marriott hotel across from the Dow Jones headquarters—a small crowd gathered. The meeting was anticlimactic, subdued. Murdoch had already been spending much of his time in Dow Jones's headquarters. He knew the details of every budget. He had his own office and had arranged to remove much of the top layer of Dow Jones's management, including Rich Zannino, who had been so helpful in making the deal happen.

The meeting concluded quickly. "This has been a difficult and for many a sad set of discussions," said Peter McPherson. "I thank you for attending this last meeting of Dow Jones."

As the fewer than one hundred attendees streamed out of the conference room, Jane MacElree stood at the doorway, dressed in yet another multicolored wool jacket, with tears wetting her round cheeks. Her daughter Leslie and son Mike stood together. Displaying the family discord that had long been bubbling under the surface, Elefante, Lisa Steele, Martha Robes, and her husband sat apart from the Hills. Dow Jones's directors filed downstairs to have lunch with their lawyers and advisers after the meeting, to thank them for their services during the deal and convene their last board meeting. The Bancrofts dispersed, to nowhere in particular.

At eleven thirty that day, the makeshift theater of Murdoch's arrival began. Gary Ginsberg called Robert Christie, Dow Jones's vice president of communications. "Can you keep a secret?" he asked. "Rupert wants to address the staff at two thirty this afternoon. Can you set it up?"

Christie did what he could to prepare for the new boss's arrival. He pushed four boxes of printer paper together in a corner of the ninth-floor *Journal* newsroom and set up additional phone lines so foreign and domestic bureaus could listen in. An e-mail went out to the *Journal*'s staff that afternoon, giving them roughly a half-hour to assemble. Murdoch had arrived in the building and was up in Rich

Zannino's office with Ginsberg, Robert Thomson, and Leslie Hinton, the newly named CEO of Dow Jones who had worked with Murdoch for nearly fifty years, in Australia, the UK, and now here in New York. Ginsberg, wanting to imbue the moment with some historic significance, snapped photos of the men as they waited to address the newsroom. They eventually filed downstairs, Murdoch leading, followed by Hinton, Thomson, and Ginsberg. They walked into the newsroom, which was packed with *Journal* reporters, Dow Jones business managers, security staff, and maintenance crews. All had gathered to hear what Murdoch had to say. Brauchli stood off to the side, uncertain whether he would be called on that day. "What if they ask me to say something?" he asked a colleague.

The last time the room had approached such a capacity was the previous May when Peter Kann addressed the newsroom in his retirement speech. At the time he told the admiring crowd: "The best protection for honest, independent journalism is in an independent company under the stewardship of a family that views publishing and the *Wall Street Journal* as a public trust as well as a financial investment. These days, of course, there is an external challenge to that independence. The Bancroft family is showing some resistance. The drawbridge is still up. So far, so good."

Seven months later almost to the day, Rupert Murdoch had a different message. As he stepped onto the boxes, tan against his white shirt, he looked quickly at the piece of paper he had folded in his left hand.

"Naturally it's very exciting for us," he said, looking out over the crowd.

> Maybe it's more a day of nervousness for a lot of you, but I hope it's also a day of excitement because it is a new day in the history of this company. We've come here to expand it, to develop it, and, where possible, to improve its product. I know that change is often difficult or creates nervousness. If it's particularly nervousness then certainly let us know. We're very accessible people.
>
> But I just wanted to say that we do know and understand the tremendous values of Dow Jones and particularly of course of the *Wall Street Journal* and the very high bar you have set yourselves.

If anything you will find us trying to set a higher bar. So we want to see a better paper. It's already a great paper but everything can always improve. And we'll be there encouraging you and helping you in every way we can.

Our aim is pretty simple. We have to entertain, inform, enrich all our readers in their lives and in their businesses. We must be the preeminent source of financial information and comment in the world. And we must put ourselves beyond there being any doubt in that regard.

This last bit hung in the air. "We have to *entertain*, inform, enrich all our readers." The message was simple and unobjectionable enough, but the order of delivery struck many in the newsroom. Where Peter Kann had warned the group against "mixing news and entertainment," Murdoch wanted them first to entertain. Kann warned them against "pack journalism" and the journalism of "buzz and hype." Murdoch wanted to lead the pack and create the buzz. Murdoch hadn't mentioned a word about holding companies accountable. He continued with the part of his speech that Thomson had drafted for him:

This really is a moment of great opportunity in the world. We are seeing—we don't see it in New York—but outside in the world, there are a hundred million people a year coming out of dire poverty and joining the world economy, causing tremendous creation of wealth and capital formation and desperate desire—need, also —for information. It's up to us be out on the frontline providing that information in the most helpful way and the most reliable way possible.

As we go forward you'll probably find, particularly on the management side but all across, an ever increasing concentration on globalization in the whole world and digitization. In spite of that, for many, many years to come, the *Wall Street Journal* will be a key frontispiece to everything we do. So thank you very much. I'd like to pass you over to Les Hinton.

The newsroom applauded, and Hinton stepped up onto the boxes and delivered a brief, encouraging speech before stepping aside for

Thomson, who had been standing behind Hinton with his half-glasses balanced on the tip of his nose. He had looked over his notes as Hinton spoke and stepped onto the boxes, offered a brief smile, and then delivered the first warning shot to the reporters who stood before him. He enjoyed provocation and elaborate speeches and took pleasure in the opportunity to strike fear into the hearts of his new charges.

"We as journalists all know that the world is not only changing but changing exponentially," he began. "And while it's right to be respectful of the past, these days, it is certainly fatal to be haunted by history.

"He who stands still, will be overrun. And yet the global demand for journalism of integrity, quality, of perspicacity and of immediacy has never been greater. So I have no doubt that as long as there is a willingness to create and to change that the *Wall Street Journal* and Dow Jones will have success beyond its recent imaginings. And we are genuinely looking forward to sharing in that success with you. Thanks very much."

Thomson would be Murdoch's messenger. Despite his fearsome reputation, Murdoch disliked direct conflict and would allow Thomson to carry out the more difficult assignments. Murdoch quickly stepped forward again. He would, as he knew how to do, lighten the mood: "Well, I think that's all we have to say so you'd better get back to work and make sure you're not scooped tomorrow."

18

Chiefs

I N JANUARY, the *Wall Street Journal*'s top editors came from across the country and around the world to New York for the biennial ritual at the paper, the bureau chiefs' meeting. In years past, this meeting collectively shaped the direction of the paper and, in turn, the country's thoughts about business and commerce. Chiefs could air pettier concerns as well, push their agendas, and show off in front of the crowd. The three days were like a family gathering at Thanksgiving, where each editor inevitably fell back on his or her assigned role—the curmudgeon, the gadfly, the intellectual, the fashion diva. The group would argue and grumble, and everyone would return home feeling oddly reassured that despite all the discussion of new priorities for the year, little about the newspaper would in fact change.

To open the meeting, Brauchli had arranged a dinner for the attendees and asked Murdoch to speak. Before the dinner, the group assembled for cocktails at seven. Because the *Journal* needed to be printed and distributed across the entire country, the paper's deadlines were early. Reporters filed stories at 5:00 p.m. for the early, "two-star" version of the paper that served a large chunk of the nation, then updated their stories for the three-, four-, and five-star versions of the *Journal*. At seven in the evening, many of the *Journal*'s reporters were still furiously updating breaking stories for later editions to make sure they weren't shamed the following morning by a competing story in the *New York Times*. For this special occasion, however, the bureau chiefs left their offices—some had flown from halfway around the world—and put their deputies in charge for the next couple of days. They were having dinner with Rupert Murdoch, and very few things were more important than that. So on Wednesday, January 9, 2008, the bureau chiefs streamed across the street from their nondescript Battery Park City newsroom, across West Street, and over to the New York Marriott Financial Center. Murdoch had made the same trek, waving off his chauffeur's offer of a ride and offering the car to Dot Wyndoe, his faithful assistant.

When Murdoch entered the small, windowless ballroom where the chiefs had gathered, he could barely get past the door. He was stopped immediately by one of the editors, who was trying to impress Murdoch with his smart commentary. Patient and convivial with his new staff, Murdoch chatted while Les Hinton went to fetch him a drink. The three men—Murdoch, Hinton, and Robert Thomson—were the celebrities in the room. It was almost a month since they had addressed the newsroom from their makeshift stage. Eyes darted toward them as the others in the room attempted their own separate conversations.

As the group sat down for dinner, Brauchli stood to introduce Murdoch. He began with a story about Murdoch's grasp of the details of newspaper production—he had walked into a printing facility and immediately spotted the capability of the plant to produce and ship regional coverage—and praised his new boss. "He is someone who is interested, knowledgeable, and passionate about newspapers," Brauchli said from a raised podium in front of the round tables of editors, "and as you know that's not exactly a common quality among people in business these days . . . We're fortunate he can be here to talk to us."

Murdoch was on his best behavior and thanked Marcus for his generous introduction. "I consider myself extremely lucky to find myself the head of Dow Jones at this particular time," he began, as if he had happened on the post by chance. He praised the company's heritage and traditions and told the crowd that the assets of the company went far beyond the *Journal*. There were also Newswires, *Barron's*, the company's Indexes business, MarketWatch, and Factiva to consider. All were capable of "great expansion," he said. "But first we should take stock. Print and especially newspapers are in trouble for many reasons we have to face and be honest about. Circulation is appalling," he said, for reasons that started twenty years ago—"a change in lifestyle, women going to work, all that sort of thing"—and of course there was the Internet. But Murdoch was not going to lose this opportunity to tell the editors how they were implicated in this decline. "If I may be so bold as to say that in this country newspapers have become monopolized. They've become—some of them have become pretty pretentious and suffer from a sort of tyranny of journalism schools so often run by failed editors." At this, the crowd laughed, perhaps approvingly, perhaps a bit nervously. "But circulations have all sunk even more than the figures would suggest," Murdoch continued. "Let me just tell you before we congratulate ourselves too much tonight that the single-copy sales of the *Wall Street Journal* since 2000 have fallen 55 percent."

Murdoch had done his homework and come armed to the dinner. He would not allow the self-satisfaction of this crowd to continue for long. "You go across the country and the fall-off in readership of news on printed paper is pretty dramatic . . . I think there are many reasons for this but they're the facts of life." And then he presented his solution, in the same calm, almost bored tone he often used when speaking publicly. "Of course our first priority is to urgently make the *Wall Street Journal* more attractive. We must go to a wider circulation and get more readers per copy, as well as improve everything we already do . . . As far as we're concerned, of course, it involves a lot of change," he said. "I'd like to take the opportunity to compliment Marcus on the changes he's already made." Brauchli had begun to put more news on the front page. Just that morning, which was the day after the New Hampshire primary in which Hillary Clinton and John McCain had won their parties' respective primaries in those states, Brauchli had put the news on the front page and coupled it with a feature on McCain's comeback from his blistering defeat eight years before by George W. Bush. Murdoch praised the McCain coverage and then moved on to one of his favorite topics.

"Talking of opportunity, and I don't want to get into a flaming match, but there is of course the lamentable state of the *New York*

Times." Murdoch said he saw the *Times* as the *Journal*'s main competitor. Over at the *Times,* they were bracing for Murdoch's attack on their business. The *Times* had set up a war room with the guiding principle "What Would Rupert Do?" The *Times* had a weakness, Murdoch explained. "One of the great frailties, I think, of that paper is that it seems to me their journalists are pandering to powers in Manhattan. You know"—he paused for dramatic effect—"reporters are not writers in residence." Stories in a newspaper were not magazines or books; they had to be more direct and less complex. This message was directed as much to the editors in the room as to the *Times* editors in midtown. Murdoch made that explicit: "This is true for the *New York Times* and I'm sure that most of you can see the need for some streamlining at home right here."

He then outlined the strategy he had used countless times before in Britain to attract greater readership through newsstand sales. "We must be proud of what we do, proud enough to project it more boldly than we have in the past on the newsstand. Retail sales will be an increasingly important part of our strategy. We must entice, engage, and excite readers or else we will lose them. A new reader caught at the newsstand is the best possible prospect for a long-term subscriber." Murdoch had his playbook and he would not alter it for the United States, where most papers, and certainly the *Journal,* relied mainly on subscriptions for circulation. As the Detroit bureau chief commented to his colleagues that night, "We don't even have newsstands in Detroit." But Murdoch was unfazed. He would follow the same playbook he always had.

The bureau chiefs had an opportunity to ask Murdoch questions. He started off easy. In response to a question about the competitive dynamic with the *Financial Times,* Murdoch replied, "The whole company is very vulnerable. Let's hope that some crazy megalomaniac buys it and wrecks it." The room erupted in laughter, a release of nervous energy. He backed off his previously stated desire to make WSJ.com free, calling his prior analysis "much too simplistic." He answered a question about how he felt about the *Journal*'s front page and its longer features.

"There was a feeling in the past that people get all their news on the Web and we just do analysis," he said, referring to Brauchli and

Crovitz's pet project *Journal* 3.0. "I think we have to have news and analysis and we have to break hard news. And I think when there is very big news such as last night, don't run away from it. Go with it. I'd like to pick up the paper and say, 'Gosh, I must read that—did that really happen?' And then let's get the facts of the stories, the key facts, in the first paragraph and then go to the analysis. When you talk about long-form journalism, one of the things I would say is just remember the readers and how much time they have. And don't confuse the time you spend on a good story with the need for length in writing it. A story is a story and should be told in as few words as possible."

At this lecture, many of the chiefs looked at each other, thinking, "*He's* telling *us* how to write a story?" He sounded very much like an editor talking to a cub reporter, in a tone that seemed misplaced given the speaker and his audience. He told the editors that long stories were best put in the paper on the weekend, which brought him back to his favored topic: the *New York Times*. "The Sunday *New York Times* is by far the worst edition of the week. Even what used to be their strength with the color magazine is not what it was. It's just massive, gray, and written way before midday on Friday before they leave for the Hamptons." Again, the editors laughed, but it was becoming clear to them that his impression of the *Times* staff was interchangeable with his impression of the editors in front of him.

The questioning continued. Would Murdoch make the *Journal* less of a business paper? It would still be "mainly" business, he said, but he had greater ambitions than that. "I think people in business, in law, and people with money—investors—and for that matter people in academia, too, we should be *the* paper, the absolute number-one paper in this country." As for the chiefs' concern that the *Journal* would join in the pack mentality of other media, Murdoch said, "The fact is that this year so far the political season has really caught the imagination of the public . . . There's something out there that's stirring people and we can't afford to ignore that." The notion was counter to what the editors of the paper had done for years, which was ignore the most obvious headlines and go for those that lurked in the corners of a major news story.

After a time, Brauchli cut off the questions and dinner was served. The chiefs talked at their tables, trying to remain optimistic about the future that lay before them.

Two days later, Rupert Murdoch looked out at the row of editors lined up against the wall like captured prisoners of war, ready to recant their prior allegiances and adopt a new oath of loyalty.

Shuffling toward the front of the room, they were going over in their minds what they would say in their two minutes in front of the assembled group. The meeting had been moved to the India House in lower Manhattan. Murdoch wasn't on the agenda; it was the editors' time to talk. But Murdoch had shown up that morning in what was a surprise to most of those assembled. That he attended the meeting at all was a signal of how much he was personally invested in this latest purchase. Robert Thomson had delivered his message the day before, warning the group that from conceptualization to publication, a story's life should not last "the gestation of a llama," or 350 days. Now, on the third day of the meeting, each editor was to outline his (most of the editors were men) bureau's priorities.

There were two types of editors at the *Wall Street Journal*. There were the editors who controlled "bodies," and there were editors who controlled "real estate." The editors in charge of bodies had journalists reporting to them. These were the bureau chiefs, whose job was to pitch their charges' stories and lobby forcefully for their underlings. The other group was the page editors. They decided which stories would appear on the coveted Page One and which would be relegated to the inside pages of the paper. The inherently oppositional forces of those two groups had cultivated one of the greatest newspapers in the world. That bizarre and yet delicate ecosystem had been built over a century. Outsiders, like the victorious News Corp. executives, focused on the ecosystem's peculiarities and waste.

This year, the meeting wasn't a pleasant family gathering filled with ritualistic squabbling. As they gathered on the second-floor conference room of the India House, they were preparing for their moment in front of the new boss.

Managing editor Marcus Brauchli had directed the bureau chiefs to present four priorities in two minutes—thirty seconds per topic. Some took insult from the directive. They had just heard Murdoch's disdain for stories that were too long. Already they were meant to show they could be brief.

Despite the fact that they were top editors at the premier business publication in the world, many of the assembled had few options to find jobs outside the paper. Journalism was a shrinking field. There were fewer papers in the world than when they started out. Maybe it was true that there were more Web sites and blogs, but few of those had demand for middle-aged editors prized for their experience and news judgment. This crowd was a captive work force. At another time they may have faced their new owner with a righteous protest, but that kind of romantic resistance was a luxury they could no longer afford. That Friday morning in January, they were meek, easily disheartened, and scared. They were auditioning for the jobs they already had.

Murdoch was growing weary. He sat through presentations from page editors, bureau chiefs, deputy managing editors, and news editors—all these layers of management. What did they do all day? From his seat in the third row of tables, Murdoch spent most of his time at the meeting quietly conferring with his newly appointed publisher of the paper, Robert Thomson, his tour guide. Murdoch trusted Thomson to recognize the pomposity of the assembled crowd, to break through the rigid traditions that these journalists were clinging to out of fear or laziness or both. The two had been whispering to each other during several of the presentations. As was his custom, Murdoch had a pen in his hand and was scrutinizing the day's *Journal*. The presentations continued, about such topics as computer-assisted reporting, writing an investigative "leder," reporting and writing "scoops of thinking," a type of story the *Journal* prided itself on dominating. Murdoch was not impressed.

Now it was time for the bureau chiefs to stand before the group and present their priorities. Brauchli had been excited about the idea. "Let Murdoch and his lieutenant meet the editors at the *Journal*," he thought. "Show them how smart and down-to-earth these editors are. Show Murdoch that the paper isn't made up of the media elite he so despises. Let him see the good midwestern roots at the core of the paper, its work ethic, its heart. This will convince him not to gut the paper. Let Murdoch inside and he will be impressed with us. We will change him. We will be the exception." But as the editors lined up, they began to have second thoughts. The plan to introduce Murdoch to the brilliance and humility of the *Wall Street Journal*'s staff seemed foolish, even disastrous. So much for the celebration of the greatness of an iconic institution. Instead, Brauchli had put on a parade of humiliation where the conquered were being made to sing for their new master. The only consolation to the editors: Murdoch barely looked up to hear them speak.

19

Taking Bullets

BRAUCHLI VALIANTLY CONTINUED onward, putting the paper out every day and second-guessing himself more often than that. His busied himself with keeping Murdoch and Thomson out of the newsroom. He was in a race to change the paper in a way that satisfied them, yet Brauchli insisted that neither man meddled in coverage. "I had more contact with the previous publisher than the current one," he told colleagues. But avoidance took more energy than engagement, and in his furious rush to keep them out of his affairs, Brauchli appeared constantly preoccupied.

On February 4, News Corp. released its quarterly earnings for the first time as an official owner of Dow Jones. That day, the company reported a 24 percent increase in operating profit, though its net income rose fractionally—just 1 percent. Thomson strolled by Brauchli's office and said, in a stage whisper, "Operating profit, operating profit, operating profit." Brauchli was initially puzzled but then realized that Thomson must be referring to the earnings release. Brauchli brought Thomson into his office and explained that the *Journal* always emphasized net income first in its stories. That figure took into account taxes, depreciation, and all the other costs that affected a business's performance, and the paper considered it the most important figure in a company's earnings release. Any other number allowed a corporation to include and exclude various charges and other figures that could massage the earnings to make them appear rosier.

"Oh, don't change the standard, then," Thomson replied. "Just be consistent." The following day, Brauchli was amused to see the *New York Post's* story on the topic led with a "record" increase in operating income.

On February 13, a snowy day not long after the bureau chiefs' meeting, Thomson stood in Brauchli's ninth-floor office with a request from the boss. "Rupert thinks I should have an office on nine," he said, almost sheepishly. Until then, Thomson had resided on the executive eleventh floor and had to descend two floors on the elevator to see the news desk on the ninth floor.

Brauchli swiveled in his chair to face out his wall of windows overlooking the newsroom, where beyond his assistant's desk there lay a swath of empty carpet and no desks or reporters or editors. Brauchli's grand redesign of the newsroom hadn't yet begun, and there was still a large chunk of the newsroom that wasn't being used.

"Gee, there's no space down here," he said to Thomson, with a barely perceptible smile.

"Look, it's not what you think," Thomson said. "He doesn't want to make me editor." With his stooped carriage and ever present black suits, Thomson cut an unusual figure in the newsroom, but he could be unexpectedly charming. Thomson was ultimately responsible, in Murdoch's eyes, for the paper, though Brauchli didn't see it that way. Thomson didn't want to have to continue to answer to Murdoch that he had no desk on the newsroom floor.

"To be honest, he wants us to be seen more in the newsroom. He thinks we should be visible," Thomson said.

"Does he want me to quit?" asked Brauchli.

"No, no," said Thomson, attempting to smooth things over and yet deliver a message. "He just wants things to move faster. You and he are moving in the same direction; it's just a matter of speed."

"I have to look after the culture and the staff, too. I can't do it all at once," Brauchli said, pausing. "You have to protect me."

"I take a lot of bullets for you, to be honest," Thomson shot back. Brauchli's face flushed.

He recovered quickly, accustomed as he was at this stage to the battering of his position. He suggested Thomson take over a vacant conference room near where the reporters for the financial magazine *Barron's* sat. The room was the second-to-last office on the way out of the *Journal's* ninth-floor newsroom, between the *Journal's* graphics department and the *Barron's* office space.

"If you take that," Brauchli said, always strategizing, "I can make the case you are in between the two publications and not in the *Journal* newsroom." Thomson agreed to the arrangement but warned Brauchli, "Never tell Rupert I'm not in the *Journal* newsroom."

Of course, Murdoch needn't be told something he could witness with his own eyes, and the symbolism of it enraged him. Murdoch wanted his man on the newsroom floor, someone he could call to hear the latest news of the day. He didn't pay more than $5 billion to see his closest intimate stashed away in a closet nowhere near the reporters. That move, simple and petty, helped usher in what came next.

Murdoch still hadn't adjusted to the formality of the Dow Jones staff he had inherited, nor they to his unexpected outbursts. In a March 2008 meeting, Murdoch dropped by to listen to the paper's plans to promote yet another redesign, due to launch April 21 with some of Brauchli's proposed changes. When told he should listen to the paper's public relations plan, Murdoch said it wasn't necessary. "We don't need to talk about this," he said. Public relations was something Murdoch had never fully trusted. He thought it was a waste of time and, worse, a way to tip your hand to a competitor.

"You really should hear what Bob has to say," urged Kelly Leach, who worked on strategy for Dow Jones, referring to the ever affable vice president of communications, Robert Christie. Earlier in the week, the *New York Times* had run a lukewarm story on the paper's overhaul of its "Marketplace" section. "Usually my philosophy is we get ahead of the story," Christie ventured, "so we're not in a reactionary mode."

"Fuck the *New York Times*," Murdoch growled, suddenly surly. "I don't care what the media says."

"But Rupert," ventured Leach, "we know our advertisers aren't committed on incremental advertising spend—"

"We're going to do this our way and not give them a road map," Murdoch replied, beginning what became a longer-than-expected rant. "We're going to build a fantastic newspaper. I don't give a fuck what the media says," he continued.

Finally, Leach edged back into the conversation. "We've been doing market research of our readers and their opinion of the *Journal* has diminished since News Corp. announced it was going to acquire Dow Jones."

Then Rupert Murdoch, who had been simmering under the surface, exploded. "We're going to build a fucking great paper and I do not give a fuck what New York or the media has to say about it! We'll build the world's best paper!" This must be what truly energized him. He didn't want these nervous midlevel people around him, questioning every move. He wanted them to be aggressive and have fun and be a little more like one of the team.

20

Resigned

ON AN UNSEASONABLY COOL April morning, Murdoch, looking buoyant, boarded his 130-foot Boeing jet, spacious enough in a standard model to accommodate 125 people but shuttling only 5 that day. Given Murdoch's plans, his mood might have convinced those who called him cold-blooded of the accuracy of their description. Maybe it was the prospect of change, not the task ahead, that was energizing him.

Murdoch passed distractedly down the long corridor lined with blond wood and past the bedroom, tastefully decorated with a beige bedspread and ivory pillows and blankets. He shuffled past the private meeting room with a long conference table surrounded by seven seafoam-green leather easy chairs. The flight attendant, Peggy, busied herself arranging the pillows and otherwise tidied up. Idle hands, her activity suggested, need not apply.

Murdoch threw himself down on a plush seat at the back of the plane, which was among the largest on the private tarmac. "Oh, the Arabs' planes are bigger," he casually offered to Gary Ginsberg, his spokesman, who was waiting for him. Added fuel tanks on this model allowed him to travel ten hours without stopping—nice for trips back to his native Australia, where he traveled at least once a year and which, after all these years away, still remained the continent on which he felt most at ease.

Today, the trip was less ambitious. They were headed to Washington, DC, to a dinner honoring Murdoch at the Atlantic Council—a nonpartisan think tank that aspired to promote civilian dialogue among NATO member countries. Spain's former prime minister José María Aznar, a fellow conservative and News Corp. board member, had suggested Murdoch for the award, and while skeptical of the organization, Murdoch wanted to help his friend. Such awards were obligations for him and the dinners that accompanied them almost lethal. The Distinguished Business Award event would normally have been no night to remember, but he would be there, smiling occasionally and feigning interest in the proceedings. At least he would be sitting next to Henry Kissinger, which might prove entertaining.

The night before the plane trip to DC, Murdoch took his two youngest daughters, ages six and four, out to dinner. "A big adventure," he said. "Dinner with Daddy." The domestic evening of dinner with the girls behind him, Murdoch was on the plane to DC, about to make his move. He would show that the *Journal* was under his control. Four months after Murdoch's deal for the *Journal* had closed, Marcus Brauchli, the managing editor of the paper, was about to leave the picture.

"It'll all be finalized in two hours," Murdoch said to Ginsberg.

Many times the News Corp. "pirates" had signaled the arrival of the new order with the tossing of figureheads. Often Murdoch explicitly fired them, but many times they got the message and jumped before they were pushed. The only consistency was that they left. Dorothy Schiff was supplanted at the *New York Post*, *New York*'s Clay Felker was ejected, Harry Evans of the *Times* of London was suddenly redundant. Murdoch made no concessions to sentiment or even familial association. As everyone knew, Murdoch had allowed News Corp. executives like Roger Ailes, the former Nixon speechwriter, to undermine his tattooed and athletic elder son, Lachlan, whom Murdoch had trained from his earliest days to take over at the company. Ailes prevailed—he'd won the old man's affection by building Fox News. At Dow Jones, it had been similar. Zannino offered to leave his post but simultaneously said, "'I'll hang around and help or be available if you like,'" Murdoch remembered. "But I've taken up offers like that in the past. And then I moved in, and always by the afternoon of the first day, I'm telling the guy to put his hat on and get out."

For almost a year, Brauchli had a lame-duck tenure, delicately attempting to protect himself from his new boss's encroachments. Not for a day had Brauchli appeared truly in charge. His limited reach wasn't a shock; he'd seen all of this coming and was holding out as best he could. Shortly after Murdoch's bid for the *Journal* became public, Brauchli sighed, saying to a friend, "I work my whole career to get this job and now I'm working for *Murdoch?*"

On the plane, Murdoch was dressed in a chalk-stripe gray flannel suit with a white spread-collar shirt and a red patterned tie. He scanned the morning's *Journal* and looked with disappointment at his new toy.

"It's starting to look like a real newspaper," attempted Ginsberg, hoping to draw out his boss on the paper. The reaction was muted.

Murdoch's brow furrowed. His white handkerchief peeked out of his front breast pocket, like the white roots that betrayed his pale brown dyed hair. "The stories could be better, but it's a start."

This morning, April 21, 2008, was the first day of the official redesign that was inching the paper in the direction where Murdoch wanted it to move. Previously the old *Journal*, with its airless but important appearance, had seemed beyond time's changes, newsstand appeal, and even questions of readability. It seemed designed for those so seriously and closely intertwined in the events described that not even a nuance could be sacrificed. The paper's front page had contained three lengthy feature stories every day down its sides and middle, like columns adorning the front of an ancient temple. In lieu of sensational photos, the page showcased stately ink-drawn portraits of the business figures it featured. Even before Murdoch, the temple had been under siege: breaking news, color, and photos, the province of the populist papers, had nosed their way into those sacrosanct spaces.

The changes Brauchli and others had rushed to make were evident in that morning's paper, which displayed a new sports page, more political coverage, shorter stories, and bigger headlines. The unusual vertical design that had graced the front page of the *Journal* for most of its history had all but disappeared. The day before Pennsylvanians were to vote in a primary for either Hillary or Obama, political stories—accompanied by large color photos—dominated the front page. A four-column headline stretched over them, announcing in tall, bold letters: "Latest Attacks Roil Democrats."

The notion that the *Journal* could be a second read, famously espoused by the legendary midcentury *Journal* editor Barney Kilgore, was no more. No one had time to read two publications. And anyway, Murdoch didn't want to be second at anything. As smaller papers around the country faltered, Murdoch wanted to pick off their readers. Turning to the second section of the *Journal*, "Marketplace," he mused, "I think we'll change it from 'Marketplace' to 'Business.'"

He paused briefly, then said, "I don't know." Then he abruptly shot down his own suggestion. It seemed that Murdoch wasn't exactly certain what he wanted to do with the paper he had coveted for twenty years. At first, his judgments had looked haphazard; he demanded the paper make its Web site free and then would reverse himself once presented with Dow Jones's research on the money such a decision could cost the company. He was an improviser.

Though the paper wasn't what he wanted it to be yet, he was casual, confident, and unconcerned. The *Journal* would evolve, each move making possible the next, and in time a new personality—breathless, naive, and attention-getting—would greet readers who once considered the paper the province of carefully considered judgments and old blue suits. "More graphics, with more color; just you wait," he murmured.

He opened the *Financial Times*, London's *Journal* equivalent, which Murdoch had attempted—and uncharacteristically failed—to buy years before. He glanced through, looking for lessons. As he scanned the pages, he noted the preeminence of reports from behind the scenes. He loved colorful quotes. Murdoch was a fan of full access and on-the-ground reporting. He didn't want his reporters analyzing; he wanted them pounding the pavement, telling him what the important people had to say about important things.

"See, they have very strong reporting on Obama and Clinton. In the *FT,* you hear word for word what they're saying, they have somebody with them, you can tell." He took a quick look at the *Journal.* "Our story," he said, pausing. "Typical overediting." But then he pulled back, not wanting to be too harsh. "You could argue it either way."

As he was no longer the renegade never invited to dinner, Murdoch now found himself a tourist attraction for the obsequious politicos and dignitaries on global jaunts. They knew, as he did, that enemies and opponents were best kept on a first-name basis. He enjoyed their entreaties. He wasn't afraid of making his own. Right now, Murdoch wanted a sit-down with Obama, and Ginsberg wanted to firm up a meeting between his boss and the young candidate who was closing in on the Democratic nomination. Hillary Clinton was expected to win in Pennsylvania, but Obama was the star and had the momentum.

Murdoch made a point of establishing friendly relationships with politicians in his adopted homes. When Hillary Clinton stepped up to become senator from New York, Murdoch made a bridge to her as a fellow pragmatist. She was planning to run for president and didn't hold grudges. The *Journal*'s editorial page never made such allowances. It had hounded the Clintons for everything but their fashion decisions and devotion to fast food. In a particularly vicious attack in June 1993, the editorial page singled out Vincent Foster, deputy White House counsel and a former law partner of the then First Lady, with the headline "Who Is Vincent Foster?" Other editorials about Foster and his role in the Clinton White House followed. On July 20, 1993, Foster was found dead of a gunshot wound to the head. With him was a suicide note of sorts, reading, "The WSJ editors lie without consequence." But Hillary let it all go and came to the table. Her reward was what seemed to be, at the top of the primary season, Murdoch's support.

Hillary wasn't the stock to buy at this juncture. Murdoch, intrigued by Obama and his surprise win in the Iowa caucus, had started to distance himself from Senator Clinton. Months earlier, in January, Murdoch's *New York Post* endorsed Obama over the former first lady, disappointing those in the Clinton camp who had pieced together the rapprochement with Murdoch. Ginsberg, who had worked for the Clintons years earlier, had reached out to Obama numerous times, but to no avail. Obama-ites, including Al Gore and others, said the candidate was interested in talking to Murdoch. Yet no meeting was forthcoming. The latest intermediary, former U.S. senator Tom Daschle, had broached the subject to Ginsberg, who decided on the plane to gauge his boss's interest in pursuing a meeting.

"We don't want to be supplicants," Ginsberg said quietly to Murdoch.

"On the other hand," replied Murdoch, looking toward the window that morning on the plane, privately exploring an altogether different angle, "we don't want him to win the presidency thinking we are bitterly hostile."

Just before 10:00 a.m. as the plane lifted off, Murdoch's thoughts turned to his comments for the lunch with Atlantic Council members that day. He went over his address for the gathering. Like the dinner speech, these words were written by recently retired Bush speechwriter William McGurn. Murdoch had just hired him as his speechwriter; in a pleasant felicitous synergy, McGurn's column debuted on the op-ed page of the *Journal* that morning.

His carefully organized pages in hand, Murdoch asked Peggy, the flight attendant, for some coconut water, one of his favorite health boosters. Murdoch was always looking for a way to maintain his energy, to stay youthful, to not slow down. It was one of the habits that betrayed his awareness of growing older, a bit of reality he successfully ignored. Wendi had banned dessert as part of an effort to keep Murdoch slim. Peggy placed a lowball glass in the gold-rimmed built-in coaster in front of her employer, who stood up and raised it. "It's a magic potion. No calories, and packed with all sorts of . . ." He trailed off, snapping his fingers together, trying to remember the name. "Electrolytes," he finally resolved, heading down the hallway to his private meeting room as the plane passed over New Jersey.

Two weeks before, on April 7 to be exact, Marcus Brauchli sat in the dingy ninth-floor conference room of Dow Jones's headquarters in Battery Park City. He had arranged for the chiefs of domestic and foreign bureaus to call in that morning to hear a discussion of the paper's proposed direction. Around the table, deputy managing editor for news coverage Bill Grueskin, Page One editor Mike Williams, and deputy managing editor Alix Freedman all sat with him. The New York chiefs also gathered to hear a new way to think about the paper. Brauchli hand-picked Grueskin and Williams for their jobs. Each, like Brauchli, possessed a desire to change the paper and the confidence to think they were the right men to do it. Freedman was the longest-serving deputy M.E. of the three and the only one to survive Brauchli's management shuffle intact. She was now the anointed keeper of the *Journal*'s ethical standards.

Murdoch's outspoken statements that there were too many editors at the paper—he had repeated his amazement that stories in the *Journal* were touched "an average of 8.3 times" before appearing in print—fueled anxieties that were already running high. Fear of firings (what was a Murdoch takeover without a bloodletting?) accelerated as the new era announced itself in not-so-subtle ways. Traditional "leders," the long, narrative, front-page stories that were a *Journal* trademark, were disappearing in favor of shorter news stories. Brevity was always desirable these days. So was anything political. Coverage of the presidential primaries dominated the front page in a paper that had originally made its name with enlightening features on business and the economy. This revolution had originally been instigated by Brauchli, but it was Murdoch's message that had been heard loud and clear around the *Journal* empire.

Engaging and charming one-on-one, Brauchli fell apart in front of crowds, cracking obscure jokes and making casual remarks that sometimes left permanent scars. Brauchli was a constant planner, often weighing how to get his way while giving his audience the perception that they had gotten what they wanted. His promotion strained this strategy. He had too many constituents to please all of a sudden, including Murdoch. He was determined to win over Murdoch and, at the same time, carefully counter him.

In the past few months Brauchli had appeared pale and gaunt, constantly rushing to get somewhere else but never quite arriving. The editors who worked for him could barely get a moment alone to discuss a story—he was too preoccupied with the task of preserving his publication to run it. Most dangerous, though, was his lack of combat training; he had no notion of the tested and gradually perfected tactics that allowed Murdoch to plot a murder while smiling at the face of the chosen victim. Brauchli read up on his subject. Andrew Neil had written in his book *Full Disclosure* that Murdoch had courted and then shunned him when he was the editor of Murdoch's *Sunday Times*. Brauchli, like Neil, felt he would be the exception, the one to make it work with Murdoch.

As the meeting began, the stressed-out Brauchli attempted to articulate his editorial philosophy, which he hoped would not be too distant from his new employer's vision of what the paper should be. "Every story on Page One has to compete for space and length," he said. This represented a break from the *Journal*'s past. No longer would feature stories dominate the page. Williams, the Page One editor, explained this further: the front page would be more responsive to news. He had already sent out memos to the staff urging them to write shorter stories and be punchier in their writing. Bureau chiefs chafed at their glibness. Grueskin, formerly the head of the paper's Web site, urged more news breaks and online packages.

But Brauchli had a credibility problem. This latest direction for the *Journal* was the polar opposite of what he and Crovitz had championed the entire previous year.

Now, in 2008, as he pushed a message in the meeting that the *Journal* would cover more politics and general news, he wasn't admitting even to himself that the previous redesign of the paper promoted exactly the type of story his new boss despised. Murdoch wanted straight news stories, and Brauchli found himself in the difficult position of backtracking. His new message undermined the old one. This is what his life had become, a series of misfired communications and bureaucratic gatherings. The non–New York bureau chiefs listened via conference call as Brauchli led the meeting. The people in the room could sometimes hear them snickering.

Toward the end of the meeting, Brauchli checked his BlackBerry and saw that he had a message from Thomson. He told the group he had to excuse himself and go to another meeting. Brauchli returned the call. "We have to go and talk to Les," Thomson said, referring to Leslie Hinton.

The two men walked to Hinton's office; he had just returned from a trip to China.

"*Ni hao*," Brauchli said, Mandarin for "hello." Hinton didn't smile.

"There's no easy way to put this but we want you to step down as managing editor. We don't think things are working out. We'd like to make a change." Neither Hinton nor Thomson went into detail or explained why. Brauchli knew they were merely handing down a verdict arrived at by their boss.

Murdoch's influence often began with installing a like-minded editor. As a student of history, Brauchli shouldn't have been surprised. Plus, so many of his colleagues were already missing: the eleventh-floor executive ranks had been decimated. Stuart Karle, the beloved newsroom lawyer who had edited the *Columbia Daily Spectator* when Brauchli was a reporter, recently had been fired. Brauchli had imagined this grim scenario a hundred times, even going so far as to liken himself to a soldier in Iraq who sees officers shot and wonders if the next bullet is for him.

Suddenly, he heard himself say, "I think it would be impossible for me to remain as editor if I don't have the support of the owner." His twenty-four years of climbing ended abruptly with that sentence. "I'll do whatever I feel is in the best interests of the *Journal* as an institution, including stepping down if necessary. But I think you're making a mistake."

Thomson chimed in. "Don't worry. We can take care of you financially."

"We'll figure it out," Brauchli replied, and then decided to get a lawyer. He soon hired Robert Barnett, the always cheerful, $975-an-hour Washington power broker who represented both of the Clintons, Bob Woodward, Lynne Cheney, Alan Greenspan, and Queen Noor of Jordan on their book deals. Barnett went to work; Brauchli went ahead with plans for a trip to Asia and the *Journal*'s California bureaus while Barnett handled the details of his "resignation."

That night, Brauchli and Thomson went out for a drink at Moran's Irish bar, one of the regular newsroom post-deadline watering holes nearby. "This makes no sense," Brauchli said. He had been making changes to the paper, doing much of what Murdoch wanted, he thought. Thomson knew his boss too well: "The precipitating fact is the change in ownership. It's obvious."

Brauchli had been telling people in the preceding weeks that editorships weren't like rent-controlled apartments. "There are no squatters' rights," he would joke. He had been cast out of the job he had worked to obtain for a quarter of a century. His only option now that he had agreed to go was to negotiate how much his silence would be worth to News Corp. He would say that it was his choice to leave, but he had some leverage.

The plane had landed, and now, speeding along the highway in a black Suburban to downtown Washington, Murdoch and Ginsberg never turned from their cell phones. At some point Ginsberg noticed an e-mail from Marcus Brauchli about a planned breakfast. "That's weird," Ginsberg said, almost to himself. "I just got an e-mail from our friend M.B.," he told Murdoch, who was up in the front seat next to the driver.

Murdoch paused, looking puzzled. These initials meant nothing to him. For a moment, he seemed to have no memory of the man whom he had considered it necessary, at some earlier moment, to fire. "Who is that?" Murdoch asked.

Pushing himself forward from the back seat of the SUV past a faulty middle seat that was stuck and folded in half, Ginsberg started a whispered consultation with Murdoch, who was on the phone again after Ginsberg's last syllable.

It was 11:29 and Murdoch's attention had suddenly shifted. "Sam? Congratulations," he said in a suddenly cheery tone. Sam Zell, real estate magnate and fellow billionaire, had purchased the Tribune Company, publisher of the *Los Angeles Times* and the *Chicago Tribune* and the owner of television stations and smaller papers. The tortured auction of Tribune was further confirmation of the newspaper industry's slide. Using very little of his own money, Zell financed the acquisition with debt that he was now struggling to pay off. To recoup a few hundred million, he had decided to sell the Long Island newspaper *Newsday*, a paper neither Murdoch nor Zell cared much about. Murdoch's interest in *Newsday* was only as a property that might prop up one of its competitors, his beloved *New York Post*. Combining the printing and distribution of the two papers would save him the $50 million a year he lost at the *Post*. It was a beautiful deal for him and his friend Jimmy Lee at JPMorgan, who had been integral to both the buyout financing of Zell's Tribune acquisition and a primary Murdoch adviser on the Dow Jones transaction. In the *Newsday* purchase, Lee had paired two of his best clients. (Murdoch never won the prize. *Newsday* went to the Dolan family, who controlled the cable company Cablevision. The Tribune purchase turned into a disaster for Zell. The company filed for bankruptcy in December 2008.)

At eleven thirty the car was halfway to the hotel and Murdoch picked up his phone again. It was Les Hinton. Hinton remembered fetching Murdoch sandwiches back in Adelaide when the two were working at Murdoch's first paper, the *Adelaide News*. Now there was this day's work to organize around a slight unpleasantness.

Murdoch's pledge not to interfere with the "editorial independence" of the *Journal* was being tested. Though many within News Corp. had found it mildly insulting to have to sign an agreement that implicitly said Murdoch was unfit to run a respectable paper, Murdoch was willing to weather such slights. They were minor, temporal; they always faded. Murdoch thought the separation between a newsroom and its owner was another false conceit of American newspapers, particularly those of the East Coast establishment variety. But if they helped him get what he wanted, he was willing to sign on to an artificial set of rules he would inevitably circumvent.

In this case, Murdoch had agreed to a five-person "Special Committee" designed to protect the *Journal* from editorial interference by the owner. The five members would each be paid $100,000 to go to four meetings a year. They would be on call for the managing editor and editorial page editor of the *Journal* in case either felt Murdoch was stepping across the line and inappropriately influencing the paper's coverage. The paper had previously been left to flourish without prying from the family. On any given day, the Bancrofts didn't know what was set to appear in the following day's *Journal,* nor did Dow Jones's business executives. The journalists were isolated and allowed to carry out their work uninterrupted, mostly happy to ignore the quickly eroding business prospects of Dow Jones.

"My own feeling is that I'll tell the Special Committee," Murdoch said. Meanwhile, Ginsberg, in the back of the car, was working his own angle, on the phone with Robert Thomson: "It's going to break tomorrow. It's really going to be bad if it breaks somewhere else," other than the *Journal.* Murdoch and Ginsberg were chatting, not to each other, but each working toward the same goal.

They rode for a few minutes in silence, until Ginsberg's cell buzzed with a text message from *Journal* editor Nik Deogun telling him the paper had caught wind of the situation and was soon going to put a story out on the wire. Grimacing at this inconvenience, Ginsberg called Thomson to discuss it. "Tell him to hold it and we'll give it to him exclusively," Ginsberg said, referring to Martin Peers, the *Journal* editor overseeing the story. "Tell them to hold it until we have a signed deal."

The black Suburban pulled into the driveway of the Ritz-Carlton and Murdoch stepped out of the car. He walked into the lobby and leaned against the front desk. "Rupert Murdoch; I'm checking in," he said. The pretty woman behind the desk smiled knowingly at this celebrity, quickly producing his swipe card for the elevator. The bellboy was starstruck. "Thank you very much, Mr. Murdoch, and it's a pleasure to meet you," he said eagerly.

Murdoch walked into his eleventh-floor Ritz-Carlton suite, booked for the night though he would stay for only a few hours that afternoon, and threw his coat down. Ginsberg and Bill McGurn followed, setting their bags down in the foyer. "It's huge," Murdoch commented as he lumbered toward the bedroom as if he were unaccustomed to such luxury.

Immediately, Ginsberg was on his cell phone again, dialing Robert Thomson, attempting damage control. The paper that Murdoch owned seemed intent on showing the world that it still had some spine. It wouldn't be scooped on its own news *again.* Standing by the window in the suite's marble foyer, Ginsberg put his cell phone on speaker as Murdoch approached. "Tell him to hold it and we'll give it to him exclusively," Ginsberg said to Thomson.

"Tell them to hold it until we have a signed deal," said Murdoch, wearily. This would be an annoyance for him, for this news to break before he had alerted the appropriate people. The contract that they had been haggling over with Brauchli's lawyer, Bob Barnett, for two weeks would be signed in a matter of hours, and then Murdoch wanted to personally call the members of the Special Committee to preempt any potential revolt in their ranks. "Can't we just say that this thing's been written and he's *going* to sign it?" Murdoch yelled, clearly accustomed to revising reality so the facts served his needs. But he had bent this one as far as he could. They had to wait for Brauchli to arrive in Washington and sign the contract.

"Marcus doesn't get off the train for another damn two hours?" Murdoch asked, incredulous. Ginsberg shook his head.

"I'm going to call him right now and say I'll call you at five and we can go over the story then," Ginsberg said. Murdoch, frustrated by these strictures, this tight timetable, was irritated the story couldn't be contained.

"They don't answer to News Corp.," Thomson's voice, tinny from the cell phone reception, told Ginsberg. "We can't tell them not to run a story."

Thomson, aware that his boss was losing patience, stressed to Ginsberg that Murdoch had to make the calls to the Special Committee before anything was announced. "He absolutely must call the Special Committee."

"And what do I do about the *Journal*?" asked Ginsberg.

"Just say, 'Give me a window and I'll give you the story.'"

"What publisher doesn't make the decision what to publish?" Murdoch said over the sound of the cell phone conversation. He stalked through the living room and past the marble fireplace to the bedroom.

Ginsberg called Martin Peers and promised he would give him the story later, when he could. "I'll make sure you don't get scooped," he said.

Murdoch returned to the living room and paced in a small circle, looking over the comments he would make at lunch. He held a single page of lined notebook paper in his hand, covered with his handwritten scrawl.

After lunch, Murdoch returned to the Ritz-Carlton suite, loosened his tie, and dropped onto the plush chair by the phone in the corner.

Brauchli had not yet arrived in Washington. It was two fifteen, and Ginsberg dialed Thomson. "[Brauchli] could have been down there six hours ago," Thomson said, his voice frustrated and weary. Just that morning, instead of leaving early for DC, Brauchli had stayed in New York to keep up appearances. "We attended a meeting for WSJ .com and attempted a witty repartee to give the appearance of nothing happening," Thomson continued.

No one commented. Brauchli was out, essentially fired. Not in so many words, of course. No top executives were fired in modern corporations. Murdoch had another way of saying thanks for the memories. "OK," Murdoch said, pausing again. "But I don't see the purpose it serves" to go to the meetings, to pretend all was well.

Thomson sighed. "I don't either. Unless it is being seen as a trouper to the end, for whatever psychological purpose that would serve." Thomson continued, intent on the reason for the call, the instructions for Murdoch to complete the task. "What's implicit is an air of finality. That the discussion is over and as a courtesy, we are informing you. What Marcus has slightly in his head is that it isn't final until the Special Committee meets. They are under the impression that someone from News Corp., Mark [Jackson, Dow Jones's general counsel], is making the calls. What they don't know is Rupert is making the calls." If Murdoch made the calls, it would carry more weight. It would be harder for them to object. It would give Murdoch the outcome he wanted.

In the meantime, Rupert made other calls to Long Island congressmen, to smooth his way through acquiring Tribune Company's *Newsday*. Like a Great White, he had to keep moving to survive. After those calls, he dialed Jimmy Lee. "Did you have the conversation with the *Journal* about our subject of common interest?" Murdoch asked, wondering if word of his interest in *Newsday* had been leaked to his media outlet. "No, not yet," said Lee. "But it's OK. It's all been sent over and I talked to Sam [Zell]." He spoke quickly, bringing a smile to Murdoch's face, like a father indulging his precocious child.

At 4:27, the phone in the hotel suite rang again. The contract with Brauchli had been signed. Murdoch went immediately over to the phone on the desk at the window. He dialed the numbers of the members of the Special Committee. "I can't get anyone," he drawled softly after a round of unsuccessful calls.

Ginsberg, across the room on the couch, offered the cell numbers of the Special Committee members. Most worked, connecting Murdoch to a group of people he reassured with rare unctuousness, working off a script prepared for him by his general counsel Lon Jacobs.

He first tried Lou Boccardi, a respected journalist and a former CEO of the Associated Press. "Lou, this is Rupert Murdoch," he said. "Fairly urgent I speak to you. I'm temporarily reachable at 202-835-0500, room 1112. If you don't reach me, I'll try you back. It's fairly urgent I speak to you."

"Is Dean Phillips [Susan Phillips, dean of the George Washington University business school] there? Hi. Sorry to bother you. I'm calling the members of the committee as a courtesy to let you know the managing editor, Marcus Brauchli, has resigned." Pause. "He's been very careful to say we've behaved scrupulously but he feels it's time to move on." The plan would be to have a call at midday the next day.

"It's all very civil and friendly. I just thought I would tell you instead of you reading it. OK." Murdoch laughed. "I just thought we'd have a chat tomorrow and have him on the line."

Phillips thanked him for calling. "Not at all," he replied. "He's a very nice fellow. It's all been done in a very civilized way. Thanks so much. Not at all. Bye."

One down, four to go.

Murdoch repeated the same script with Jack Fuller, a *Chicago Tribune* Pulitzer Prize winner who went on to become the president of all of Tribune's newspaper operations. The call was quick and painless.

"Well, I got two," Murdoch said after hanging up.

Next, Murdoch updated Thomson on the calls to Phillips and Fuller. "We're going to send messages to their BlackBerrys to call here," Murdoch said.

Retrieving more cell numbers, Ginsberg called them out.

Murdoch placed a call to Tom Bray, the chairman of the committee and a former *Detroit News* editorial page editor who had written for the *Journal*'s own editorial page. "Tom, sorry to bother you. This is to tell you the sad news [at this, Ginsberg chuckled] that Marcus Brauchli has resigned. It's all very civilized and friendly . . . No, we don't have a replacement. But the idea is for Robert Thomson to go through the staff for someone for you to nominate.

"Let's talk tomorrow . . . the idea would be to have a midday conference . . . We're all very much of one mind," Murdoch said. And then he remembered Thomson's instructions—*an air of finality.* "Except that it is done . . . Sorry to worry you with it."

Two to go.

"Lou? Rupert Murdoch here. Sorry to bother you. Just a call to tell you that Marcus Brauchli has resigned, all in a very friendly way. The idea is to get Robert Thomson to supervise until we can find another candidate to present . . . It's all very friendly and he said we've behaved scrupulously . . . He'll stay as a consultant for six months . . . in setting up an Asian business channel."

But this call was longer than the rest. Lou Boccardi was Brauchli's pick for the Special Committee. "What did Marcus say?" Boccardi asked. Murdoch replied: "He's going to say he'd be more comfortable, everybody'd be more comfortable that the new regime have a new editor . . . I have no doubt that the *New York Times* will make trouble with it for a day or two, but I'm not too bothered by it."

Click.

Finally, the task was completed, though the last member, Nicholas Negroponte, hadn't been called yet. Negroponte had been Murdoch's choice for the committee and was not a Brauchli loyalist. The *Journal* had scrutinized Negroponte's charity, One Laptop per Child, in a front-page story by investigative reporter Steve Stecklow not long before for struggling to distribute its promised laptops to the world's neediest children. Negroponte had privately expressed concern to Brauchli about the story. Brauchli glibly responded, "Oh, that's the first of a five-part series."

"On me?" Negroponte asked, incredulous.

"No, on each member of the committee," Brauchli deadpanned.

Murdoch did not expect Negroponte to object to the Brauchli resignation.

After all the calls, Murdoch announced, visibly relieved, "There's always a bit of nervous tension around things like that."

A moment later he picked up the phone to report back to Thomson. "I've spoken to everybody," he said. "We got them on their cell phones." Les Hinton was in the background, hovering to make sure Rupert's work was done. "Hi, Les. Everything's fine."

What was the reaction? Hinton asked. "Surprise, shock, horror," Murdoch quipped. "No, no horror. And we're all OK for a midday call tomorrow . . . I've said Marcus would be on the phone and all of us, too." But what had he told them? "I said it's been very friendly. Scrupulous. And I made a statement praising him."

Next came an uneventful call to Paul Gigot, the powerful and established editorial page editor of the *Journal,* who had not been deeply involved in the independence agreement. Like his colleagues on "the page," he believed in the rights of the owner. He wasn't immediately thrilled about the Murdoch takeover, but he wouldn't brook any protest or hand-wringing over it from his staff. If an employee didn't appreciate being owned by Rupert Murdoch, that employee was free to quit. Free markets, free people, as the slogan of the newspaper's editorial page had it. Gigot was serious, well known, and widely respected. Still, Murdoch couldn't pronounce his name correctly. Instead of "Jhee-go," Murdoch reversed the soft and hard g's, pronouncing Gigot's last name as "Gee-jo."

After the call to Gigot, Murdoch finally called Negroponte. He hung up, that task completed. "They may as well earn their fifty grand," he said, referring to the $100,000 a year that the members of the committee were paid.

The press conference for the evening's Atlantic Council honorees was starting downstairs, and Murdoch was running late. "But what's it going to be? Blair going on about the world?" Murdoch laughed, relaxed and allowing himself to be candid, without false praise or modesty. Tony Blair and Murdoch were both getting awards that night. Blair would receive the Distinguished International Leader Award and Murdoch the Distinguished Business Award.

"Ah, they can wait," Murdoch said. Murdoch retied his tie, straightened his flyaway comb-over, which had begun to stand straight up, and made his way downstairs to greet Blair in the Ritz-Carlton's "green room" before the press conference. Unexpected but old allies, they shook hands warmly, patting each other's shoulders. Fred

Kempe, head of the Atlantic Council and a former *Journal* editor, moved between them excitedly, trying to make them feel comfortable and welcome. He went over the format, prepping the two men and saying he hoped to discuss their respective speeches. "Rupert, you have some pretty strong words for Europe. I mean, 'Europe no longer has either the political will or social culture to support military engagements.' That's strong. I expect we'll get a lot of questions about that." But Murdoch's mind was elsewhere.

"I might get a local question because Obama said something about me today," he offered, almost proudly.

"What did he say?" asked Blair.

Obama, campaigning among a few dozen voters that day in Blue Bell, Pennsylvania, had answered a question about media consolidation and freedom of the press by saying that voters have a right to be concerned when "Rupert Murdoch has his eyes on a lot of different media outlets."

"Oh, it was just about media consolidation, et cetera, et cetera." Murdoch shrugged dismissively. And then for his punch line: "I thought about asking him if he knew about the existence of the Internet."

Blair guffawed, his shoulders thrown back, reveling in the audacity of his old supporter. "So that's your idea of letting him down gently, eh? Really whack him!" Blair had been the object of Murdoch's attention before; he knew the power the man could wield. While Blair was still chuckling, the three men walked out of the room to greet the press.

Just as he had been doing the morning of his forced resignation two weeks previously, Marcus Brauchli listened that morning of the Atlantic Council dinner as the top editors at the paper discussed the day's stories. He realized he would never be there again. This part of his life was ending. After he left the paper, he would not be able to even read the *Journal* for weeks; it was too painful. As time passed, he saw how much his identity had been intertwined with the paper's. He had built his life around his assignments, and a reasonable chunk of his wardrobe was emblazoned with Dow Jones logos. He had called his father in Denver, a lawyer and columnist for the left-wing magazine *CounterPunch*, for advice as he negotiated his departure. He had no choice but to leave—the question was how he would make his exit. If neither side spoke out against the other and Marcus resigned quietly, he would walk away with upward of $6.4 million. Brauchli was due $3 million regardless of how he left Dow Jones— that sum was his regular severance as an executive of the company, plus the stock options that he had accumulated and negotiated for when he took the managing editor job. The additional $3.4 million came from his lawyer's negotiations with News Corp. The amount was a pittance for Murdoch, but enough to make Brauchli abdicate his position. He accepted Murdoch's offer to stay on as a "consultant" to the company for six months. He knew he would be attacked by fellow journalists for taking money rather than fighting Murdoch. Brauchli reasoned that to stay and fight would damage the *Journal*'s brand. He honestly hadn't felt that Murdoch meddled in coverage. If he went to the Special Committee, what would he say? That he wanted to keep his job? He didn't feel he had a concrete complaint. No one had told him to run or not run a story. Besides, he hadn't seen an editor who had successfully gone to war with his paper's owner and won.

On his last day, Brauchli kept up appearances, as Thomson and Murdoch had perceived. Brauchli was determined to depart with dignity. He would hold his head up but he wouldn't fight, despite his critics' urging. Although most companies whisked departing executives out quickly, Brauchli played his part up to the moment of his departure, even keeping a meeting with editors Alan Murray and Almar Latour to talk about the redesign of WSJ.com, the *Journal*'s Web site. That morning, he and Thomson exchanged quips and the usual banter, all the while knowing that Brauchli had just a few more hours at the top. Brauchli interviewed a job candidate and headed to the airport to catch a shuttle to Washington, DC.

He arrived at the Ritz, checked in, and carried his bags up to his room. He changed into his tuxedo and walked downstairs for the reception, feeling awkward to be dressed up so early. No one else was in black-tie attire at that early hour, aside from Fred Kempe's wife, who was, in effect, the hostess of the evening. He milled around awkwardly for a moment, and then almost immediately a huge crowd swelled out of the doors where Murdoch's press conference had just concluded. Rupert eyed Brauchli and walked over. "Oh, are you planning to stay over?" Murdoch asked. Yes, Brauchli replied. "Well, you should come home with us on the plane tonight instead." As the exchange concluded, a photographer snapped a picture of them together, grinning into the camera, the victor and the vanquished. Of course it had been no match at all.

Murdoch headed through the growing crowd to make his way up to the penthouse to change into his tux. He wore a modern black tie, not a bow tie, a change for a traditionalist like Murdoch, one of many since marrying Wendi. When he returned to the VIP cocktail hour downstairs, he was, as usual, stopped at almost every turn. Murdoch did not seek out people at a cocktail party. He didn't have to. Everyone came to him. Even in a crowd such as this—Colin Powell, Henry Kissinger, Sir Howard Stringer, José María Aznar—Murdoch stood out.

In previous years, the Atlantic Council's fete had drawn a few hundred attendees, but Murdoch's presence boosted the guest list. The settings had been carefully done, with white orchid centerpieces arranged atop shimmering deep blue tablecloths. Murdoch sat between Kissinger, who would present him with his award after dinner, and Jimmy Lee, his banker friend. When Murdoch asked Jimmy if JPMorgan could be a host sponsor to the event, Jimmy agreed under the condition that Murdoch underwrite Jimmy's awards ceremony later that year, at the New York Public Library.

The guests started their meal with roasted lady apple, stuffed with blue cheese mousse, on a bed of mache lettuce, pickled red onions, dried cherries, and Brie wrapped in phyllo pastry. Murdoch picked at his meal with the Ritz-Carlton–branded silver, while Jimmy Lee, in a low voice, gave him the rundown on the deal they had agreed to with Sam Zell. There was always another deal. The two were also strategizing about a possible Yahoo! tie-up. The Vidalia-onion-crusted filet arrived next, suitably rustic with pattypan squash and baby turnips. The guests' chatter grew louder as they downed their glasses of 2006 Simi Chardonnay and Steele Pinot Noir.

When Kissinger introduced Murdoch, Brauchli's BlackBerry buzzed with a call from Bill Grueskin, his deputy. He ignored it. A moment later, just as Murdoch stood to take the stage, Grueskin sent Brauchli an e-mail, and he looked at his small screen. It was a story from Time.com: "*Wall Street Journal* M.E. to Resign."

Wall Street Journal M.E. That was him. The real action of the evening was happening on the small screen in front of him and not on the stage where his boss was speaking. Nine hundred other people were listening to Murdoch thank Kissinger for his kind introduction. "Your words remind me of the definition of a diplomat: a man who always remembers his wife's birthday—but never remembers her age . . ." For Brauchli, the joke and the polite laughter were taking place in another world, one he seemed to be departing with such mixed feelings. Murdoch, not yet aware of the headline, seemed unconcerned with the havoc he was wreaking in Brauchli's career. He later explained to Brauchli that it had to happen this way, but it was a problem of physics. "Two people can't occupy the same job at the same time."

Murdoch didn't seem to notice the furious BlackBerry activity between the two tables of *Journal* editors at the dinner. They were hungrily anxious for news of their own future. Murdoch continued: "Today, we can be tempted to bask in our achievements—and wax nostalgic about all we have been through. But this is no time for nostalgia . . ."

Seated next to Brauchli was John Bussey, the intense and hard-charging Washington bureau chief of the *Journal*. As foreign editor, he had been Brauchli's boss for years when Brauchli was chief of the China bureau. He had made Brauchli's life miserable. It was with not a small amount of pleasure that Brauchli leapfrogged Bussey to become the managing editor of the *Journal*. His first instinct was to return the pain Bussey had inflicted on him. In his first (and only) major reorganization of the editing ranks, Brauchli offered Bussey a pay cut. But shortly after, he reversed himself and offered Bussey the high-profile Washington bureau chief job. Brauchli wanted to place a strong *Journal* person in the position, to establish "the facts on the ground," knowing that the DC bureau was about to be an object of obsession for Murdoch.

Ironic, then, that it was Bussey who turned his BlackBerry screen to Brauchli with raised eyebrows and questioning shoulders. "Is this true?"

"*Wall Street Journal* M.E. to Resign."

Brauchli responded only with a sheepish, evasive smile. He couldn't say anything. So he sat among his colleagues, some of whom ran in and out of the ballroom to call back to the newsroom for details of his departure, while Murdoch lectured. Bussey, a company man above all else, set aside the past differences and e-mailed the top editors in New York to tell them to stop e-mailing Brauchli, who had turned off his cell phone. The moment the last speaker left the stage, Brauchli darted out of the ballroom, eager, now that the word was out, to get away.

That night, after the dinner, Brauchli took Murdoch up on his offer for a ride home. Brauchli boarded the private plane, which carried Murdoch, Ginsberg, speechwriter Bill McGurn, and longtime Murdoch investment banker Stan Shuman, who had navigated Murdoch's path in the United States, helping him buy the *New York Post* and other properties. Murdoch, propped up on cashmere pillows, bow tie loosened, watched Bill O'Reilly from the mammoth flat-screen TV that overlooked the conference table where all his guests sat. Murdoch dipped in and out of the conversation. No one spoke a word about Brauchli's resignation. The small talk revolved around China, Passover (Ginsberg had been observing the Jewish holiday and was avoiding leavened bread), and the progress of the short flight back to New York. When Murdoch occasionally lost interest, he turned toward the television and turned the volume up so he could hear a bit better. As O'Reilly bellowed from the screen, Murdoch's guests looked at one another, sometimes smirking at the bellicose television host. Murdoch, seemingly unaware, turned away from the show to comment on it: "Has a good rhythm, doesn't it?" he said, to polite nods. Peggy, the flight attendant, distributed bottles of water and brought out small plates of almonds for the guests. Murdoch had offered everyone a drink, but there were no takers.

21

Thomson's Journal

FTER BRAUCHLI LEFT the paper, Thomson initially tried to tread lightly on the news floor of the *Journal* and keep up the appearance that he was searching far and wide for a replacement managing editor. Resentment in the newsroom toward Brauchli—who had left his post quietly with a chunk of money in his pocket—was palpable. In his first move as the "acting" managing editor of the paper, Thomson held a series of meetings with reporters and bureau chiefs to make himself the friendly face at the head of the newsroom, the calming influence who would offer clear communication from on high. It was a direct response to criticisms that Brauchli didn't communicate anything, even as the paper's expectations—of its writers, its editors, and its own readers—were transformed.

In that spirit, Thomson gathered in the last week in April with the reporters from the paper's "Money & Investing" section, the squarest, most buttoned-up of all the paper's cliques, the group that became passionate about arcane *Journal* articles the reporters across the newsroom floor in the "Weekend" section used as stuffing in their Prada boots after a rainstorm. They were the core of the paper. At any other paper in the country they would have been relegated to a business-section ghetto. At the *Journal,* they were the hard-nosed experts. They were also an exceedingly nervous bunch.

Perhaps for these reasons Thomson started with them. The reporters gathered in a conference room. The meeting started off with a bitter irony. Thomson discouraged the attendees from taking notes or making recordings. He was excruciatingly aware of the press the *Journal* received and didn't welcome unauthorized leaks. Nik Deogun, the group's chief, who had proved himself able in guiding Thomson through the *Journal*'s minefields, introduced Thomson. He hadn't prepped Thomson entirely in *Journal* sensitivities, however. Thomson started off with a series of slights that would leave an imprint.

"I think a journalistic culture based solely on one story or two stories in the paper today is skewed in the wrong direction," he began. "Journalism is a lot more complicated and a lot more diverse than that. And I think people have to be doing several things, several types of stories at the same time. And that's a challenge, but that's a challenge every journalist around the world at every news organization is facing." He was referring to the paper's "leders," the Page One feature stories *Journal* reporters spent weeks if not months reporting and writing before handing them off to the paper's legendary Page One staff. That group of editors existed in an unapproachable ivory tower in the corner of the newsroom, quiet and removed. Leders were the main measure by which reporters were judged. Failing to successfully produce them—and in relatively large quantities—could kill a career. Hitting one memorable one could have the opposite effect in that it would allow the lucky (and talented) reporter to coast, as some occasionally did, for months after the publication of a noteworthy effort. The vast majority of the staff fell somewhere in between the career-ending and career-making Page One existence. They also broke news on a regular basis, producing in-depth feature stories in their downtime while they were waiting to have their calls returned. Juggling both types of stories was not a new notion for the paper's reporters. That Thomson thought so was a sign of how little he had become acquainted with the newsroom over the past four months since the acquisition had officially closed and he had become the paper's publisher.

His impression of the *Journal* had been forged during his years as the editor of the U.S. edition of the *Financial Times*, when he had a crack mergers-and-acquisitions reporter who beat the *Journal* on a series of stories. But the scoops may well have not happened at all, so little attention did the *Journal* pay them—or at least that was Thomson's impression. When the *Journal* did follow the stories, it failed to credit the *Financial Times*. Such arrogance enraged him.

Even so, he had made quite an effort to be noticed back then, booking his writers for television appearances and enjoying the additional attention the *FT* was getting through its marketing push. A series of Dan Aykroyd television spots for the *FT* sought to soften the paper's stodgy image in the United States. Thomson had a flair for self-promotion and a competitive spirit, two aspects of his personality that must have attracted Murdoch early on. Now he was here at the *Journal*, where he was once utterly ignored, at the helm of a newsroom that would no longer brush him aside.

His audience got immediately restless. "I don't understand," piped up one reporter seated around the conference table in the meeting. "I mean, Marcus left for a reason. He wasn't doing what you wanted him to do. But I still don't have a clue what you're going to do now that he wasn't already doing."

Thomson quickly brushed aside the question of Brauchli—"History will reveal what happened last week with Marcus, but he behaved extremely professionally"—and got to talking about the changes he wanted to make. "A year ago we were looking at something called 3.0 and that was about how headlines would start with the word *how*. We've reversed that now. That is a very fundamental change." He kept returning to the theme: "You will learn that there will be strategic change. And it will be change where you all are participating in the debate, the news desk, or the bureau chiefs." He went on, "I can't be specific, but it will be change of quite a different sort from what people are used to."

The meeting continued, and reporters asked him whether *Journal* reporters would become wire service reporters (the answer was a resounding no) and how the front page was going to change. Then came a question that was close to Thomson's heart. "One of the things we worry about a little bit in the newsroom is that we're being sent forward into a U.S. version of the *Financial Times*," said an unsuspecting reporter. "I was wondering how you see us vis-à-vis the *FT* and how you see the *FT*."

The question gave Thomson a chance to expound on his—and Murdoch's—belief that British papers were more competitive than American ones and therefore better. The *Journal,* by developing an acute sense of itself, didn't concern itself with bridge collapses in Minneapolis; that was what the other papers were for. Murdoch wouldn't tolerate that. "In 1998 and 1999, the odd thing was the people at the *Journal* didn't feel enough pain," Thomson said. "They thought, 'We're the *Wall Street Journal.'*" The choice of dates would have been meaningless to the assembled crowd unless they remembered that those were the years Thomson was running the *Financial Times* in New York.

Thomson continued, expounding on why the *Journal* should be more ambitious in its coverage: "Why should the *New York Times* own international coverage?" he asked. He then outlined for the reporters how to be more receptive to pain: "Journalists should be nervy. Journalists should be edgy. If journalists aren't nervy or edgy they're in the wrong profession. You need to wake up every morning wondering if someone's stealing your story. That's part of the culture that's inherent in the profession, or the craft, depending on how you define it," he said. He told them the paper was poorly organized before he arrived: "One of the problems previously was that you weren't quite sure where to find stories in the *Journal.* It's more manageable now at the paper. You know where to find things."

Deogun, who had been at the meeting but largely silent, weighed in from time to time. He provided backup evidence for Thomson's assertion that stories in the *Journal* were too long. Dow Jones had conducted research recently that showed that only 40 percent of the readers of the "Money & Investing" section turned past the front page of the section to read beyond the jump. "So," he said, "that's pretty sobering."

The meeting continued, with the resentment growing on both sides. Finally, Jim Browning, a union activist and a veteran *Journal* reporter, spoke up. "I apologize, and I hope I don't sound disrespectful, but I was dumbfounded a few minutes ago to hear you saying that you felt that people at the *Journal* didn't feel they competed with anybody, and that people felt that stories that hadn't appeared in the *Journal* hadn't been written about. I have to tell you that maybe I'm lying, but I think if you talk to Nik or Mike or to Ken [the group's leadership] or any other people who have helped edit the news we put in the paper, if you ask them, they would take issue with that. I would take strenuous issue with that. In all the years that I've been here the credo of the paper has been that if we aren't first with all of our news, then something is very, very wrong. And if somebody is scooped on a significant story here, I can assure you that for many, many years since 1979 when I joined the paper, and I think for many years before that, we all felt—" He paused, clearly exercised. "I mean, I just wonder where in the world did you get that notion? Anything we can do to sit down with you and discuss that thought, we'll do, because my worry is that if people are making decisions on the theory that there was a lack of competitive vigor at the paper, and that the people running the paper and the people reporting the news didn't feel competitive every day, well, what worries me is that may be a misconception. Did I misunderstand you or . . . ?"

Thomson jumped in. He had to stop this rant or it would overtake the entire discussion. "Well, I wasn't talking about the vast majority of the paper. Look, I had noticed this when I was competing with the *Journal* when I was in midtown. I certainly did not mean to cause offense." Thomson was talking quickly now. "That is exactly the right attitude that the *Journal* should have, and I know a great many people do, but there were people here that didn't share your passion or share your concern," he concluded in an attempt to defuse the tension. "And it certainly wasn't meant to be a characterization of any individual or any department, but more a general warning about the need for competition, frankly, in an age of ultra-competition." The meeting couldn't end quickly enough at this point. "Thank you all very much," he said. "I think you've put out a great paper."

If Thomson tracked the coverage of the *Journal,* he was none too pleased by the report on the gossip site Gawker the day after his meeting with the "Money & Investing" section. "Civil War at the *Wall Street Journal*" the headline read, outlining the most explosive parts of the meeting and delivering a who's who of the inside players in a newsroom that was wholly unaccustomed to such attention.

Nik Deogun, according to Gawker, was a "potential quisling," and Paul Steiger "was beloved but is now being talked about like a greedy bastard." Steiger's wife, Wendy, was pictured with a screen grab from her "bosom-revealing blog." The gossip may have been shrugged off in a newsroom more inured to such darts, but the *Journal* had always labored outside a certain media glare. How exciting could gossip about stock market reporters be? Now, with a dash of Murdoch, even a small editorial meeting was noteworthy. The mean-spirited glee took *Journal* folk by surprise.

After one such article in this period that suggested Thomson was not just the acting managing editor but the permanent head of the newsroom (an observation obvious to any but the most wishful of old-school thinkers), Thomson e-mailed deputy managing editor Bill Grueskin late on a Sunday night and asked him to call. As the man in charge of the news coverage at the paper, Grueskin was the closest thing it had to a nominal leader. Thomson wanted to assure Grueskin that he wouldn't interfere with the running of the paper while he was only acting managing editor. "Believe me, if I were managing editor, you'd know it. I'd be in there every day," he said, a message meant to be reassuring but one that had, in the end, the opposite effect.

A week after news of Brauchli's departure broke, Thomson's figure appeared in Grueskin's doorway, holding a mock-up version of the next day's paper with a hand-drawn bar graph Thomson had sketched just moments before. The graph displayed the day's news of newspaper circulation for the past six months among the country's largest papers, a data set that had been released earlier that morning by an industry group. The data indicated that among the top ten newspapers in America, only the *Wall Street Journal* and *USA Today* showed modest increases in circulation, while the rest of the papers' circulation numbers continued to slide. Newspaper circulation figures were dutifully reported in the *Journal* every six months. The story was the same almost every time, ran between five hundred and a thousand words, appeared on the inside page of the paper, and was greeted with little more than a shrug of resignation from the editors and staffers who paid attention to it at all.

This Monday afternoon, Thomson was energetic. The bar graph he had drawn, which on its x axis tracked the rate of growth of circulation and on the y axis listed the nation's largest papers including the *New York Times*, the *Los Angeles Times*, the *New York Daily News*, and Murdoch's own *New York Post*, showed the results, which framed the meager growth of the *Journal* in a positive light only through comparison with its peers. "Even the *New York Times* was down," Thomson enthused to Grueskin, taking obvious glee in the pain of the *Journal*'s main competitor. Thomson suggested the graphic could run on the front page of the paper.

Grueskin, a thirteen-year *Journal* veteran, was a no-nonsense, glib newspaperman with a dry wit. He knew there were a lot of close ethical calls a newspaper editor would be forced to make on any given day when determining how to cover a given news event, but this one—the question of whether to trumpet the *Journal*'s own good news on the front page of the paper in contrast to a competitor's misfortune— wasn't even close. This was a *New York Post*–like tactic of self-promotion, he thought, one that belonged in the realm of the marketing department, not the paper's newsroom. He told Thomson his opinion (omitting the dig at the *Post*) and directed him to the appropriate person in the marketing department who might handle such a matter. After a brief quizzical look, Thomson retreated from the office. The exchange was perfectly pleasant, but Grueskin kept Thomson's scribbled chart, in case the difference of opinion became more complicated. Two days later, Thomson returned with a copy of the day's paper with a full-page color ad touting the *Journal*'s rise. Grueskin would resign from his job a month later.

The *Journal*'s modest circulation increase had been cemented before the deal had even closed. During the destabilizing interregnum in the moments of what Brauchli had called "preemptive capitulation" (a term he did not apply to himself but that others did), Dow Jones's marketing department had arranged an additional $17 million in spending to boost the paper's circulation in the period following the close of the deal, a tidy sum that would guarantee the perceived success of the upcoming changes to the "new" *Wall Street Journal*. By the time Leslie Hinton, Murdoch's hand-selected CEO of Dow Jones, took the helm of the company, the campaign had been scaled back, but a portion of the money had already been spent on hefty direct-mail campaigns and granting subscriptions to frequent fliers. Of course, Murdoch's tactics weren't unique to him, and there wasn't a paper in the country that hadn't bulked up its circulation. But a successful businessman knew the importance of the impression of success, and Murdoch wouldn't risk losing a game of perception in this newspaper battle.

22

One of Us

I N ABOUT A MONTH, Thomson arrived at the conclusion that he was, indeed, the best man to take over the *Journal* newsroom. He moved into Brauchli's office (finally attaining a prominent ninth-floor spot) days after the short-lived managing editor vacated it. Even though it was obvious to anyone who knew Murdoch that Thomson would be the paper's next managing editor, speculation about other candidates had persisted inside the *Journal* newsroom in the weeks preceding the announcement. The speculation illustrated a newsroom's capacity for self-deception in the face of the uncomfortable reality that this Murdoch takeover was proceeding exactly like every other. Murdoch was not going to make an exception for the *Wall Street Journal*.

Journalists are, typically, a self-loathing bunch. Driven as they are to see the flaws in other people and institutions, their eyes often train on themselves, uncovering the weaknesses in their own and colleagues' stories and reporting styles. Self-recrimination ran rampant at the *Journal* in the weeks and months after Brauchli's resignation. The *Wall Street Journal*, despite being one of the most powerful papers in the world, retained the defensive status of a runner-up to the *New York Times*. Though it sold double the number of papers the *Times* did, and was the newspaper of choice in the heartland, it was less important in the corridors of New York and Washington. Murdoch obsessed about replacing the Grey Lady with his paper. Rallying his band of pirates had always been one of Murdoch's easiest tasks. News Corp. executives and editors often used the phrase "one of us," as if they were members of the mob. Thomson wasn't an old-school Murdoch hand like the *New York Post*'s Col Allan or Dow Jones's Leslie Hinton, but he was able and willing to wage guerrilla warfare against his rivals. While he took swipes at the *Times* at every opportunity, through his alliterative digs—he once labeled the uptown rival "sanctimony central" and on the same occasion said the paper was full of "preening, posturing, and pretentiousness"—the rallying didn't give the troops back at 200 Liberty a surge of solidarity with their new boss. For Thomson was still waging his own war inside the paper, against his own staff, to shake them out of what he would happily call the complacency of editors who stayed too long in their posts, preening for one another and writing only for prize packages. "I mean no disrespect to Paul Steiger," he would say, as he launched into one of his screeds, "but I think it's good for editors to not stay in their jobs too long."

Dow Jones plunged into a period of high anxiety. The staff waited for the influx of Aussies to start and for the old *Journal* heads to roll. Outside the walls of the *Journal*, Thomson's style of boosterish support for the paper began, and he lashed out at the *New York Times* repeatedly in a Fleet Street–style attack that cheered Murdoch and drew confused head shaking from those inside the *Journal*. Perhaps they had been trained to be too gentlemanly over the years with their midtown rival, but the *Journal* prided itself on its passive aggression toward competitors. Under Steiger, understatement ruled the day. Though the newsroom had stopped recruiting primarily from the Midwest for its leaders, the sensibility still reigned. Murdoch, of course, wanted nothing of understatement. His game was one of splash and headlines, not subtleties and nuance.

Murdoch appeared at the Dow Jones–sponsored "D: All Things Digital" conference in Carlsbad, California, at the end of May and sounded off, once again, that the average story at the paper was touched by a "ridiculous" 8.3 editors. None of the reporters at the paper could figure out where he got such a hyperbolic figure. Papers, Murdoch said, would survive by writing stories people wanted to read instead of stories to win Pulitzer Prizes. Editors began to adjust to this familiar refrain.

Oddly, a period of calm followed. The expectation of a violent bloodletting and daily rumors of imminent layoffs gave way to low-level anxiety and a general feeling of hopefulness that perhaps things wouldn't be so bad after all. Thomson put what he called a troika of editors in place to run the newsroom, with another veteran as his direct deputy who would run the paper when he wasn't around. The triumvirate comprised Nikhil Deogun, Deputy Managing Editor, International; Matt Murray, Deputy Managing Editor, National; and Mike Williams, Deputy Managing Editor, Page One. Mike Miller, the former *Journal* Page One editor, became Thomson's senior deputy.

The *Journal* editors and reporters realized they couldn't dig in their heels and resist the changes Thomson clearly wanted. No longer would stories last the gestation of a llama. They wouldn't be overwrought or slowly and painstakingly researched. They would be energetic and full of news. The formula sounded appealing until the editors and the staff slowly began to realize that the *Wall Street Journal*, the paper founded by Dow and Jones and built by Clarence Barron and revolutionized by Barney Kilgore, hadn't gotten to its vaunted status by being a lazy, diminished product that couldn't handle a major news story. There was something in the ecosystem that worked, albeit imperfectly, and the tearing and scraping away that Thomson had done over the past months had destabilized the soil.

As the reporters were growing accustomed to writing shorter stories and scrapping long-term leder projects for news stories, the biggest downturn since the Great Depression hit the *Wall Street Journal* newsroom when it was in the midst of its own crisis.

23

Urgent

O<small>N SEPTEMBER</small> 15, 2008, the *Wall Street Journal*'s main story on Page One began simply, "The American financial system was shaken to its core on Sunday." Over the weekend, some of the most vaunted names on Wall Street had crumbled. Lehman Brothers, denied a bailout by the federal government, was teetering on the brink of liquidation. Merrill Lynch, on the verge of collapse itself, had agreed to be bought by Bank of America. The largest insurance company in the world, AIG, was desperately trying to raise cash to avoid ruin. Ten major commercial and investment banks pooled $70 billion to create a lending facility for their ailing brethren.

The turmoil in the markets marked the first time since September 12, 2001, that the editors of the *Wall Street Journal* thought the events of the day warranted a headline that ran across the entire width of the front page. (Prior to that, the only other banner headline of the sort announced the attack on Pearl Harbor.) Across six columns of the paper in huge, bold font, the paper announced: CRISIS ON WALL STREET AS LEHMAN TOTTERS, MERRILL IS SOLD, AIG SEEKS TO RAISE CASH. Then, the unusual became quotidian: the rest of the week the *Journal* carried similar paper-spanning headlines.

The week also marked the first time that Rupert Murdoch sat in on the paper's morning news meetings. He said little and attended only a few, but his presence alone was remarkable. Never had a Bancroft requested or received an invitation to go to a news meeting. Peter Kann rarely saw the inside of a *Journal* news meeting. Yet, after all the concerns—and denials—that he would meddle in coverage, there Murdoch was. Murdoch found great entertainment in being at the table of the nation's top financial newspaper while the nation's financial system was collapsing. "Nobody could fail but to be excited by the whole thing unraveling," he later remembered.

The paper spent the next few months in a convulsion of newsgathering. The journalists broke plenty of news, but the paper, which had adopted a new editing "hub" under Thomson that September, was a mess. The "hub," designed to centralize the power of the news desk and break some of the tyranny of the bureau chiefs who oversaw groups of reporters, had a rocky beginning. Stories that were filed to the editors through the new system were often lost. The paper's notoriously early deadlines, which Murdoch had said repeatedly he hoped to move later so the *Journal* could be more competitive, moved earlier instead so the "hub" wouldn't miss "lockup," the hour when the paper needed to be sent to the printers to avoid costly delays and missed deliveries. "Most of us were able to get our college papers out more effectively," one reporter joked.

Word came down from Thomson that reporters needed to be more "productive." The top editors began paying more attention to byline counts for reporters, a measure of how many stories a reporter produced for the paper. Leders sat on the Page One desk for months, usurped by news of the market's fluctuation on a given day. Veteran reporters said that reporting daily on the dips and rallies of the stock exchange with banner headlines across Page One made the *Journal* seem naive. These hurried and perfunctory dispatches failed to explain for readers why the entire system was wobbling. Slowly, the supply of leders started to dry up. "Incentives have consequences," reporters said to each other, as they scurried to please their editors by penning brief news stories for the following day's paper.

Not everyone was despairing of the *Journal*'s new direction. On June 26, 2008, Ivanka Trump stopped by to talk to Robert Thomson and declared cheerily, "I just love what you've done with the front page!" Tina Brown praised Murdoch's influence: "I think he's put muscle into it, flair and focus," she said.

News Corp. editors engineered some of the chaos intentionally. Murdoch's newsrooms were often chaotic and boisterous, exactly the opposite of the *Journal* newsroom, which staffers often compared to an insurance company. That atmosphere confirmed to Thomson the plodding, overly planned nature of the *Journal*. With his reorganization, he wanted to rattle the reporters and editors, turning the paper into something more recognizable to both him and his boss.

The world was gripped by financial collapse, but the *Journal* often focused inward on its own tumult. The paper didn't step back to explain how the world got to where it was. To do so would have taken it away from the most urgent news of the day. The paper still managed fantastic reconstructions of key events, the midnight meetings in corporate boardrooms and the desperate brinkmanship of business titans and government appointees—the "tick-tocks" for which they were famous. The paper published remarkable stories on the downfall of Bear Stearns and the management lies at Lehman Brothers. But the readers of the *Journal* were left without a sweeping explanation of the systemic causes of the crisis. The paper didn't muster coverage to match the historic nature of the moment. Thomson, who had decried the culture of the *Journal*, now had to reap what he had sown: the newsroom was in a state of confusion with no strong editorial voice leading the coverage.

"Sending the staff to chase news like so many hamsters on a wheel is not the same as editing a great newspaper. Neither is festooning page one with the news everyone else already has," the *Columbia Journalism Review* lamented in December 2008, for a piece entitled "In the Crisis, the *Journal* Falls Short."

Though he knew from the moment Murdoch won the paper that he would play a significant role in the *Journal*'s future, Thomson hadn't actually planned to be the *Journal*'s editor. He had his eye on bigger targets. He thought he would climb within the ranks of News Corporation. He had, he told people, already been the editor of the *Times* of London. At the *Journal*, Thomson grew lonely for the camaraderie of his old colleagues. He remained distant and difficult to discern for the *Journal*'s editors. "It's almost a year in, and we're tired of being on probation," one said.

Thomson's impression of *Journal* editors and reporters as out of touch was cemented at the Democratic National Convention in Denver at the end of August. The *Journal*'s Washington bureau chief, John Bussey, had suggested he and Thomson have dinner one night. Instead of arranging a dinner surrounded by other journalists and potential sources, Bussey, always mindful of budget restraints, took Thomson to a pancake house in suburban Denver. The Australian dined on a stack of plain, undressed pancakes and retired to the hotel. Just when the evening seemed like a complete failure, his cell phone rang. "Hey, we're here with some of Obama's top aides and they want to meet you," the voice on the other end said. It was Gerard Baker, the British-born *Times* of London's U.S. editor. Thomson joined Baker for an evening of drinks and schmoozing, leaving Bussey alone. "*Journal* reporters should drink more," Thomson later joked.

Baker was known for his right-leaning columns in the *Times*. After Michelle Obama said that her husband's candidacy made her proud of her country for the first time, he wrote a column headed, "Obama: is America ready for this dangerous left winger?" In another column, he satirized the enthusiasm surrounding Obama's candidacy, likening him to a messiah, and read the piece aloud on Fox News's right-wing *Hannity & Colmes* show.

Thomson wooed Baker to the *Journal* shortly after the Democratic convention, demoting his existing deputy, Mike Miller, and the rest of the *Journal* editors a notch. Thomson told people that he brought Baker over because he didn't feel any of the *Journal* editors were senior enough for the deputy post. He told the *Journal* editors, when announcing Baker's hiring, that he missed Baker's wit.

Though leders had been dying a slow death, Thomson issued their obituary with a memo in March 2009 to the news staff outlining his plans for the *Journal* to cooperate more fully with Dow Jones Newswires. While the staff of the paper had always contributed to varying degrees to the newswire, Thomson had something more dramatic in mind. He wanted the *Journal* reporters to finally see that their storytelling wasn't at the top of the pecking order at Dow Jones. In an acerbic memo to staff, he wrote:

Dear All,

There is no doubt that co-operation between Newswires and Journal journalists has improved markedly over the past year, but true fraternity remains more nascent than mature. Our structure must complement the needs of all Dow Jones readers and reflect the contemporary value of what is crudely called "content." A breaking corporate, economic or political news story is of crucial value to our Newswires subscribers, who are being relentlessly wooed by less worthy competitors. Even a headstart of a few seconds is priceless for a commodities trader or a bond dealer—that same story can be repurposed for a range of different audiences, but its value diminishes with the passing of time.

Given that revenue reality, henceforth all Journal reporters will be judged, in significant part, by whether they break news for the Newswires. This is a fundamental shift in orientation which will also require a fundamental change in the inaptly named Speedy system. The Speedy was designed with a simple objective: the urgent dissemination of breaking news unearthed by WSJ reporters. Apart from being an important facet of the Newswires service, the system was intended to enhance the newspaper's reputation as the world's leading source of financial, business and general news. In the age of digitally compressed content, the Speedy should have been a defining advantage for Dow Jones—but, alas, too many of these items were written in a way which neither made sense to Newswires users nor maximized the value of the news they sought to convey.

The system is in need of revolution, not reform. We must all think of ourselves as Dow Jones journalists and, at the least, have some comprehension of the life-cycle of a news story and its relative worth to our readers around the world. Not all content demands to be free and our content, in particular, has a value that is sometimes better recognised by our readers than our journalists. That we have multiple opportunities to generate income from this content is in stark contrast to many other revenue-challenged news organizations, which have not sold their soul—they have merely given it away.

With these objectives in mind, we are sending Speedy to the knackery and saddling up a successor, the URGENT. New nomenclature alone will not generate news, so there must also be basic changes of principle and practice at the Journal. A guide to the new system will be published next week and we are aiming to launch on April 15. In coming days, please raise any relevant issues with your bureau chief or editor. There is much angst-ridden, vacuous debate about the fate of American journalism—this is an important practical measure to secure the long-term future of journalists at Dow Jones.

Robert

Reporters speculated, rightly, that Thomson directed the memo not solely to them, but to an audience of one sitting in midtown: Rupert Murdoch. The tone of his missive exemplified the culture war waging every day in the minds of Thomson and his boss.

Days after the memo, two of the *Journal*'s strongest investigative reporters in Washington, Glenn Simpson and Sue Schmidt, announced their resignations. They were the latest in a series of departures of prize-winning journalists frustrated with the *Journal*'s changed priorities. Simpson, a *Journal* veteran, specialized in complex stories about terror financing. In one such story in February 2002, the *Journal* said that Saudi Arabia, at the behest of the United States, was monitoring bank accounts of prominent Saudi businesses and individuals to determine whether they were being used to siphon money to terrorist groups. A Saudi Arabian company mentioned in the story, Abdul Latif Jameel Company Ltd., and its general manager and president sued the paper.

Having spent millions of dollars on its defense, the *Journal* lost in trial and on appeal, winning only when the case reached the House of Lords. That ruling changed British libel law, which had required newspapers being sued to prove the truth of the allegations they had printed. In the United States, by contrast, the burden of proof falls on plaintiffs to demonstrate reckless disregard for the truth. The Jameel ruling strengthened the ability of the media in Britain to report stories in the public interest, as long as they act responsibly.

Jameel later sued the *Sunday Times* of London over a different story. In that case, the *Sunday Times* settled.

When Simpson had met Murdoch in the *Journal* newsroom in 2008, he was introduced as the investigative reporter who wrote a lot of stories about the financing of terrorism and wealthy Arabs who allegedly finance terrorism. "It was then noted that I had caused several of these wealthy Middle Eastern oligarchs to file libel cases against the *Journal*, all of which we prevailed in . . . one of these cases actually set a new precedent for freedom of the press in the UK," Simpson later remembered. "At that point Murdoch had a glimmer of recognition. 'Oh, yeah, that same guy sued us at the *Times* of London,' he said, 'but we just fixed it.'" Then Murdoch turned and walked away.

Shortly after Simpson's and Schmidt's departures, another *Journal* feature writer, Josh Prager, said he was leaving the paper because he and the *Journal* were no longer a "good fit." Prager wrote less than a story a year. His pieces were long, never relevant to the news of the day, and their subjects were totally unexpected: the family saga behind the royalties from the children's book *Goodnight Moon;* the story of how the New York Giants stole signs from the Brooklyn Dodgers during the game when Bobby Thomson hit his "shot heard 'round the world"; the identity of a previously anonymous Iranian photographer whose photo of assassinations during the Iranian revolution had won the Pulitzer Prize.

Prager's departure note attacked Thomson directly, saying, "The worship of byline and word counts and all that is 'urgent' has doubtless stifled the boundless creativity of the Journal staff. I hope the paper will address this problem. Implementing some version of the rule at 3M that lets employees spend 15 percent of their time on 'projects of their own choosing' would benefit morale and yield wonderful stories."

For Murdoch, these departures were just the noise associated with a staff sorting itself out. As his editor, Thomson, would note, if people weren't happy, they were free to leave.

The journalistic culmination of the year came when the Pulitzer committee announced its prizes. In a year of the most important business and financial events of all the editors' and reporters' life-times, the *Journal* had been shut out. The paper hadn't won a prize the year before, either; the prize had eluded the *Journal* ever since Murdoch took over. In the previous ten years, the paper had won at least one Pulitzer in all but two years.

The reaction from News Corp.'s executives was clear: the journalistic establishment was out to get Murdoch. Baker told reporters they deserved to win, but that the journalism profession hated Murdoch too much to reward him. News Corp.'s mindset was confirmed.

Epilogue

RUPERT MURDOCH was waging wars on all sides. He had gone to battle with his own staff within the *Journal*. He took the fight to the *New York Times*. He threatened to sue the BBC. He came to blows with the White House. He invited the conflicts and thrived on them. What would he do, after all, without a competitor to batter? The Murdoch juggernaut was working, and the collateral piled up.

Indeed, the feud Rupert Murdoch promised Arthur Sulzberger Jr. after Barry Diller's party came as promised and inflicted casualties on both sides. Of course, both men were battling a common enemy in the Internet, which easily did them more damage than what they inflicted on each other. But as their own fortunes faded, they fought each other even more fiercely than before.

In the wake of Murdoch's deal for Dow Jones, Sulzberger's company lost $60 million and cut one hundred newsroom jobs. The Times Company's shares traded below $8 for most of 2009, making Murdoch's $60 a share for Dow Jones seem even more unreal than it had back in 2007. To survive the onslaught, the Sulzbergers canceled their generous dividend payments, a test of loyalty the Bancrofts surely would have failed. Murdoch lost an estimated $5 billion of his personal net worth, cut his own pay by 28 percent, and eliminated 3,700 jobs at News Corp. He wrote down $3 billion of his company's $5.6 billion investment in Dow Jones, a move that was as explicit an admission of error as anyone could ever hope to get from him. Murdoch began renting out his *Rosehearty* yacht for $350,000 a week. Sulzberger and Gail Gregg divorced. News Corp. stock, above $20 a share at the time of the Dow Jones deal, sank below $6 in the spring of 2009. The *Journal* alone lost $87 million in a year.

But Murdoch was unbowed. In the summer of 2009, Murdoch moved the *Journal* and Dow Jones Newswires to his midtown News Corp. headquarters at a cost of more than $60 million. The location, in the heart of the city, improved upon the old Battery Park ghetto. The restaurants were superior and powerful sources were closer at hand. The newly designed offices were sleek, with understated gray carpets, glass-walled conference rooms, chrome accents, and a news "hub" overseen by Thomson and his deputy, Gerard Baker. Nicknamed the "death star" by *Journal* reporters, the hub showcased mammoth screens that hung above the desks of *Journal* editors broadcasting the Fox Business channel. The new offices highlighted the favored status of the paper versus the *New York Post,* for which Murdoch's affections seemed to have faded. Still, as some *Journal* reporters walked past the "Fox Nation" billboards in the lobby of the headquarters, their hearts sank.

That fall, the *Journal*'s online circulation edged up to round out the paper's overall circulation at 2.02 million, surpassing *USA Today* to become the largest paper in the nation. It was a crowning achievement for Murdoch, a debt he owed to former Dow Jones CEO Peter Kann. (Because people paid for the online *Journal,* it was the only paper in the country permitted to officially count its online circulation as part of its overall circulation number.) In the same period, the *Post*'s circulation declined more than 20 percent. Never mind that the *Journal*'s print subscriptions had declined 3 percent in the two years since Murdoch had agreed to buy the paper; the bundled online and print subscriptions secured increased overall circulation for the *Journal* and big headlines for Murdoch when the results came out.

At the same time, the *Times* and the *Journal* expanded their fracas to the West Coast. Both papers launched regional editions in the San Francisco area in October and November of 2009, to pick up the readers who had defected from the ailing *San Francisco Chronicle.* Simultaneously, the *Times* said it was launching a regional edition in Chicago; the *Journal* quickly said it would follow. To hit the Sulzbergers and the *Times* where they most valued it, Murdoch announced plans in October 2009 to hire a group of reporters to cover local New York news. The fight to be the nation's national paper was happening just as Murdoch had hoped it might.

But the real threat was not the Sulzbergers and their devotion to the *Times* no matter what the cost. Murdoch faced the Internet, and it was an enemy he wasn't quite sure what to do with. He had long ago abandoned his plan to make WSJ.com free. And though he had once seen the paid subscription wall around the *Journal*'s Web site as a barrier to his grand expansion of the paper, in May of 2009 he embraced a vision of a paid online *Journal* with a vehemence that even Kann had never mustered. Murdoch promised that the company would start charging for the content at all of its newspapers by the summer of 2010. Several months later, as his newspapers around the world struggled to find a model to charge readers for their online content, Murdoch became an outspoken proselytizer for paying for the news. He talked of online "content kleptomaniacs" and told his Sky News Australia channel that the people "steal our stories, we say they steal our stories—they just take them." He publicly threatened to cut off Google News's access to News Corp.'s stories to encourage people to pay for his content.

Still, the 180-degree change in Web philosophy showed Murdoch's keen ability to alter his argument when it suited him. The problem with this shift: what was Murdoch's content worth? The question cast doubt on all that he had built. If the *Journal,* the paper he had found dry and timid and gray, was the only newspaper he owned that people were willing to pay for online, what did that say about the wisdom of his business strategy of pumped-up headlines and color photos? Would people pay for Murdoch's brand of breathless news? The company's early research seemed bleak. Apart from the *Journal,* Murdoch's papers weren't unique enough for people to want to pay for them online.

As he struggled for a business model he seemed increasingly erratic in his public statements. He backed up his commentator Glenn Beck's assertion that President Obama was a racist: "He did make a very racist comment about blacks and whites and so on," Murdoch said. When asked why there was not more civility in public discourse, Murdoch blamed politicians like New York governor David Paterson, whom he called "a very nice, honest man, who's blind, and can't read Braille, and doesn't really know what's going on."

Two years after Rupert Murdoch had officially made the *Journal* part of his empire, the paper bore his stamp. One of the great icons of American journalism had been transformed. The famous front page had become more common. The process had begun years before, but now, each morning, Page One carried the big news of the day. Stories were shorter. The *Wall Street Journal* sent reporters out to cover local natural disasters, mass shootings, and minor political scandals. Features that had gestated for months and had been precisely edited for song and nuance were gone. There were fewer investigations. The signature *Journal* "tick-tocks" lacked the old rigor. Joe Nocera, business columnist at the *New York Times* who had pilloried the old Dow Jones management, titled a piece in August "Wall Street Journal, R.I.P." He noted how little business coverage was in the front section and how much less distinctive the paper had become. "Most painful for me," he continued, "are the memories I have of the rollicking Wall Street Journal narrative that was such a staple—a behind-the-scenes story about some shenanigans inside a company that only The Journal would ferret out and tell. Nobody else in journalism wrote those stories on a regular basis, and now that The Journal has largely stopped writing them I fear they are going to disappear, like an ancient dialect that dies out."

Many other outside readers, including some of the leading voices in journalism, praised the paper or professed not to see any changes. Eugene Roberts, the legendary former executive editor of the *Philadelphia Inquirer*, admitted, after originally being skeptical of Murdoch, "I've been impressed with what I've seen so far." The *Washington Post*'s Walter Pincus said the *Journal* was better under Murdoch. Harold Evans, the former *Times* of London editor famously ousted by Murdoch, said, "The *Journal* is a much improved newspaper."

And eventually, there was the question of balance. At the *Journal*, Robert Thomson intoned that *Journal* reporters had the "objective of objectivity." He attacked the *New York Times* as a liberal outlet that made no effort to be balanced. "At the *New York Times*, you have news with a skew. Or a skew with news," he said. The comment seemed eerily similar to Fox News's "fair and balanced" stance versus the "liberal" CNN.

By the fall of 2009, it no longer took a careful and obsessive reader to notice changes. "Taliban Now Winning" a front-page story in August screamed. Reporters at the paper were aghast, though they noted that the story itself was more nuanced and in many ways contradicted the banner headline. "State Death Taxes Now the Latest Worry" announced another in August on the front of the paper's "Marketplace" section. The loaded "death tax" phrase was used six times in the story to describe estate taxes. The headlines grew cruder and more insistent. "Politicians Butt In at Bailed-Out GM" blared a story in October.

When President Barack Obama announced his decision to drop plans to deploy a ballistic-missile defense shield in Central Europe, the *Journal* initially headlined the story "Allies Roiled by U.S. Missile U-turn." The headline took a momentary *cause célèbre* of Obama's Republican critics and turned it into the story of the day. Obama's decision was attacked, the story said, "by Republicans in Congress and Bush-era defense officials" and drew "immediate cheers in Moscow and criticism elsewhere." But the story didn't back up the headline. It merely demonstrated that Republicans, not U.S. allies, criticized the decision, and in an unusual step, the paper corrected its headline to read more accurately, but less sexily, that "Allies React to Missile U-turn." The same day, the paper's other front-page headline read "Bankers Face Sweeping Curbs on Pay." The story was a much less exciting account of the Federal Reserve mulling pay guidelines. But, as media critics noted, the grab-you-by-the-throat headlines were classic Murdoch.

As Obama staked the first year of his presidency on passing health care reform and the media focused on the debate in all its permutations, *Wall Street Journal* readers read stories about the flaws of the health care systems in other countries. One outlined how in Britain, dogs had more choice of doctors than people. Another told of a woman in France who gave birth in a fire truck because the hospital near her house had been shut down due to the country's high health care costs. The story noted, "France's woes provide grist to critics of

Mr. Obama and the Democrats' vision of a new public health plan to compete with private health insurers. Republicans argue that tens of millions of Americans would leave their employer-provided coverage for the cheaper, public option, bankrupting the federal government."

Readers couldn't see or know that editors were frequently altering stories in subtle ways. Reporters at the paper noticed that quotes criticizing Republicans or praising Obama were cut. Small editing decisions changed the news—as the *Journal* reported it—every day. Reporters began to sense that top editors were ordering stories to fit a political agenda. "As News Corp. has consolidated its control of the paper they have increasingly come to demand enterprise journalism that serves the interest and viewpoints of the News Corp. management," Glenn Simpson said. "The upper ranks are now dominated by conservative and partisan editors who aren't shy about making their views known."

When Ted Kennedy died, the *Journal* led its obituary with conservative talk-radio host Rush Limbaugh, who derided the "slobbering media coverage" of Mr. Kennedy's death that ignored his past "bad behavior." Mr. Kennedy had been someone who "uses the government to take money from people who work and gives it to people who don't work," Limbaugh said.

Sometimes individual decisions seemed small and utterly justifiable. After all, news stories were always edited quickly, and there were numerous ways to write about any news event. But when every decision seemed to move in one direction, the reporters took note. Thomson ordered a story on how litigation adds to health care costs. The editor on the piece said it had to be edited within "an inch of its life" to ensure that it wasn't politically biased. Thomson repeatedly objected to another story on how business tax breaks were costing the government more than Congress realized. The story never ran. Tax proposals from Obama were described in a news article as an "assault on business," but the phrase was eventually removed for late editions of the paper after one of the reporters raised objections to the language. Thomson objected to a story on Fannie Mae's and Freddie Mac's roles in the housing crisis as "too anti-Republican." In a news meeting, he once offhandedly commented that the housing crisis was "all the fault of incompetent borrowers." Political reporters

often heard requests for more stories on Republicans. Education reporters were told by their editors to write their stories as if "the most
conservative reader in the world" were reading over their shoulder.

Thomson dismissed criticisms of political bias, saying that people
determined to see a right-wing slant in a Murdoch paper would see
it, regardless of the facts. He felt his *Journal* was being praised everywhere except for a strange group of "Columbia Journalism School"
types who felt News Corp. had cheapened the *Journal's* brand. He
said this group, not his colleagues, were the ones bordering on amoral
behavior. Not paying attention to a paper's financial health was the
greatest crime.

In the fall of 2009, Gerard Baker, Thompson's number two, had
joined Thomson in the task of policing the newsroom for left-leaning
ideological bias. Baker maintained that he was tough on both Democrats and Republicans, and strove only to provide balance and rigor
in the *Journal's* stories. He said his editing leaned against the prevail-
ing left-of-center bias prevalent in most newsrooms. The former columnist for the *Times* of London openly mocked Barack Obama and
what he saw as the turgid style of American journalists. After several months, he and Thomson had identified reporters in the *Journal* newsroom they felt were too far to the left. Slowly, the old bureau
chiefs were replaced with new ones whom the two men trusted. The
old news meetings changed, and the stories on Page One were discussed last, not first. Editors selected front-page photos. At one such
meeting, in the long conference room on the sixth floor opposite the
hub television screens, Baker groaned when told of a photo of Barack
Obama touring Beijing's Forbidden City: "Not Obama again."

In the 2009 off-year congressional elections, Baker began to show
inordinate interest in a minor race in a conservative district in upstate New York. The Republican establishment figure, Dede Scoz-
zafava, faced a challenge from Doug Hoffman, an upstart from the
right wing of her party. Political commentators saw it as a symbol of
the damaging civil war within the party, but right-wing pundits, often appearing on Fox News, heralded the challenger as the standard-
bearer of the ideological purification of the party. When the *Journal*
ran an early front-page story on the race, Thomson and Baker were
incensed that a draft of the story contained, as he saw it, too many

quotations from Democrats. The quotes were cut. Come the election, the Democrat won, upending the hopes of the insurgent wing of the GOP. Afterward, Baker told people in the newsroom not to draw too many lessons from the election, adding that the Republicans would likely retake the seat the following year. (He cautioned against reading too much into all the surprise wins, including Republican victories in Virginia and New Jersey.)

At the height of the health care reform debate in the fall, a Washington area think tank, the Lewin Group, conducted a study suggesting that the Democratic health care proposals would lead to a catastrophic influx of new patients on the government-funded health plan, crippling the federal budget. The study estimated that a hundred million people would flow into a government-funded health plan if a public health care option were passed. Baker ordered up a story.

The health reporter pursuing the piece quickly ascertained that the Lewin Group was not a nonpartisan think tank but was owned by UnitedHealthcare, the health insurance giant—clearly not an unbiased source of information. It turned out that even this front group for an insurance company was going to have to back off its outlandish number, bringing its estimate down to thirty million, a figure more in line with that of the Congressional Budget Office.

The *Journal*'s health care group prepared a story. At 5:30 p.m. on a Sunday, Baker got a look at it. No longer did the story highlight a sensational figure that might damage President Obama's chances to pass a health care bill. He ordered the story held. Baker shrugged that the *Journal*'s readers wouldn't be interested in a story from such a compromised outfit.

Editors protested. The story editor argued that *Journal* readers would be very interested in precisely such stories that pulled back the spin and counter-spin of the debates governing politics and industry. Baker prevailed.

While the *Journal* was being transformed, Marcus Brauchli was remaking a newspaper of his own as executive editor of the *Washington Post*. Rich Zannino joined a private equity firm. The Bancrofts felt exceedingly lucky to have exhibited such impeccable timing. The family was ever divided on the direction of the paper. But on their financial well-being, the Bancrofts were of one mind. "Thank God we sold when we did," said Christopher Bancroft, in a sentiment echoed by others in his family. Many of them received cash from Murdoch, and sidestepped the market's gyrations in the months following the deal.

Lisa Steele sent Rich Zannino a Christmas card, thanking him for saving her family "from ruin." Elisabeth Goth divorced Robert Chelberg and started riding competitively again, winning two Reserve World Championships in 2009. She thought the paper looked better than ever. The Hills, alas, were still dissatisfied. Leslie Hill continued to feel uneasy about the sale. She couldn't get over her distaste for Murdoch. Her mother, Jane MacElree, worried about the paper's new look. "I certainly don't think it's changed for the better," she said.

Rupert Murdoch, of course, begged to differ. "We produced a better paper," he said. "I'm sorry but it's as simple as that."

Acknowledgments

I could not have written this book without the *Wall Street Journal*.

Not only would I have been deprived of a main character and a narrative thread, but I would have been without the professional home that taught me everything I know about recognizing a good story and then telling it. I joined the paper at twenty-four as a news assistant in Paris. It was, as my friend Matthew Rose had promised, like being paid to go to journalism school.

Writing about the people and place where I learned so much—and where I had personal relationships with many of the book's subjects—was particularly challenging. I endeavored to treat this story as I'd been trained to do, with rigorous objectivity, intellectual honesty, and fairness. The readers' interests were paramount, and I hope they feel well represented.

Peter Kann created an atmosphere where inspiring journalism flourished. His wife, Karen House, was personally generous to me when she ran the paper's international editions. Fred Kempe, Tom Kamm, and Greg Steinmetz gave me my earliest opportunities at the paper, and I will always remember their patience and generosity.

Barney Calame and Stuart Karle taught me the rigorous and unwavering ethical standards that defined the *Journal*.

Nik Deogun hired me to come to New York and looked out for me on many occasions. He worked with me on my last assignment, to cover Rupert Murdoch's bid to buy the paper. That story gave me the immense privilege of working directly with Paul Steiger, who oversaw the paper's coverage of the deal. I am indebted to the team of editors and reporters who worked with me on that story: Mike Siconolfi, Rich Turner, Martin Peers, Susan Pulliam, Matthew Karnitschnig, Dennis Berman, and Susan Warren. Matt Murray and Margaret deStreel were gracious under tremendous deadline pressure.

I am grateful to Marcus Brauchli for granting me leave to write this book and promising he would take me back no matter what I wrote, as long as it was true.

Thanks to my former colleagues, including Geeta Anand, James Bandler, Lisa Bannon, Rebecca Blumenstein, Ellen Byron, Robert Christie, Michael Connolly, Gordon Crovitz, Kevin Delaney, Jesse Drucker, Jennifer Forsyth, Robert Frank, Alix Freedman, Alessandra Galloni, Bill Grueskin, Dan Hertzberg, Larry Ingrassia, Paul Ingrassia, Dave Kansas, Dan Kelly, Kate Kelly, Almar Latour, Peter Lattman, Merissa Marr, Mike Miller, Alan Murray, Emily Nelson, Bruce Orwall, David Sanford, Suzanne Sataline, Sam Schechner, Steve Stecklow, Brian Steinberg, Joseph Stern, Kim Strassel, Suzanne Vranica, Mike Williams, and Rich Zannino.

My friend Julia Angwin, who juggled a newborn and a book project just a year before I did, was always ready with much-needed encouragement and advice.

Special thanks to the Bancroft family and their advisers, too numerous to name here, who generously shared their time and the stories of their family.

I am grateful to Rupert Murdoch and his family for agreeing to talk to me for this book. Thanks to Gary Ginsberg and Teri Everett for their help with my research; to Robert Thomson for his wit; and to Lon Jacobs, Jimmy Lee, John Nallen, Arthur Siskind, Andrew Steginsky, and many other current and former News Corp. employees and advisers who were helpful to me.

Thanks to Neena Lall for her early transcriptions, Kate Ryder for her research assistance, and especially Nadia Mustafa for her meticulous fact checking. Meredith Angwin provided sage comments on an earlier version of this manuscript. Daniel Okrent, Norman Pearlstine, Ken Auletta, and James Stewart gave me early advice that was extremely useful. Christopher Dickey and Michael Elliott helped me get to the *Journal,* and for that I am grateful.

I couldn't have started, much less finished, this book without the wise counsel and encouraging words of my agent, David Halpern. Kathy Robbins and everyone at the Robbins Office, including Ian King and Rachelle Bergstein, were enormously supportive at every step. George Hodgman at Houghton Mifflin Harcourt was this book's champion. No author could ask for a more passionate or hilarious editor. Special thanks to Andrea Schulz for her encouragement and advice. Barbara Wood was a meticulous copyeditor. Thanks, too, to Larry Cooper and Loren Isenberg at Houghton Mifflin Harcourt for their attention to the manuscript.

My friends have been a source of sanity: Jenny Carchman, Claudia Campo, Nell Casey, Caroline Cooper, Valerie Lincy, Christina Lowery, Betsy McPherson, Kendra Percy, and Nita Rao. Special thanks to Lexi Reese, Saira Rao, and Lisa Turvey, who were on speed dial.

Thanks to my in-laws, Erica and Peter Eisinger, for enduring long discussions of book titles. Sarah Eisinger accompanied me on many soul-searching walks around the park.

My warmest gratitude goes to my parents, James and Susan Ellison, whose unconditional love instilled in me the confidence and work ethic required for a book like this. My mother spent six weeks taking care of my newborn daughter so I could finish the manuscript. My amazing brother, J. P. Ellison, his wife, Lauren Case, and their children, Meredith and Henry, have provided constant love and savvy Web design. The Ellison and Miller aunts, uncles, and cousins were wonderful cheerleaders, especially my aunt Nancy Miller and cousins Carrie and Gretchen.

To my daughter, Iva: Every author should have such a joyous interruption of the writing process. And, especially, to my husband, Jesse Eisinger, without whom I would never eat a proper meal, much less write a book. Any mention here couldn't possibly reflect my deepest love and thanks.

Sources

This book is based primarily on firsthand reporting consisting of hundreds of interviews with Bancroft family members and advisers; Murdoch family members and advisers; current and former News Corp. executives; and current and former Dow Jones executives. My coverage of News Corp.'s takeover of Dow Jones began in the spring of 2007 as an assignment from the editors of the *Wall Street Journal*, where I worked for a decade and where I was the media reporter at the time of Rupert Murdoch's formal bid for Dow Jones. This book would not have been possible without the foundation of that reporting and the extraordinary effort of my fellow reporters and talented editors at the *Journal*. However, I re-reported this book in its entirety, and I had no financial ties to Dow Jones or News Corp. as I wrote it.

While I received cooperation from all of the significant players in the narrative, this is not an authorized account. It has not been vetted or cleared by News Corporation or Dow Jones.

Because the *Journal*'s initial reporting on News Corp.'s offer for Dow Jones formed the basis of my knowledge of the events, I have listed the bulk of the paper's articles on the topic here, by date:

"News Corp. Duo Set to Lead Dow Jones as Zannino Resigns," December 7, 2007
"Bancrofts Bicker, Miss a Deadline, Lose Board Choice," November 7, 2007
"Dow Jones Didn't Get a Viable Rival Offer," September 8, 2007

"Member of Independent Dow Jones Panel Has Ties to News Corp.," August 3, 2007

"Murdoch Wins His Bid for Dow Jones—Bancroft Family Agrees to $5 Billion Offer After Deal on Fees—A New Owner for Journal," August 1, 2007

"Dow Jones Deal Gets Closer as Talks Turn to Fees—Fund Would Cover Some Family Costs to Gain Key Votes," July 31, 2007

"Bancrofts' Jockeying Over Murdoch Deal Goes Down to the Wire," July 30, 2007

"Bancroft Wrangling Intensifies—As Bid Deadline Looms for Dow Jones, Splits in the Family Remain," July 28, 2007

"Relative Uncertainty: As Sale Decision Nears, Family Split Persists—Murdoch Deal Pits Heirs Against Parents; Call for a 'Leap of Faith,'" July 25, 2007

"Dow Jones Board Member Quits in Protest—German Publishing Heir Cites News Corp. Deal; Net Falls 27% on Charges," July 20, 2007

"For Bancrofts, Decision Time Is Near on Sale of Dow Jones—News Corp. Seeks to Know 'Promptly' If Deal Is Supported," July 19, 2007

"SEC Plans Suit Against Dow Jones Director," July 19, 2007

"Dow Jones Board Approves Sale—Vote Could Pressure Family; Christopher Bancroft Leaves Meeting Early," July 18, 2007

"Dow Jones, News Corp. Set Deal—Tentative $5 Billion Pact Gets Board Vote Tonight; Family to Meet Thursday," July 17, 2007

"Key Bancroft Aims for a Long Shot—Second Family Member Scrambles to Stop Sale of Dow Jones to News Corp.," July 16, 2007

"Dow Jones Makes Late Push to Find Other Buyers," July 9, 2007

"Dow Jones Pact Would Protect Three Top Editors," July 3, 2007

"Bancroft Heir Pursues Alternative to Murdoch," June 29, 2007

"News Corp. Awaits Reply from Bancrofts," June 28, 2007

"News Corp. Nears Dow Jones Pact—Agreement on Protection of Editorial Independence Would Pave Way for Sale," June 26, 2007

"Dow Jones Deal Talks Intensify," June 25, 2007

"Dow Jones Board Takes Over Talks on Firm's Future—Deal with News Corp. Becomes More Likely; 'Fish or Cut Bait' Mood," June 21, 2007

"GE and Pearson Discuss Joint Bid for Dow Jones—Talks Signal Alternative to News Corp.'s Offer Could Be Taking Shape," June 18, 2007

"Dow Jones Scenarios Highlight Divide," June 14, 2007

"Dow Jones Moves to Cover Executives in Event of a Sale," June 8, 2007

"In Murdoch's Career, a Hand on the News," June 5, 2007

"Murdoch May Make Concessions, Up to a Limit, in Dow Jones Talks," June 4, 2007

"Family Dynamics: Behind the Bancrofts' Shift at Dow Jones," June 2, 2007

"Bancrofts Open Door to a Sale of Dow Jones," June 1, 2007

"Dow Jones Board Won't Act as Bancrofts Deliberate," May 17, 2007

"Dow Jones CEO Zannino: The Man in the Middle," May 14, 2007

"Dynasty's Dilemma: For Bancrofts, Dow Jones Offer Poses Challenge—Murdoch Bid Tests Family's Cohesion; Sell 'Grandpa's Paper'?" May 12, 2007

"Clearer Timeline of Murdoch Offer Emerges," May 10, 2007

"Dow Jones Ex-Chief Praises Family's Stance," May 8, 2007

"Ex-Dow Jones Executives Oppose Murdoch's Bid," May 7, 2007

"At Dow Jones, Focus Is on the Bancroft Family," May 3, 2007

"Key to Company's Fate Is the Bancroft Family; Firm 'No' or a 'Maybe'?" May 2, 2007

"Murdoch's Surprise Bid: $5 Billion for Dow Jones," May 2, 2007

PROLOGUE

My description of the party aboard Barry Diller's yacht is based on interviews with numerous party guests.

The history of the Bancroft family is based on extensive interviews with various members of the family as well as several books, including Lloyd Wendt's *The Wall Street Journal: The Story of Dow Jones and the Nation's Business Newspaper* (Skokie, IL: Rand McNally & Co., 1982), Richard Tofel's *Restless Genius* (New York: St. Martin's Press, 2009), and Jon Meacham's *The Beginning of the Journey* (New York: Dow Jones, 2002). In addition, a number of articles were useful, including Marshall Loeb, "Words to Profit By," *Time,* December 7, 1998; Stephen Foley, "A Tale of Wealth and Intrigue: The First Family of Wall Street," *Independent,* June 9, 2007; and Susan Pulliam, Dennis K. Berman, Matthew Karnitschnig, and Sarah Ellison, "For Bancrofts, Dow Jones Offer Poses Challenge," *Wall Street Journal,* May 12, 2007.

The Bancrofts' fear of becoming "just another rich family" was reiterated to me in several interviews with family members and initially appeared in Joseph Nocera, "At Dow Jones, It's All About Family," *New York Times,* August 20, 2005.

Background on the Sulzbergers came from their friends and acquaintances. Other useful sources on this subject include Susan E. Tifft and Alex S. Jones, *The Trust: The Private and Powerful Family Behind the New York Times* (Boston: Back Bay Books, 2000).

The history of the Murdoch family and Keith Murdoch's role in Gallipoli are based on interviews with Murdoch family members and longtime Murdoch family associates. Other useful sources on this subject include the National Library of Australia, "Despatches from Gallipoli; Scenes from a Remote War: Sir Keith Murdoch," http://www.nla.gov.au/gallipolidespatches/2-2-1-murdoch.html.

The influence of Murdoch's *Sun* in London is outlined in the National Readership Survey, http://www.nrs.co.uk.

CHAPTER 1

The Bancroft family trust structure was laid out for me by several family members and advisers. The most detailed newspaper article done on the trust structure was Matthew Karnitschnig, "Bancroft Trusts' Lawyers Hold Key to Dow Jones," *Wall Street Journal*, July 2, 2007.

To describe the ascension of Peter Kann and Karen House at Dow Jones, I interviewed current and former Dow Jones executives, as well as Kann and House, for whom I worked during much of my tenure at the *Journal*. In addition to those interviews, I found *Vanity Fair*'s "In the Company of Sharks," by Robert Sam Anson (August 1997), useful for its description of that era as well as an artifact itself of the disdain with which most media watchers viewed Kann and House at the time. For details on Kann's history at the *Journal*, I used a collection of stories and memorabilia his former colleagues at the *Journal* assembled for him as a retirement gift.

Financial information on the company came from company filings and the reporting on Dow Jones's performance in various publications, including the *Journal*, the *New York Times*, and *Fortune* magazine.

CHAPTER 2

To describe Elisabeth Goth's campaign after her mother's death, I relied on interviews with Bancroft family members. In addition, Joseph Nocera's February 3, 1997, article in *Fortune* magazine, "Disgruntled Heiress Leads Revolt at Dow Jones," was indispensable. It not only reported Elisabeth Goth's unhappiness at the time, but it made news itself, as it was the first public account of Bancroft family unrest. Nocera's follow-up piece (with reporter associate Maria Atanasov), "Attention, Dow Jones: Ms. Goth Wants Results Now!" which appeared in *Fortune* on March 2, 1998, also proved useful.

The description of Chris Bancroft's wife was based on interviews with him as well as press articles at the time, including Paul Tharp and Zachery Kouwe, "A House Divided: Bancroft Heirs Split on Murdoch's $5B Offer," *New York Post*, May 4, 2007.

My description of Herbert Allen's Sun Valley conference was drawn from interviews with various people who have attended the conference, as well as several books that have reported on the atmosphere of the gathering, including Alice Schroeder, *The Snowball: Warren Buffett and the Business of Life* (New York: Bantam, 2008).

My account of the state of the Murdoch family at the time of the Murdochs' meeting with Jimmy Lee in Sun Valley was based on interviews with family members as well as Michael Wolff, "Fox Family Values," *New York*, August 17, 1998.

My characterization that the Murdoch children had reached a consensus that Lachlan was Murdoch's heir apparent was based on interviews with the children as well as press accounts at the time, including Cathy Newman, "Murdoch Vows to Keep Up Cut-Price Newspaper War," *Independent,* November 13, 1997.

CHAPTER 3

The proposed change in Dow Jones's bylaws to lower the threshold at which Bancroft super-voting shares would convert to common shares is outlined in the company's 2005 proxy statement: http://www.sec.gov/Archives/edgar/data/29924/000119312505054765/ddef14a.htm.

Roy Hammer's comment to *Fortune* magazine appeared in this article: Julie Creswell, "Dow Jones: Does the Family Finally Want Out?" *Fortune,* May 16, 2005.

The decline in the *Journal*'s revenues in the first quarter of 2005 is based on the company's annual report, "Value and Values," Dow Jones & Company Annual Report, 2005.

The jump in the *Journal*'s stock price after Zannino's appointment was announced can be found in "Dow Jones and Company Incorporated (DJ) Daily Prices from 15-Dec-1986 to 13-Dec-2007," http://www.dj.com/Investor Relations/Overview.html.

My description of the correspondence between Jim Lowell, the lawyers at Hemenway & Barnes, and the Bancrofts, and the ensuing e-mail exchange among the Bancroft family members, is based on interviews with family members and advisers and e-mails I reviewed from that time.

Wendi Murdoch's role at News Corp. and her history leading up to her marriage to Rupert Murdoch were outlined in John Lippman, Leslie Chang, and Robert Frank, "Meet Wendi Deng: The Boss's Wife Has Influence at News Corp.," *Wall Street Journal,* November 1, 2000.

CHAPTER 4

My description of Richard Zannino's appointment as CEO was based on numerous interviews with current and former Dow Jones executives. Zannino's quote "I know what will happen if we screw up the *Journal*" appeared in Brian Steinberg and Joe Hagan, "Dow Jones Taps Richard Zannino As New CEO," *Wall Street Journal,* January 4, 2006.

My description of Lachlan's departure from News Corp. was based on interviews with current and former News Corp. employees. In addition, I found several articles from that time to be useful, including Steve Fishman, "The Boy Who Wouldn't Be King," *New York,* September 11, 2005.

Anna Murdoch's description of her recovery from her divorce as "coming out of a deep mental illness" appeared in *Australian Women's Weekly* in July 2001 and was reported on extensively by the UK press, including in Christopher Zinn, "Anna Murdoch Mann: 'He Was Hard, Ruthless and Determined,'" *Independent,* July 27, 2001.

CHAPTER 5

My description of Billy Cox III's role as his cousin Elisabeth's coconspirator was based on interviews with a number of family members and family advisers who remembered that period well. Because Billy's comments in the press caused so much angst within his family, I also relied on several articles, including Joseph Nocera's previously cited "Attention, Dow Jones."

My description of the differences between the Bancroft family's trust structure and the Sulzberger family's trust structure was based on numerous interviews with advisers to both of the families as well as public company filings from the *New York Times* and Dow Jones. The most detailed discussion of the Sulzberger family's trust appears in Tifft and Jones, *The Trust*.

My description of the state of the newspaper industry at the time of Rich Zannino's conversation with Jimmy Lee is based on the totality of negative news coming from newspaper publishers at that time as outlined in their own SEC filings and circulation figures, as well as "The State of the News Media 2006: An Annual Report on American Journalism," Project for Excellence in Journalism, http://www.stateofthemedia.org/2006.

My description of Dow Jones's interest in Business Wire and Warren Buffett's subsequent purchase of the business was drawn from interviews with former Dow Jones executives as well as press accounts of Buffett's purchase, including Dan Fost, "Buffett Seals the Deal: Business Wire Is Latest Addition to Billionaire Investor's Portfolio," *San Francisco Chronicle*, January 18, 2006.

CHAPTER 6

My description of Tony Ridder's attempt to appease investor Bruce Sherman before caving to pressure to sell Knight Ridder is based on Knight Ridder's own filings, including a November 10, 2005, 13D filing (http://yahoo.brand. edgar-online.com/EFX_dll/EDGARpro.dll?FetchFilingHTML1?SessionID= VcxtINVjuQgXtfT&ID=4007412), as well as press accounts, including Charles Layton, "Sherman's March," *American Journalism Review*, February/March 2006.

Hassan Elmasry's dissatisfaction with the New York Times Company's management was outlined in an article I wrote for the *Journal* in 2007: "How a Money Manager Battled New York Times: Mr. Elmasry Escalated Efforts Over Two Years; Letters to the Chairman," *Wall Street Journal*, March 21, 2007.

CHAPTER 7

John Malone's exchange of News Corp. shares for control of DirecTV was outlined by News Corp. in a company announcement, "News Corporation Completes Exchange Agreement with Liberty Media Corporation: Largest Buyback in Company's History," February 27, 2008, http://www.newscorp.com/news/news_370.html.

Gordon Crovitz's note to *Journal* readers appeared in L. Gordon Crovitz, "A Report to Our Readers: Welcome to the Newspaper of Tomorrow," *Wall Street Journal*, January 2, 2007.

Marcus Brauchli's quote about *Journal* 3.0 appeared in Howard Kurtz, "Wall Street Journal Names New Editor," *Washington Post*, April 19, 2007.

The reception of *Journal* 3.0 in Dow Jones's executive suite was outlined to me by Rich Zannino and several other Dow Jones board members. The reception in the blogosphere was outlined in Edward B. Colby, " 'Shrinky-Dink' WSJ Debuts, Bloggers Muse," *Columbia Journalism Review*, January 2, 2007.

Paul Dacre's salary as the editor of the *Daily Mail* is outlined in the company's annual report, "Daily Mail and General Trust plc Annual Report," September 28, 2008, http://www.dmgt.co.uk/investorrelations/reportsandpresentations.

CHAPTER 10

My description of the fissures in the Bancroft family during the summer of 2007 are based primarily on interviews with individual family members. Some of those divisions were initially reported by me and my colleagues at the *Wall Street Journal* at the time, including in Matthew Karnitschnig, Sarah Ellison, and Susan Pulliam, "Bancroft Wrangling Intensifies: As Bid Deadline Looms for Dow Jones, Splits in the Family Remain," *Wall Street Journal*, July 28, 2007.

David Faber's initial break of the News Corp. offer for Dow Jones appeared on CNBC *Morning Call:* "CNBC's David Faber Reports News Corp Made Unsolicited $60 a Share All Cash Offer for Dow Jones," May 1, 2007.

The *Journal* article by Martin Peers, prepared prior to the Faber story and released afterward, appeared on Dow Jones Newswires, "Dow Jones Receives $60/Share News Corp Bid," May 1, 2007.

The Bancroft family's initial statement that they were "evaluating the proposal" was released by Dow Jones the day the offer became public: "Dow Jones Confirms Receipt of Unsolicited Acquisition Proposal from News Corporation," May 1, 2007, http://penplusbytes.blogspot.com/2007/05/dow-jones-confirms-receipt-of.html.

The large turnover in Dow Jones's shares on May 1 was reported widely the day of the offer and is verifiable on a number of free online databases. The turnover was also reported in the *Journal* itself: Susan Pulliam, Gregory Zuckerman, and Karen Richardson, "Dow Jones: The Premium Question—Murdoch's Lofty Offer Could Deter Rivals; Buffett Unlikely to Bid," *Wall Street Journal*, May 2, 2007.

Andrew Ross Sorkin's piece on Murdoch's offer appeared in "What to Do When Rupert Calls?" *New York Times*, May 6, 2007.

CHAPTER 11

The family's statement that it would "consider strategic alternatives available to the company, including the News Corporation proposal," initially appeared on WSJ.com, "Bancrofts' Statement on Dow Jones Bid," May 31, 2007.

For my account of the conference call in which Zannino, Crovitz, the Bancroft family board members, and Dow Jones editors initially discussed an editorial independence agreement, I relied on interviews with the participants. Harold Evans's recollection of Murdoch's dismissal of the *Times* of London's editorial agreement initially appeared in Evans's book *Good Times, Bad Times* (Philadelphia: Coronet Books, 1984).

CHAPTER 12

For my description of Marty Lipton, I relied on interviews with people who have worked with him as well as his corporate biography, "Martin Lipton (Partner, Corporate)," http://www.wlrk.com/Page.cfm/Thread/Attorneys/Sub Thread/Search/Name/Lipton%2C%20Martin (Wachtell, Lipton, Rosen & Katz Web site).

My account of Rupert Murdoch's experience in China is based on a variety of interviews with current and former News Corp. employees, including Peter Stothard, the former editor of the *Times* of London. I also relied on several press accounts, including William Shawcross, "Murdoch's New Life," *Vanity Fair*, October 1999. Particularly useful was Bruce Dover, *Rupert's Adventures in China: How Murdoch Lost a Fortune and Found a Wife* (Edinburgh: Mainstream Publishing Co., 2008).

James Murdoch's speech attacking the Falun Gong was widely reported at the time in a number of newspapers and criticized in the *Wall Street Journal*: Tunku Varadarajan, "Bad Company: Rupert Murdoch and His Son Genuflect Before Chinese Communists," March 26, 2001.

CHAPTER 13

The *Journal* story outlining Murdoch's relationship with his editors throughout his career appeared as "In Murdoch's Career, a Hand on the News: His Aggressive Style Can Blur Boundaries; 'Buck Stops with Me,'" by Steve Stecklow and Aaron O. Patrick in London, Martin Peers in Sydney, Australia, and Andrew Higgins in New York (June 5, 2007).

Murdoch's frustration with the delay in receiving an editorial independence proposal from the Bancroft family was relayed to me by a number of his associates. His comments to Reuters appeared under the headline "Murdoch: No Plans to Raise Dow Jones Bid" by Gabriela Baczynska (June 27, 2007).

Murdoch's unscripted interview with the *New York Times* appeared under the headline "Murdoch on Owning the Wall Street Journal," by Richard Siklos and Andrew Ross Sorkin, May 4, 2007.

CHAPTER 15

For Murdoch's lawyer's assertion that the mogul looks at reporters "as furniture," I relied on Sarah Bernard and Aaron Latham, "My God, What Trouble You Could Cause!" *New York*, July 6, 2008.

The *New York Times* and the *Washington Post* both covered the Minneapolis bridge collapse on their front pages: Libby Sander and Susan Saulny; Pat Borzi, Karron Skog, and Carla Baranauckas contributed reporting, "Bridge Failure in Minnesota Kills 7 People," *New York Times*, August 2, 2007; and Joe Kimball and Elizabeth Williamson, "Interstate Bridge Collapses into Mississippi River in Minneapolis," *Washington Post*, August 2, 2007. The same day, the *Journal* noted the collapse in a brief item in its "World-Wide" column for non-business news.

The *Journal* followed a day after with a story exploring the collapse's implications for infrastructure in the United States: Christoper Conkey, Daniel Machalaba, and Douglas Belkin, "Bridge Collapse Could Spur Infrastructure Fixes," August 3, 2007.

CHAPTER 17

Murdoch publicly discussed his view that he wanted to make WSJ.com free at an investor conference in September 2007. His comments were widely reported, including in the *Journal:* Sarah Ellison, "Murdoch's Choice: Paid or Free for WSJ.com?" September 19, 2007.

CHAPTER 18

My account of the dinner prior to the bureau chiefs' meeting is based primarily on my own observations of the cocktail party and dinner on the eve of the meeting. My account of the meeting itself is based on interviews with bureau chiefs and others who attended the meeting.

In addition, I relied on various internal *Wall Street Journal* memos, including a December 17, 2007, e-mail—"Bureau Chiefs' Meeting Agenda"—from Donna Davis to the *Journal*'s bureau chiefs.

CHAPTER 20

I spent April 21, 2008, with Rupert Murdoch. Most of the events described in this chapter are based on my own observations of that day.

The dimensions of Murdoch's Boeing Business Jet were taken from the Boeing Business Jets Web site, http://www.boeing.com/commercial/bbj.

The circumstances of Rich Zannino's departure from Dow Jones were relayed to me by both Zannino and Murdoch and a number of current News Corp. executives and former Dow Jones executives. Murdoch's comment that he has "taken up offers like that in the past" came from an interview I conducted with Murdoch.

Murdoch commented on the *Journal*'s front page that day (April 21, 2008), including on the article "Latest Attacks Roil Democrats."

The *Journal*'s editorial coverage of Vincent Foster spanned several articles, including "Who Is Vincent Foster?" June 17, 1993.

Foster's note about the *Journal* editors was widely reported at the time, including in Jason DeParle, "A Life Undone—A Special Report; Portrait of a White House Aide Ensnared by His Perfectionism," *New York Times*, August 22, 1993.

Andrew Neil's account of his editorship at the *Sunday Times* is outlined extensively in his book *Full Disclosure* (London: Macmillan Publishers Ltd., 1996).

My description of the day Brauchli learned that News Corp. wasn't happy with his editorship is based on interviews with current and former News Corp. employees as well as several editors at the *Journal*.

The details of the duties and compensation for Dow Jones's editorial committee were outlined in "Meet the Editorial Committee: Our Task Under the News Corp.-Dow Jones Merger Agreement," *Wall Street Journal*, December 14, 2007; and "Text of Dow Jones Editorial Agreement," *Wall Street Journal*, August 1, 2007.

CHAPTER 21

My description of Robert Thomson's round of discussions with the *Journal* newsroom after Brauchli resigned is based on interviews with current and former *Journal* reporters as well as some press coverage at the time, including John Koblin, "Hands Still Wringing at Journal as Robert 'Head of Content' Thomson Takes Reins," *New York Observer*, May 6, 2008.

Thomson's view of the *Journal* was relayed to me by several people familiar with his thinking.

Gawker's coverage of Thomson's meeting with the *Journal*'s "Money & Investing" section appeared as "Civil War at the Wall Street Journal" by Nick Denton, Gawker, April 30, 2008.

Thomson's interactions with Bill Grueskin were relayed to me by Grueskin.

Dow Jones's campaign to boost circulation to coincide with Murdoch's takeover was described to me by a former Dow Jones executive, who said, "It was a plan to create artificial success . . . This is exactly what we planned to happen. What you don't see is how much marketing money is spent to get there."

CHAPTER 22

Thomson's appointment as managing editor of the *Journal* was widely reported and outlined in "Statement on New WSJ Editor," *Wall Street Journal,* May 20, 2008.

The speculation about who would take over the *Journal* newsroom appeared in a number of publications, including "Rupe Melding with UK Tabloid Editor?" Mediabistro.com, May 19, 2008.

Thomson's characterization of the *New York Times* as "sanctimony central" and his statement that the paper was full of "preening, posturing, and pretentiousness" were relayed to me by a number of *Journal* bureau chiefs present for his presentation to them at the bureau chiefs' meeting in January 2008.

Thomson's statement to a group of *Journal* reporters that editors should not stay in their jobs too long was relayed to me by a *Journal* reporter who heard the statement directly from Thomson.

Murdoch's assertion that the stories in the *Journal* were edited a "ridiculous" number of times was made publicly at the D: All Things Digital conference in May 2008, http://d6.allthingsd.com/20080529/video-rupert-murdoch-on-politics-obama-and-mccain/.

CHAPTER 23

The *Journal*'s story that declared that the "American financial system was shaken to its core" appeared under the headline "Crisis on Wall Street as Lehman Totters, Merrill Is Sold, AIG Seeks to Raise Cash" by Carrick Mollenkamp, Susanne Craig, Serena Ng, and Aaron Lucchetti, September 15, 2008.

The *Journal*'s history of rarely using banner headlines was relayed to me by Robert Christie, vice president for communications at Dow Jones.

Murdoch relayed his excitement about sitting in on the *Journal*'s news meeting in September 2008 in an interview I conducted with him on November 10, 2008.

Reporters' quips about the disorganization of the *Journal* newsroom after News Corp.'s takeover and the new incentives News Corp. instituted in the newsroom come from interviews with current *Journal* reporters.

Ivanka Trump's comments to Thomson about the *Journal*'s front page were relayed to me by several eyewitnesses.

The *Columbia Journalism Review*'s assessment of the *Journal*'s performance during the financial crisis appeared under the headline "In the Crisis, the *Journal* Falls Short: The Newspaper Is Missing the Moment," by Dean Starkman, December 24, 2008.

Thomson's announcement of his senior deputy Gerard Baker was widely noted in the press. His e-mail announcing the appointment appeared as "WSJ Announces Editorial Leadership Changes," PoynterOnline, June 19, 2008, http://www.poynter.org/forum/view_post.asp?id=13417.

My account of a *Journal* editor's frustration with still being "on probation" with Thomson came from an interview with that editor.

Robert Thomson's memo to Dow Jones's reporters urging cooperation between the *Journal* and Newswires was sent as an e-mail to Dow Jones reporters and was picked up by Talking Biz News, "WSJ ME Thomson: Reporters Will Be Judged on Whether They Break News," by Chris Roush, March 19, 2009.

The coverage of Thomson's memo linked several reporters' departures to the changes News Corp. had instituted at the *Journal,* including Jeff Bercovici, "'Historic' Memo Leaves Feathers Ruffled at 'WSJ,'" Portfolio.com, March 24, 2009.

Josh Prager's goodbye e-mail was picked up by a number of outlets, including Politico.com: Michael Calderone, "Prager Leaves Journal: 'The paper and I were no longer a good fit,'" April 3, 2009.

Gerard Baker's comments about the Pulitzer committee were relayed to me by several reporters with whom Baker spoke directly.

EPILOGUE

Joseph Nocera's comments about the *Journal* originally appeared in an online column in the *New York Times* on August 29, 2008.

Various commentators voiced their impressions of the *Journal* in a piece by Scott Sherman in the May 11, 2009, issue of the *Nation* entitled "Has the 'Journal' Lost Its Soul?"

Robert Thomson's comments about the *Journal* and the *New York Times* initially appeared in a July 3, 2008, interview with *BusinessWeek,* "The Wall Street Journalist," by Jon Fine.

Index